WINDOWS REGISTRY FORENSICS

WINDOWS REGISTRY FORENSICS

Advanced Digital Forensic Analysis of the Windows Registry

Second Edition

HARLAN CARVEY

AMSTERDAM • BOSTON • HEIDELBERG • LONDON
NEW YORK • OXFORD • PARIS • SAN DIEGO
SAN FRANCISCO • SINGAPORE • SYDNEY • TOKYO
Syngress is an imprint of Elsevier

SYNGRESS.

Syngress is an imprint of Elsevier
50 Hampshire Street, 5th Floor, Cambridge, MA 02139, USA

British Library Cataloguing-in-Publication Data
A catalogue record for this book is available from the British Library

Library of Congress Cataloging-in-Publication Data
A catalog record for this book is available from the Library of Congress

ISBN: 978-0-12-803291-6

For information on all Syngress publications
visit our website at https://www.elsevier.com/

Working together
to grow libraries in
developing countries

www.elsevier.com • www.bookaid.org

Publisher: Todd Green
Acquisition Editor: Chris Katsaropoulos
Editorial Project Manager: Anna Valutkevich
Project Manager: Priya Kumaraguruparan
Designer: Matthew Limbert

To Terri and Kylie; you are my light and my foundation

CONTENTS

ABOUT THE AUTHOR

Harlan Carvey is a senior information security researcher with the Dell SecureWorks Counter Threat Unit—Special Ops (CTU-SO) team, where his efforts are focused on targeted threat hunting, response, and research. He continues to maintain a passion and focus in analyzing Windows systems, and in particular, the Windows Registry.

Harlan is an accomplished author, public speaker, and open source tool author. He dabbles in other activities, including home brewing and horseback riding. As a result, he has become quite adept at backing up and parking a horse trailer.

Harlan earned a bachelor's degree in electrical engineering from the Virginia Military Institute and a master's degree in the same discipline from the Naval Postgraduate School. He served in the United States Marine Corps, achieving the rank of captain before departing the service. He resides in Northern Virginia with his family.

ABOUT THE TECHNICAL EDITOR

Mari DeGrazia is a Senior Security Consultant with the Verizon RISK team, which provides Incident Response services on a global scale. During her tenure with Verizon, Mari has investigated high-profile breach cases and computer security incidents. Prior to Verizon, Mari worked civil and felony criminal cases as a digital forensics examiner which included testimony as an expert witness. Mari has a Bachelor's of Science in Computer Science from Hawaii Pacific University as well as various certificates related to Digital Forensics. She is currently pursuing her Masters of Science in Digital Forensics.

PREFACE

I am not an expert. I don't know everything. In particular, I do not and have never claimed to be an expert at analyzing Windows systems nor in analyzing the Windows Registry. What I have done is taken all that stuff I've got written down over the years, in different places, as well as stuff I've found online, stuff I've found after running malware in a VM and creating a timeline, etc., and put it into what I thought would be a logical structure. I then decided to call some of this stuff "chapters," and I sent them to Mari to review and tech edit. She sent them back, I looked at her comments, decided that she was right in most cases, and sent the chapters into Syngress. They made it into a book. That's a process, and it doesn't make me an expert at anything, especially digital forensic analysis.

When I wrote the first edition of this book, I mentioned in the preface that by 2010, I had met a good number of forensic analysts who had little apparent knowledge of the value that the Windows Registry can hold. As 2015 draws to a close and I am submitting the manuscript for the second edition of the book, the same holds true. Data within the Windows Registry can provide a great deal of context to investigations, illustrating user access to files, devices that have been attached to the system, applications that have been executed, and users that have been added to the system. Configuration settings maintained with the Registry will inform the analyst as to what they can expect to see on the system; did deleted files bypass the Recycle Bin, was the page file cleared at shutdown, and what is the effective audit policy for the system? I've used information from the Registry to determine that a user intentionally infected a system with a remote access Trojan (RAT) and then attempted to "clean up" after removing the malware. Prior to sharing my findings, the popular notion was that systems infected with that RAT were the result of spear phishing.

Throughout this book, I have maintained a good deal of information specific to Windows XP and 2003 systems, because they are still out there. However, I've included more information regarding Windows 7, as well as 8, 8.1, and Windows 10 systems, where possible. There are things that we still don't know about Windows 7 systems, and at the time of this writing, Windows 10 is still somewhat new. However, it's likely that by the time the book is published and on the shelves, that holiday season would have resulted in a large number of newly purchased systems arriving with Windows 10 preinstalled. As such, there is still a great deal of research to be done, and even more to discover about Windows 10.

Again, I am not an expert, and I don't know it all; I have simply tried to include some of what I've encountered and experienced in this book.

Intended Audience

The intended audience for this book is anyone analyzing Windows systems. This includes, but is not limited to, law enforcement officers, military personnel, those in academia (students, professors, lab assistants, etc.), as well as investigators in full-time employment and consulting positions. IT admins and managers will find useful things in the chapters of this book.

So…yeah…the intended audience is "everyone who performs incident response and/or digital forensic analysis of Windows systems," and this also includes anyone interested in doing so.

Book Organization

This book consists of five chapters following this preface. Those chapters are as follows:

Chapter 1: Registry Analysis

In the first chapter of the book, we go over some of the basic concepts of digital forensic analysis and then present some basic information about the Windows Registry; where it can be found in the file system, nomenclature, that sort of thing. This chapter may seem somewhat rudimentary to some, but it lays a foundation for the rest of the book. Over the years, and even today, I find that there are some examiners who try to jump into Registry analysis and go from "0 to 60" without that base foundational knowledge. This understanding of Registry analysis is critical, as it allows the examiner to be discerning of not only the tools used but also of the available data itself.

Chapter 2: Processes and Tools

In this chapter, we discuss some open source and freeware tools that are available to analysts. There are viewers and data extraction tools available, and it's important for analysts to understand the strengths and weaknesses of each class of tool, as well as each individual tool, when using them.

What you won't find discussed in this chapter is the use of commercial analysis suites. The decision to go this route was a conscious one, with two guiding reasons. The first is that it's important for analysts to be aware of their analysis goals and what it is they're trying to achieve, before using an automated tool set.

The second reason is simply that I don't have access to the commercial tools. And honestly, I don't want access to them. But don't misunderstand my reasoning as to why; it's not the suites themselves that I have an issue with, it's how most analysts use them. So, again, my goal with this book is to provide a resource from which analysts can build a solid foundation.

Chapter 3: Analyzing the System Hives

In this chapter, we discuss the Registry hives that pertain to the system as a whole (not specifically to the users). In this edition, I wanted to organize the keys and values discussed into "artifact categories," in the hope of making it a bit clearer as to why an analyst would be interested in the various keys and values in the first place.

For example, one of the things I've tried to illustrate with respect to the value of Registry analysis is that even some of the stealthiest malware found needs to persist in some manner. In 2015, analysts from a computer security company published their findings with respect to extremely stealthy malware named "Moker"; they went into significant detail regarding how the malware itself was written to avoid detection and hamper analysis. However, in the comments section of their blog post, they mentioned that the malware persisted via the use of the "Run" key, which should make it trivial to detect something anomalous on the system.

I've also tried to illustrate the value of Registry analysis by discussing how system configuration settings within the Registry can impact an investigation, as well as how there are various bits of malware that leave traces in the Registry that have nothing to do with persistence (the values appear in some cases to be associated with the configuration of the malware).

Chapter 4: Case Studies: User Hives

In this chapter, we discuss the Registry hives specific to the user, and once again, present various Registry keys and values of interest to analysts broken down into artifact categories. There is a great deal of valuable information within the user's hives that can have a significant impact on an investigation. I've had occasion to examine systems thought to have been infected with remote access Trojans (RATs) through the use of spear phishing or a "watering hole attack" (also referred to as a strategic web compromise), only to find that the user had purposely infected the system. In more than one instance, I've also used data derived from the user hives to illustrate that a user or administrator had attempted to "clean up" a malware infection.

Chapter 5: RegRipper

In the final chapter of the book, we specifically discuss the RegRipper tool itself. Over the years, I'm aware that there are a lot of folks who use RegRipper but largely from the perspective of downloading and running the GUI for the tool. I don't think that what folks are aware of is that RegRipper can be a much more powerful tool, if you know a bit more about how it functions and how it can be used. My hope is that a few will not only develop a better understanding of the tool but also choose to open an editor and write their own plugins. Consider this chapter a "user manual" of sorts.

ACKNOWLEDGMENTS

I start by thanking my Lord and Savior Jesus Christ, for it is with His many wondrous blessings that this book is possible. A man's achievements are not his alone when done with the right heart, and I know in my heart that for all of the things to come together that made this book possible is a gift and blessing for which I am forever grateful.

I'd also like to thank my lovely wife for putting up with my nerdy ways and my excitement in digital forensic and Windows Registry analysis. I know that you don't get as excited as I do when I see or achieve the things I do, but I'm thankful that you let me do those things.

I'd like to thank Mari DeGrazia, my technical editor, for not only providing excellent insight and feedback throughout the process of writing this book but also for engaging in discussions with me to help sort of my thoughts about the new book out. Engagement and discussion is something sorely absent within the DFIR community, and I am thankful that folks like Mari and Corey Harrell are willing to engage in discussions relevant to our field. After all, this is the really the best way for us to grow as analysts.

I'd be remiss if I didn't thank Corey for his time and the effort he put into his autorip tool, as well as exchanges we had over artifact categories. Corey's insight into incident response issues has been invaluable over the years.

I'd also like to thank Eric Zimmerman for all of the great work he's done in the area of Windows Registry analysis, as well as in creating and updating his Registry Explorer tool. Eric has also produced and made other tools available.

A special "thank you" goes to Cindy Murphy for providing some hive files from a Windows phone. The fact is that RegRipper *does* work with these hive files; the structure is identical to what's found on Windows computers, but the keys and values, and their uses, clearly differ. More importantly, there are those within the "community" who are reticent to share any data, even from VMs, for a wide variety of reasons, and here's a member of law enforcement sharing data...simply because she can. Thank you, Cindy.

Finally, I'd like to thank the Syngress staff for making this book possible.

REGISTRY ANALYSIS

INFORMATION IN THIS CHAPTER
- Core Analysis Concepts
- What is the Window Registry?
- Registry Structure

Introduction

The Windows Registry is a core component of the Windows operating systems, and yet when it comes to digital analysis of Windows systems, is perhaps the least understood component of a Windows system. This may be due to how little information seems to have been written on the subject; however, if you spend just a little time looking around, you'll find that there has actually been quite a bit of information regarding the Windows Registry documented. This apparent disparity may be due to the fact that most of the commercial forensic analysis applications do little more than open the Windows Registry in a viewer-type application and do not provide for the application of previously developed (from the analyst's most recent case, or provided by other analysts) intelligence to the available data. Whatever the reason, my purpose for writing this book is to illustrate the vital importance of the Windows Registry to digital forensic analysis. This is not to say that the Windows Registry is the *only* aspect of the system that requires attention; nothing could be further from the truth. However, the Windows Registry can provide a great deal of valuable information and context to a digital examination, and as such, there is a particular value in addressing this topic in a book such as this one.

The Windows Registry maintains a great deal of configuration information about the system, maintaining settings for various functionality within the system (ie, may be enabled or disabled). In addition, the Registry maintains historical information about user activity; in order to provide the user with a "better" overall experience, details about applications installed and accessed, as well as window positions and sizes, are maintained in a manner similar to a log file. All of this information can be extremely valuable to a forensic examiner, particularly when attempting to establish a timeline of system and/or user activity. A wide range of cases would benefit greatly from information derived from the Registry, if the analyst were aware of the information and how to best exploit it for the purposes of their examination.

WHAT'S IN THE REGISTRY?

The first thing to keep in mind when conducting Registry analysis is that not everything can be found there. Believe it or not, one particular question that I still see asked is, "Where are file copies recorded in the Registry?" Windows systems do not record file copy operations, and if such things were recorded, I'd think that some other resource (Windows Event Log, maybe) would be far more suitable.

Not everything is recorded in the Registry, but the Windows Registry is still an incredibly valuable forensic resource.

Information in the Registry can have a much greater effect on an examination than I think most analysts really realize. There are many Registry values that can have a significant impact on how the various components of the system behave; for example, there is a Registry value that tells the operating system to stop updating file last access times, so that whenever a file is opened (albeit nothing changed) for viewing or searching, the time stamp is not updated accordingly. And oh, yeah...this is enabled by default beginning with Windows Vista and is still enabled by default on Windows 7 and Windows 8 systems. Given this, how do examiners then determine when a file was accessed? Well, there are other resources, both within the Registry and without (Jump Lists, for example) that can provide this information, particularly depending upon the type of file accessed and the application used to access the file.

A few examples of Registry values that can impact an examination include (but are not limited to) the following:

- Alter file system tunneling (specifics of file system tunneling can be found online at http://support.microsoft.com/kb/172190) behavior, or the updating of last accessed times on files and folders
- Have files that the user deletes automatically bypass the Recycle Bin
- Modify system crash dump, Prefetcher, and System Restore Point behavior
- Clear the pagefile when the system is shut down
- Enable or disable Event Log auditing
- Enable or disable the Windows firewall

- Redirect the Internet Explorer web browser to a particular start page or proxy
- Automatically launch applications with little to no input from the user beyond booting the system and logging in

All of these Registry settings can significantly impact the direction of an investigation. In a number of instances, I have found valuable data in the pagefile (such as responses from web server queries) that would not have been there had the pagefile been cleared on shut down. When examining a Windows system that was part of a legal hold (an order was given to not delete any data), it can be very important to determine if the user may have cleared the Recycle Bin, or if the system was set to have deleted files automatically bypass the Recycle Bin. The use of application prefetching, which is enabled by default on workstation versions of Windows (but not server versions, such as Windows 2008 R2), can provide valuable clues during intrusion and malware discovery cases.

These are just a few examples; there are a number of other Registry keys and values that can have a significant impact (possibly even detrimental) on what an analyst sees during disk and file system analysis. Some of these values do not actually exist within the Registry by default and have to be added (usually in accordance with a Microsoft (MS) Knowledge Base (KB) article) in order to affect the system. At the very least, understanding these settings and how they affect the overall system can add context to what the analyst observes in other areas of their examination.

REGISTRY VALUES AND SYSTEM BEHAVIOR

The Windows Registry contains a number of values that significantly impact system behavior. For example, an analyst may receive an image for analysis and determine that the Prefetch directory contains no Prefetch (*.pf) files. Registry values of interest in such a case would include those that identify the operating system and version; by default, Windows XP, Vista, and Windows 7 will perform application prefetching (and generate *.pf files); however, Windows 2003 does not perform application prefetching (although it can be configured to do so) by default. The Prefetcher itself can also be disabled, per MS KB article 307498 (found online at http://support.microsoft.com/kb/307498). This same value can be used to enable or disable application prefetching.

The purposes of this book are to draw back the veil of mystery that has been laid over the Registry, and to illustrate just how valuable a forensic resource, the Registry, can really be during malware, intrusion, or data breach examinations, to name just a few. The Windows Registry contains a great deal of information that can provide significant context to a wide range of investigations. Not only that, but there are also a number of keys and values, as we'll discuss later in this book, in which information persists beyond that deletion or removal of applications and files. That's right…if a user accesses a file or installs and runs an application, the indications of these actions (and others) will remain long after the file or application has been removed and is no longer available. This is due to the fact that much of the "tracking" that occurs on Windows systems is a function of the operating system, of the environment, or ecosystem in which the application or user functions. As such, much of this activity occurs without the express knowledge of the user or application…it just happens. Understanding this, as well as understanding its limitations, can open up new vistas (no pun intended) of data to an analyst.

Core Analysis Concepts

Before we begin discussing the Windows Registry analysis specifically, there are several core analysis concepts that need to be addressed as they are pertinent to examinations as a whole. Keeping these concepts in mind can be extremely beneficial when performing digital analysis in general.

Locard's Exchange Principle

Dr. Edmund Locard was a French scientist who formulated the basic forensic principle that *every contact leaves a trace*. This means that in the physical world, when two objects come into contact, some material is transferred from one to the other, and vice versa. We can see this demonstrated all around us, every day…let's say you get a little too close to a concrete stanchion while trying to parallel park your car. As the car scrapes along the stanchion, paint from the car body is left on the stanchion and concrete, and paint from the stanchion becomes embedded in the scrapes on the car.

Interestingly enough, the same holds true in the digital world. When malware infects a system, there is usually some means by which it arrives on the system, such as a browser "drive-by" infection, via a network share, USB thumb drive, or an e-mail attachment. When an intruder accesses a system, there is some artifact such as a network connection or activity on the target system and the target system will contain some information about the system from which the intruder originated. Some of this information may be extremely volatile, meaning that it only remains visible to the operating system (and hence, an analyst) for a short period of time. However, remnants of that artifact may persist for a considerable amount of time.

EVERYTHING LEAVES A TRACE

Any interaction with a Windows system, particularly through the Windows Explorer graphical interface, will leave a trace. These indications are not always in the Registry, and they may not persist for very long, but there will be something, somewhere. It's simply a matter of knowing what to look for and where, and having the right tools to gain access to and correctly interpret the information.

The quote, "absence of evidence is not evidence of absence" is attributed to the astrophysicist Dr. Carl Sagan and can be applied to digital forensics as well. Essentially, if an analyst understands the nature of a user's interaction with a Windows system, then the lack or absence of an artifact where one is expected to be is itself an artifact. During a recent examination, I was trying to determine a user's access to files on the system and could not find the RecentDocs (this key will be discussed in greater detail in chapter Case Studies: User Hives) key within the user's NTUSER.DAT hive file; RegRipper did not find it, and I could not locate the key manually. As it turns out, the user had run the "Window Washer" application, which reportedly "clears the list of recently accessed documents." The time associated with the user launching the application (derived from the user's UserAssist key) corresponded to the LastWrite time on the RecentDocs parent key.

While examining a system that was part of a larger incident, our team had determined that there was a malware file on the system (a dynamic link library, or DLL) but could not determine the method used to load and launch the malware. A timeline consisting of file system and Event Log events clearly showed the user logging in, the process being launched, the DLL file being accessed, and then the known file system artifacts being created. Our first thought was that there was some auto-start location or trigger within the user's NTUSER.DAT hive file, but we could not find anything. It turned out that the DLL in question was loaded as a result of some Windows shell extensions not having explicit paths listed in the Registry, and the operating system following its designated search order to locate a DLL by that name.

In both instances, the absence or lack of an expected artifact was itself an artifact, and spurred additional, in-depth analysis.

So how does this apply to Registry analysis? When a user, even an intruder who has gained access to the system, interacts with the system, and particularly with the Windows Explorer user interface (aka the "shell"), some rather persistent artifacts are created. If a malicious user logs into the system and plugs in a USB thumb drive, there is an exchange of information that occurs, and some of those artifacts persist in the Registry (the same is true when connecting to devices via Bluetooth). If the malicious user then launches applications, there will be additional artifacts created. When a user connects their system to a wireless access point (WAP), information about the WAP persists on the system. I was told by another analyst several years ago that he'd been involved in an investigation where a former employee was thought to have provided sensitive data to a competitor and then accepted employment with the competitor. An examination of the system revealed that while the employee was traveling, he'd connected his corporate laptop to WiFi at a Starbucks near the competitor's building and then to the WiFi in the competitor's offices about an hour later. A combination of the WiFi access point names and a geolocation lookup of the medium access control (MAC) addresses of the access points, along with date and time stamps, revealed important clues about the employee's activities.

Analysts need to keep Locard's exchange principle in mind during an examination because it can not only tell them that there *are* artifacts, but can also point them to where those artifacts may be located. Knowing likely sources of artifacts significantly reduces the time it takes to conduct an investigation; instead of combing through all of the data, the examiner can target those specific areas to quickly determine whether they will be fruitful or not. This sort of data collection and triage can greatly assist incident response activities as well as increase the throughput of investigations, as a whole, without sacrificing quality or completeness.

Least Frequency of Occurrence

I first heard the term "least frequency of occurrence" mentioned in the context of digital forensics at the SANS Forensic Summit during the summer of 2009. Peter Silberman (an analyst with the consulting firm Mandiant) used the term to describe malware infections on systems. His point was that in the old days, malware (and in particular worms) would spread rapidly, infecting and reinfecting systems. In short order, a system would be so heavily infected that it would become completely unusable by anyone, let alone the attacker. The result was that not only were infected systems unusable to the attacker, but the failing systems provided a clear indication to the "victim" organization that they were infected. In order to address this, malware authors began using a unique "mutex," a software programming object that allows for mutual exclusion, within their malware in order to prevent the system from becoming reinfected. Once the system was infected, the mutex would be present in memory; upon reinfection, the malware would check for the mutex and, if found, not proceed with the infection.

The offshoot of this is that the mutex is very often random (although sometimes not so random) and always unique. This became an excellent indicator of a malware infection; in fact, Kris Harms (at the time an analyst with Mandiant, who later became an analyst with Cylance) discussed during a presentation the use of the Microsoft SysInternals tool *handle.exe* to list all the mutexes available in memory for all of the running processes on the system and then sorting the output by the unique mutexes. Kris demonstrated that a quick look at those mutexes that only occurred once or infrequently across processes very often resulted in rapid and accurate detection of malware, even if the mutex name itself had been changed.

Demonstrating Kris' use of handle.exe is outside the scope of this book, but it does serve as an example of how the concept of *least frequency of occurrence* (LFO) can be used, not only for malware but also for intrusions, and therefore can also be very important to our analysis.

The point of LFO is that during the lifetime of a system, malware infections and intrusions constitute what occurs least frequently on that system. Operating system and application updates are extremely "noisy," generating a great deal of file system (file creations, modifications, and deletions) and Registry (keys being created, values updated, etc.) activity, and occurring fairly frequently. Windows XP, by default, will create a System Restore Point every 24 h (as well as under other conditions) and will also launch its Disk Defragmenter utility every three calendar days to perform a limited defrag. Windows XP also generates or updates Prefetch files whenever an application is launched. Beginning with Windows Vista, the operating systems began maintaining Volume Shadow Copies (as opposed to the Windows XP System Restore Points) in order to provide a recovery mechanism. When a user installs software from Apple (such as QuickTime, iTunes, etc.), a Scheduled Task is *created* on the system to look for updates to those applications once a week, and the user can choose to install those updates, creating and modifying files within the file system. Microsoft releases operating system and application updates monthly, and sometimes does so "out of band," or out of the regular update release schedule. What this means is that there is a *lot* of normal file system and Registry activity that occurs on a system, but in contrast, when malware infects a system, a few files (and maybe Registry keys/values) are created, and there may also be some network connections as the malware communicates off of the system. When an intruder accesses a system via Remote Desktop due to an easily guessed password, there may be several Event Log records generated (we will discuss how to determine the audit configuration on a system in detail in chapter Analyzing the System Hives), some Registry keys created or modified, and depending upon the actions they take, maybe some files created, modified, or deleted on that system. Again, with the exception of turning the compromised system into a repository for pirated movies or music files, a malware infection or intrusion will very often constitute the least frequent activity on the system. In fact, many intrusions go undetected for long periods of time, as the intruder will use very simple techniques to minimize as much as possible the artifacts left on a system. This can also be true for other types of issues, such as viewing illegal images. A file (or a few files) is added to the system, the files are viewed (as we'll see in chapter Case Studies: User Hives, some Registry keys will be updated), and then the files may be shared or deleted. All in all, adding, viewing, and deleting these files really do not constitute a considerable amount of activity, particularly when compared to operating system and application updates.

What this often means to our analysis is that during intrusions or malware infections, we wouldn't usually be looking for large numbers of files being added to the system, or of massive numbers of Registry keys or values being created, or regular or significant spikes in activity of any kind. Most often, spikes in file system and Registry activity will indicate an operating system or application software update (or much to the chagrin of the analyst, a system administrator running antivirus application scans) not a malware infection or system intrusion.

Windows Isn't Just "Windows"

What I mean by this is that the version of Windows being examined matters; in fact, it matters a great deal. From a user's perspective, the change from Windows 2000 to Windows XP was pretty significant, because what they saw on the screen and the way in which they interacted with Windows, through the user interface, changed significantly. The same can be said for the change from Windows 7 to Windows 8 and 8.1. From a forensic analyst's perspective, the changes have been even more significant; with each new release of Windows, it seems that more artifacts are available, with many of these artifacts being maintained in different formats and locations, not just within the Registry but within the file system as a whole.

Consider user searches; with Windows XP, the terms that a user searched for via the shell were maintained in subkeys beneath the "ACMru" Registry key in the user's NTUSER.DAT hive file. With Windows Vista, the search terms were saved to an XML file, and then with Windows 7, the terms were saved beneath a key named "WordWheelQuery." With Windows 8, user search terms were saved in the Registry and associated with "Search Charm" in the user interface, and apparently, with Windows 8.1, those terms are again saved in a file.

There are other significant changes between versions of Windows. With Windows XP and 2003, system events were recorded in the Event Logs, files with the ".evt" extension in the *Windows\ system32\config* folder. As of Windows Vista, the logs were referred to as Windows Event Logs and had a ".evtx" extension, a new location, and an entirely different binary format, requiring a completely different set of tools to parse them. Oh, and even more events were (and still are) being recorded by default.

There are many more such differences between the versions of Windows, and we'll go into many of those differences in this book as they apply directly to the Registry for each version.

Remnants

One of the things I really like about digging into the Registry is the amount of information that is available, often times even after a user or intruder has taken "antiforensics" steps in order to hide their activities. Often users and intruders will take steps to cover their tracks and remove indications of their activities without realizing that their interactions with the operating system (and often times, with applications) are being "recorded" automatically.

For example, I was examining a system about a year ago which had been found to be infected with a particular variant of a remote access Trojan (RAT). This particular RAT variant is usually installed as a Windows service, allowing the intruder to access the system with privileges greater than that of the system administrator. Further, this particular bit of malware is most often assumed to be installed via a "spearphishing" e-mail, in which the user is enticed to click on a link or malicious document, resulting in the installation of the RAT. In this particular case, Registry artifacts revealed that the RAT had been installed as a result of someone with physical access to the system plugging a USB thumb drive into the system (it was mounted as the E:\ volume) and launching an installer application. When the user's employer requested that they turn in the system for examination, the user attempted to remove the RAT…in fact, artifacts in the Registry revealed that the last key in focus in the Registry Editor before it was closed by the user was the key alphabetically following the name with which the RAT was installed. Additional information was extracted from the hibernation file through the use of the Volatility Framework, but the preponderance of artifacts extracted from the Registry clearly indicated that the RAT was installed and running on the system with the full knowledge (and involvement) of the user.

As I'm writing this section of the book, I'm working (as part of my day job) on an examination in which an intruder had access to an infrastructure via domain administrator credentials and

Terminal Services. I'd tried to backtrack the intruder's connections as they hopped from system to system, but they had a penchant for clearing the Windows Event Logs on some (albeit not all) systems. Even though I could not see all of the data that I wanted to, there was more than enough data in the Registry to tell me when they were logged into the system and active (days and times), as well as other systems to which they connected. Even without the Windows Event Log records, I was able to build a time-based map of the intruder's activities, showing what time of day they were active, files and resources they'd accessed, etc. I was also able to illustrate their connection to a file transfer protocol server.

Data available in the Registry can be very revealing on a number of fronts. Although the intruder had cleared the Windows Event Log and we were not able to see where they were when they logged into the system we were examining, but we could see when they were active on the system (which we could then correlate with other sources, such as domain controller and VPN logs), what they'd done, and other systems they'd connected to through the use of the Terminal Services Client as well as via Microsoft networking. All of this data remained even following the intruder's "antiforensics" steps.

Goals

Before starting any analysis at all, every analyst should carefully consider and document their goals. What are you looking for? What questions are you trying to answer? What do you hope to ultimately achieve through your analysis? We do this because this helps us understand what it is we should be doing, what data we should extract, where we should go to look for artifacts and clues, and what data can be correlated to address the issue. Too often, analysts get caught up in the "find all bad stuff" mindset (or allow customers to hem them into it) and in doing so spend hours upon hours "doing analysis," yet never actually answer the questions before them. Believe me, I understand how you'll be looking for one thing but find something else that, while interesting, may not have anything to do with your immediate analysis. Pursuing these kinds of things is called having "shiny object syndrome"; like a fish or a kitten, you're easily distracted by shiny objects. An example of this is locating all of the malware and spyware on a system, when the customer just wanted to know if a user on the system had accessed or copied a file (as in a fraud or exposure of intellectual property issue).

Your goals may vary depending upon your employer and the type of work you generally do. If you're a consultant, your goals may vary from case to case; during one examination, you may have to determine if a system was infected with malware, and if so, the capabilities of that malware (ie, what data did it extract, where was the data sent, was the malware specifically targeted at the organization, etc.). In another examination, you may have to determine if there was sensitive information (ie, personally identifiable information, credit card data, classified data, etc.) stored on the system, while another examination may pertain to violations of corporate acceptable use policies. If you're a law enforcement officer, you may be faced with a possible issue of fraud, or you may need to demonstrate that a computer owner had knowledge of and viewed contraband images.

Regardless of the type of examination, your goals are where everything starts and ends. For consultants, not answering a customer's questions can lead to serious issues, such as spending far more time on your "analysis" than your contract allows, or attempting to bill a customer when you haven't answered their questions. Our analysis goals give us direction and focus and allow us to provide those answers in a timely and efficient manner.

Documentation

Perhaps the most important aspect of any analysis, after the goals, is documentation. Forensic analysts and incident responders should document all aspects of what they do, from the acquisition of hard drives and the transfer and management of acquired images, to their analysis plan and actual case notes. Many organizations have their own acquisition methodology and chain of custody documentation, usually in some sort of form or checklist. This is a good start, but documenting case work should not stop there.

What can sometimes be missed is documentation of the overall analysis process. Before conducting analysis, do you sit down and ensure that you understand the goals of the analysis, or the questions that you're trying to answer? Whether you're a consultant working for a customer or an examiner performing work in support of law enforcement, there's usually some reason why you're sitting there with a hard drive or an acquired image. What is that reason? Most likely, it's that someone has questions that need to be answered. So start your analysis plan by documenting the goals that you're trying to achieve. From there, you can begin framing out your steps going forward and noting where you need to look, and those tasks that you need to achieve. For example, if the goal is to determine the existence of specific e-mails, you'll likely want to check for .pst/.ost files, or maybe check the Registry and determine which e-mail client was used, determine if web-based e-mail was used, etc.

Note

Many times when beginning an examination involving the use of a web browser on a Windows system, I'll see analysts start off by saying, "I'd check the contents of the user's TypedURLs key." That key, located in the NTUSER.DAT file within the user profile, contains a list of the URLs typed into the Internet Explorer address bar. But is that really a good place to start? What if there are no entries? What does that tell you? Perhaps a better place to start would be determine which web browser the user was using, or at least which web browsers were installed on the system, before targeting browser-specific artifacts.

The analysis plan can lead the analyst directly into documenting the analysis process itself. So why would we do this? What happens if at some point during the analysis process, you get sick or become injured? What happens if the analysis needs to be handed off to someone else? Another very real possibility is what happens if 6 months or a year after you complete your analysis, you have to answer questions about it? I know several analysts to whom this has happened recently. For myself, I've worked with customers who've come back with questions six or more months after accepting the final report and paying their bill…had I not had clear, concise documentation, I would have had trouble answering their questions in an intelligible manner. We've all been busy to the point where we can't remember what we had for breakfast, let alone the specifics of an examination from 6 months ago. Your case notes and documentation can be extremely important at that point, and it's best not to have to figure that out after the fact.

Another important aspect of documenting your analysis is that it allows you to go back and look at what you did, and improve the process. Documentation is the basis for improvement, and you can't improve a process if you don't have one. Your documentation provides that process. If you didn't document what you did, it didn't happen. By listing out the steps you followed in your analysis, you can see which ones were perhaps less fruitful and can be skipped or improved upon the next time, and which ones provided greater value. This also allows for other, less experienced analysts to learn from what you have done, what worked and what didn't, so that more analysts are able to achieve a similar, greater level of analysis.

Challenges of Registry Analysis

While often fruitful, Registry analysis isn't always easy, and there are two primary challenges when it comes to Registry analysis. Depending on your particular experiences, there may be other challenges, but these are the two big ones as I see them.

The first challenge to Registry analysis is that the Registry itself isn't all that well understood by responders and analysts. To be honest, I'm not even sure that there's really *anyone* who completely understands the Windows Registry! The Registry is a critical, core component of the Windows operating systems and records a considerable amount of information about the system configuration and usage, as well as user activity, particularly when the user is interacting with the system through the Windows Explorer shell. With just the operating system itself, I don't think that there's really anyone who completely understands why some keys and values have the paths and contain the structures that they do, or what activities lead to the keys or values being created or modified, let alone the structure of various binary value data. This lack of understanding by the vendor obviates any thorough knowledge and understanding by analysts and leaves the analyst to perform considerable testing to determine and illustrate how various artifacts originated on the system.

While considerable work has been performed and documented in this area, the awareness that this work is possibly incomplete persists. As new versions of the operating system are developed, locations and formats for storing data in the Registry change, as well, and some keys or values may be added, moved, modified, or simply removed. Very little is known and documented about what actions cause various keys to be modified; while some testing has been done for a very small number of keys, new questions are being posed all the time that would, quite honestly, require access to the source code to the operating system in order to completely answer. Being closed source the way Windows is, having complete access to the source code isn't likely to happen anytime soon.

Several years ago, Cory Altheide (whom I used to work with, and is now a responder for Google) and I conducted some research into tracking the use of USB devices across Windows systems. After we were done, we published our findings, confident that we'd figured out a way to determine when a USB device was last connected to a system. More recently, Rob Lee (of SANS fame) conducted additional testing and determined that what Cory and I had determined was really the first time that the device had been connected during the current (or most recent) boot session, meaning that if the system was running for several days and the USB device connected and disconnected several times, the best we could hope to show (with just the data we'd found) was when the device had first been connected during that boot session. Additional information is available in Windows Vista and Windows 7, but there simply is no comprehensive listing of actions, by a user or within the operating system, that would affect particular Registry keys.

MALWARE AND THE WINDOWS REGISTRY

Most of the time when looking for indications of malware remaining persistent on a system, I'll go right to the Registry. Not only is this a popular location for malware to use to maintain persistence, but very often new persistence locations in the Registry are discovered by analyzing a new bit of malware that's been found. The reason is that many malware authors will become aware of these locations and how to use them well before anyone else, including antivirus vendors and malware analysts.

Analyzing the Registry for new bits of malware can often be a game of catch-up, as some new means of persistence may have been discovered by the bad guys and not yet commonly known by responders and incident analysts.

To make matters worse, not only do malware authors make extensive use of the Registry so that their creations will remain persistent on systems across reboots and logins, but some have even gone so far as to place entire Windows executable files into binary value data!

The other challenge of Registry analysis is the fact that while the binary structure of the Registry remains the same across versions of Windows (ie, the core binary structure of the Registry is very much the same between Windows 2000 and Windows 7, inclusive), important keys and values change between versions, often very drastically. In many cases, this applies to the base operating system as well as to new and even existing applications. This can make it very difficult for an analyst who figures out and documents some specific Registry keys and values based on a particular version of an application and operating system, only to find those settings null and void when an updated version of the application or the operating system is released.

One example of these changes is how user search terms are maintained within the Registry. With Windows XP, you could find various search terms under a key named "ACMru." Subkeys beneath this key pertained to particular form fields that a user could submit terms to when performing searches. With Windows Vista, search terms were recorded in a file, but not in the Registry. With Windows 7, search terms are again stored in the Registry, but under an entirely different path, beneath a key named "WordWheelQuery." These keys are discussed in greater detail in chapter Case Studies: User Hives.

It is not the goal of this chapter or even this book to provide a comprehensive listing of all similar changes that occur between various versions of the Windows operating system; rather, it is enough to understand that these changes can and do occur, and it is incumbent upon analysts to keep up-to-date on analysis techniques and procedures, particularly as they pertain to the Windows Registry.

Tip

Something that is very important to keep in mind when considering whether to engage in live response activities (as opposed to acquiring an image of the hard drive and conducting postmortem analysis) is that while your actions do have an effect on the system (processes loaded into memory, files created on the system as a result of your actions, etc.), so does your *inaction*. Think about it. A live system is running, with things going on all the time. Even while a system just sits there, processes are running and actions are occurring on the system. With Windows XP, simply wait 24 h and a System Restore Point will (by default) be automatically created. Wait 3 days and the system will conduct a limited defragmentation. Windows can reach out for and install updates. All of these can overwrite data that could possibly be recovered. Also consider the fact that if someone is exfiltrating data from your systems, then while you wait and do nothing, they continue to take more data. So the question of live response really comes down to (1) do I do nothing or (2) do I take the correct actions to protect my organization as best I can under the circumstances?

What Is the Windows Registry?

So far we've talked about Registry analysis, but what is the Windows Registry? According to Microsoft KB article 256986 (found online at http://support.microsoft.com/kb/256986) the Windows Registry is a "central hierarchal database," intended "to store information that is necessary to configure the system for one or more users, applications, and hardware devices." In short, the Windows Registry is a binary data structure meant to replace the configuration and initialization (*.ini*) files used by previous versions of Windows (okay, Windows 3.1). For your normal Windows user and for most administrators, this is pretty transparent and means very little to them. Most users and administrators do not interact directly with the Registry, instead interacting with it through some sort of graphical user interface (GUI), such as the Registry Editor that is distributed with most Windows installations. Fig. 1.1 illustrates the Registry Editor on Windows XP.

As you can see in Fig. 1.1, the Registry Editor provides a user or administrator with an easy means to navigate the Registry by providing a layer of abstraction. There may be times when even an administrator doesn't go as far as using the Registry Editor, as most interaction with the Registry may be through application installation (ie, launching the installation process, which then adds and modifies Registry entries) or removal.

Many of the instructions and KB articles available from Microsoft that deal with interacting with the Registry do so by having the reader interact with a GUI component of the Windows Explorer shell, or through another application. For example, a user wouldn't

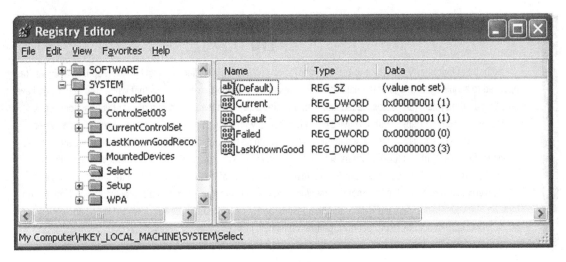

Figure 1.1 Registry Editor.

directly access the Registry to delete keys and values created when an application is installed; instead, they would likely use the Add/ Remove Programs Control Panel applet. In those instances where Microsoft does identify specific Registry keys, there is always a stern warning against directly modifying the Registry, as to do so might leave the system inoperable.

Note

Graphical tools are primarily intended to make a task easier for the user but also protect the users from themselves. The GUI prevents the user from seeing what happens "under the hood." However, that's exactly where malware authors and attackers go…under the hood. The best source of information regarding autostart locations in the Registry is the antivirus vendors; as they receive new malware samples to analyze, they begin to see what methods and autostart locations (and persistence mechanisms) these folks are using. Neither Microsoft nor application vendors provide such a breadth of information. Further, relying on antivirus vendors to let us know what they're seeing is reactive, not proactive.

Purpose of the Windows Registry

Microsoft tells us that the Registry maintains configuration information about the system, but what does this really mean? It's one thing to say that the Registry replaces the text-based .ini files of old and is a database that maintains configuration information about the system and applications that run on it, but what does that really mean to the incident responder and forensic analyst? We're not so much interested in what this means to a user or to an administrator;

instead, what we'd like to know is, what does that mean to those of us who would need to delve into this resource? Well, what it means is that there's a lot of information in the Registry that tells the operating system and applications what to do, where to put things, and how to react to certain stimulus. There are a lot of little nuances that can have a significant effect on incident response and forensic analysis that are all managed through the Registry. For example, one Registry value tells the operating system to clear the pagefile when the system is shut down, and another setting tells the operating system whether or not to enable the use of a hibernation file, while yet another value disables the updating of last access times within the file system. When you think about it, all of these values can have a significant impact on a wide range of incident response activities and digital forensic analysis.

Devices that have been connected to the system are tracked through the Registry. Information about devices is maintained in the Registry so that the devices are recognized and presented as they were previously when they're reconnected to the system; as such, this information can be extremely valuable to a forensic analyst when attempting to track the use of an iPod, digital camera, or thumb drive on a system or across several systems.

The Registry also tracks a great deal of information about a user's activities. This can be very beneficial to a forensic analyst. Let's say you sit down to play a game of Solitaire on your Windows system, and the first time you run the application, you get the default settings, with respect to how many cards are dealt and how the game is timed and scored. You change most of these settings to something else and then resize and reposition the game window. When you're done playing, you close the window and shut down the system. The next day, you come back and launch the game again, and all of your settings are still there, having persisted across a log out and reboot. This is due to the fact that the settings are recorded in the Registry, so that the next time you launch the application or game, your most recent and preferred settings are read, and the application window is presented in the location, size, and shape that you left it.

Warning

Not all applications create a presence in the Registry. For example, some peer-to-peer (P2P) sharing applications are cross-platform and Java-based, and as such don't rely on the Windows Registry to store information. Instead, they use configuration files in order to make cross-platform coding easier.

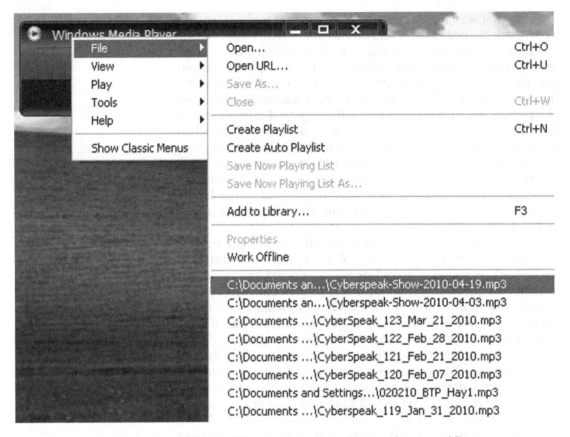

Figure 1.2 Windows Media Player File menu item showing recently accessed files.

The Registry also tracks a number of other user actions, such as clicking through the Program menu to start an application, as well as keeping track of recently accessed files that are associated with various applications, such as MS Word, Excel, Windows Media Player, etc. The user will generally see these files on the Recent Documents portion of the Program menu, or as part of a drop-down menu specific to the application, as illustrated in Fig. 1.2.

Much of the information tracked in the Registry can be associated with a time value of some sort, and as such, the Registry becomes something of a log file. As will be addressed later in this chapter, all Registry keys maintain a property called their "Last-Write time." Whenever a Registry key is modified...created, values or subkeys are created or deleted, or a value is modified...the key's LastWrite time is updated to reflect that change. This value is analogous to a file's last modification time (although, as of yet, I have been unable to locate an accessible application programming interface, or "API" that allows for the arbitrary modification of LastWrite times, as there is with file MAC times). However, this is not the only place that time stamps are maintained in the Registry. Many values contain time and date information, and often in different formats. In this way, the Registry can be considered in many respects to be a log file.

Tip

While analyzing a system to determine if a user had looked at images or videos (as opposed to a virus or worm putting those files on the system), I ran across the use of the Window Washer application, which is intended to "clean up" behind a user. In this case, the application maintained the last date and time that it had been run in its own Registry values, which I was able to correlate to other, similar data. There were two separate values, one for date and one for time, maintained as strings.

Location of the Windows Registry on Disk

From a forensic analysis perspective, an analyst does not generally interact with the Registry through the Registry Editor. An analyst will most likely interact with Registry hives files directly, through a commercial forensic analysis application, or as a result of extracting them from a file system or from an acquired image. There are a number of such tools available, several of which will be discussed in chapter Processes and Tools. However, it is important for the analyst to know where these files exist on disk so that they can be retrieved and analyzed.

The main, core system Registry hive files (specifically, SAM, Security, Software, and System) can be found in the *Windows\system32\config* folder, as illustrated in Fig. 1.3.

The files themselves illustrated in Fig. 1.3 are referred to as "hive" files, as the files contain the binary database structures or "hives." These are the hive files that maintain configuration information about the system, such as operating system version and

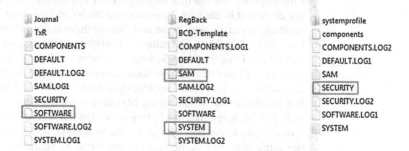

Figure 1.3 Registry hive files in the *Windows\system32\config* folder (Windows 7).

settings, local user account information, installed software and components, etc.

On Windows Vista and above systems, there is another hive file in the *Windows\system32\config* folder named "Components." While there are a number of keys and values listed in this hive file, as of this writing, I have yet to find anything significant from a forensics or incident response standpoint; however, this may change in the future as more attention is focused on this file.

With Windows 8, we found that there were several new Registry hives files in the *Windows\system32\config* folder: BBI, BCD, Components, Drivers, and ELAM. Not a great deal of information is available on the purpose of these files, but they can be opened in a Registry viewer application. However, a search on the Microsoft website reveals that "ELAM" stands for "early launch anti-malware," which is intended to protect Windows 8 systems from rootkits. From a reference to ELAM at the Microsoft Dev Center (found online at http://msdn.microsoft.com/en-us/library/windows/desktop/hh848061(v=vs.85).aspx):

> *Windows 8 introduces a new feature called Secure Boot, which protects the Windows boot configuration and components, and loads an Early Launch Anti-malware (ELAM) driver. This driver starts before other boot-start drivers and enables the evaluation of those drivers and helps the Windows kernel decide whether they should be initialized.*

My testing system was conducted on a Windows 8.1 laptop, with just MS Office 2013 installed, and little else. As such, I did not have an "ELAM driver" installed.

AMCACHE.HVE

When I first began working with a Windows 8 (and later Windows 8.1) system, one of the items about this system was "new," was the existence of a file named "AmCache.hve" in the *C:\Windows\AppCompat\Programs* folder. I initially opened this file in a hex editor and almost immediately noticed that it appeared to have a structure similar to a Registry hive file. I then opened the file in a Registry viewer application (several viewers are discussed in chapter Processes and Tools) and saw that the viewer application did, indeed, parse and display the contents of the file. After I created a Windows 10 Technical Preview virtual machine (VM) in VirtualBox, I saw that the Windows 10 system also had this file. Then, in January 2015, I noticed that at some point near the end of 2014, update installed on my Windows 7 systems (host systems, as well as testing VMs) had resulted in the AmCache.hve file being created on those systems, as well. This file is not part of what we refer to as the Windows Registry, but it does seem to contain data pertinent to forensic analysts and follows the same structure as the Registry hive files. As such, this file will be discussed in greater detail in chapter Analyzing the System Hives.

Information specific to individual users is maintained in the NTUSER.DAT hive file that is located in the user profile. For Windows 2000, XP, and 2003, the user profiles are found in the "Documents and Settings" directory at the root of the system drive, whereas for Vista and above, the user profiles are found in the "Users" directory. There is also another user hive that is merged with the NTUSER.DAT hive file on a live system when a user logs in, allowing for a unified presentation of the information from both hives. This is the USRCLASS.DAT hive, located in the user's profile, in the *Local Settings\Application Data\Microsoft\ Windows* folder on Windows XP and 2003, and in the *AppData\ Local\Microsoft\Windows* folder on Windows 7 and above. The information maintained in this hive file can vary between operating system versions; some information found in the NTUSER. DAT hive on Windows XP has been moved to the USRCLASS.DAT hive on Windows Vista and above. Many of these differences will be addressed later in this book.

REGISTRY REDIRECTION AND VIRTUALIZATION

With more modern versions of Windows, Microsoft has implemented redirection and virtualization with respect to the Registry. Registry redirection (description found at the Microsoft website online at http://msdn.microsoft.com/en-us/library/aa384232(VA.85).aspx) essentially means that on 64-bit versions of Windows, some Registry calls by 32-bit applications are redirected to another portion of the Software hive. What this means to an analyst is that some 32-bit application information (ie, those keys that are not identified as being shared between 64- and 32-bit applications) will appear in the HKEY_LOCAL_MACHINE\Software\ Wow6432Node key path, rather than in the HKEY_LOCAL_MACHINE\Software key path. Similar redirection does not occur within the Software key in the user's hive. The Microsoft Technet site provides a list of shared keys, found online at https://msdn.microsoft.com/en-us/library/windows/desktop/ aa384253(v=vs.85).aspx. Note that Registry reflection for synchronization has been disabled as of Windows 2008 and Windows 7.

Registry virtualization is a bit different, and impacts an examiner's analysis differently. Microsoft describes Registry virtualization (description found online at http://msdn.microsoft.com/en-us/library/aa965884 (VS.85).aspx) as, beginning with Windows Vista, "an application compatibility technology that enables registry write operations that have global impact to be redirected to per-user locations." What this means is that Registry modifications (writes, anything to create keys or values) that have a global impact on the system will be written instead to a "virtual store" (*HKEY_USERS\< SID>_Classes\VirtualStore\Machine\Software* key path), which translates to the USRCLASS.DAT hive file mentioned above.

Portions of the Windows Registry visible through the Registry Editor are "volatile," meaning that they are populated when the system is booted or when a user logs in and do not exist on disk when the system is shut off. This is extremely important for first responders and forensic analysts to understand, as there may be valuable data that does not exist within an acquired image and *must* be collected while the system is still running.

One example of volatile data is the *HKEY_CURRENT_USER* hive. When viewed through the Registry Editor, you can clearly see this hive, and after a little exploration, you'll find that the information in this portion of the Registry pertains specifically to the logged on user. However, when you shut the system down and analyze an acquired image, you won't find an *HKEY_CURRENT_USER* hive or any file by that name. That's because this hive is populated by using the hive for the user that's logged into the system.

For the currently logged in user, the *HKEY_CURRENT_USER\ SessionInformation* key contains a value named ProgramCount that keeps track of the number of programs you have running on your desktop. This is the count you see when you lock your workstation. However, this value doesn't exist in the user's NTUSER. DAT file when the system is shut down.

Another example of volatile Registry keys and values is the *HKEY_LOCAL_MACHINE/Hardware* key and its subkeys. This key stores information regarding the devices connected to the system (CPU, keyboard, mouse, hard drive, etc.) and their assigned resources and is populated when the system boots up.

If you open the Registry Editor and navigate to the *HKEY_ LOCAL_MACHINE\System* hive, you'll see a key named "CurrentControlSet," and most likely two others whose names begin with "ControlSet00" and end in a number. The CurrentControlSet doesn't exist when the system is shut down and is populated at boot time from one of the available ControlSets.

Note

When performing postmortem analysis of the Registry, it is a straightforward process to determine which ControlSet had been mounted as the CurrentControlSet on the live system. Simply open the System hive in a viewer and locate that Select key. Beneath that key, you will find a value named "Current," whose data is a number. If the data is "0x0001," the ControlSet mounted as the CurrentControlSet was ControlSet001 (found online at http://support.microsoft.com/kb/100010).

Yet another example of a volatile portion of the Registry is the HKEY_CLASSES_ROOT key. When the system is booted, this key is populated with the contents of the HKEY_LOCAL_ MACHINE\Software\Classes key, and when a user logs in, the

HKEY_CURRENT_USER\Software\Classes key contents are added and, according to Microsoft, take precedence of the entries from HKEY_LOCAL_MACHINE entries (found online at https://msdn.microsoft.com/en-us/library/cc144148(VS.85).aspx).

What's important to keep in mind is that there are portions of the Windows Registry that only exist in memory. Thanks to folks like Aaron Walters and Brendan Dolan-Gavitt (both of Volatility memory analysis fame), this information can be accessed, retrieved, and analyzed; the necessary tools for collecting this data will be discussed later in this book.

Tip

Understanding the version of Windows that you're analyzing can have a significant impact on your examination. For example, Windows XP maintains System Restore Points by default, which means that depending on the system being used, you may have access to a great deal of historical data. Portions of the Registry are maintained in System Restore Points (ie, not all portions of the hives are stored, as it wouldn't do well to reset a user's password to an older one when restoring a system to a previous state) and can be easily accessed during analysis. Also, keep in mind that System Restore Points are created for a number of reasons, such as driver installations, as well as simply being created every 24 h. More recent versions of Windows use Volume Shadow Copies to maintain backups of files, and accessing those Volume Shadow Copies can give you a view into the Registry in an earlier state. Understanding System Restore Points and Volume Shadow Copies can provide a view into Registry data that isn't accessible through any other means.

Finally, Windows 7 includes the ability to run XPMode, a specific Windows XP installation intended to provide backward compatibility to run older applications. Users can install applications that have trouble running in Windows 7 into the XPMode Virtual PC installation and access them via the Windows 7 desktop. This also means that on any Windows 7 system with XPMode installed, there is a second source of potentially valuable Registry hive files!

Where Else Can We Find Registry Data?

Another Registry hive file that has gained a great deal of attention since Windows 8 was released is the AmCache.hve file, found in the *Windows\AppCompat\Programs* folder. Yogesh Khatri published some interesting research to his blog (found online at http://www.swiftforensics.com/2013/12/amcachehve-in-windows-8-goldmine-for.html) regarding the AmCache.hve file in December 2013. In his initial post, he indicated that the information he was sharing was a "logical continuation" of Corey Harrell's blog post regarding the Application Experience and Compatibility feature of Windows (Corey's post can be found online at http://journeyintoir.blogspot.in/2013/12/revealing-recentfilecachebcf-file.html). What this file, formatted in the same manner as Registry hive files, appears to contain is information regarding applications that have been installed and possibly executed on the system. There is still more research to be done, but Yogesh has documented a great deal of information from this hive file, including Registry key names that appear to be MFT file reference numbers (for those systems running the NTFS file system), allowing the information to be tied back to the file system. This hive file will be discussed in greater later in the book.

On Windows 7 systems (I don't have an image of Windows Vista system to check for this), there's a file "System Volume Information" folder named Syscache.hve that follows the same format as Registry hive files, and in fact, you can extract this file from an image and open it in a Registry viewer application. At the time of this writing, there is not a great deal of public information available about this file. There is some information available at the "Windows Registry Knowledge Base" (which can be found online at https://code.google.com/p/winreg-kb/wiki/SysCache), but it largely seems incomplete. This file is likely associated with Volume Shadow Copies in some way.

Nomenclature

When working in the incident response and digital forensics field, as with many other fields, it is necessary to have and observe specificity of terminology. Basically, this is just a fancy way of saying that we all need to agree on what different things are called, and then call them that. When I took one of my first vendor-specific training courses for a commercial forensic analysis application, the instructor spent the first hour or more explaining what a "CPU," "hard drive" or "disk," a "computer system" really were. As someone with an electrical engineering degree, if you ask me to go into a room with a computer and retrieve a "CPU," I'm going to open the computer, go to the motherboard and extract that little black square thing with all of the pins coming out of it, so I really hope that you aren't expecting the entire computer.

In short, it's important that when talking about parts of the Registry, we all have to have a consistent understanding of what it is we're referring to, so that we can communicate clearly and avoid (as much as possible) confusion and misunderstandings. Fig. 1.4 illustrates the various components of the Registry, specifically keys, subkeys, values, and data. We'll go into more depth regarding the details of the binary structure of these components.

From the Registry Editor view illustrated in Fig. 1.4, "keys" and "subkeys" are the folders displayed in the left-hand pane of the

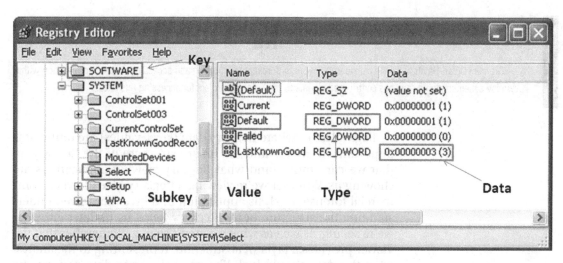

Figure 1.4 Registry nomenclature.

editor. This is an apt metaphor, in that keys can contain or point to other keys (ie, subkeys) as well as values. Keys also contain very valuable information from a forensic perspective (their LastWrite time) within their binary structure. Values, in the right-hand pane in Fig. 1.4, are much simpler and contain data of a specific type, be it a string value, multiple string values, binary, or DWORD, which is just a 32-bit binary value.

More importantly, we now have a frame of reference for discussing the Registry and Registry analysis throughout the rest of this book, and a common understanding of what a "key" is and what a "value" is, and how they relate to each other. Many times in such discussions, consistent terminology may be reversed or simply not used, and confusion ensues.

Registry Structure

Now that we've seen where the Registry "lives" within a live system, and subsequently within an acquired image, it's important to take that one step further and understand the structure of the Registry itself, as we may find vitally important information in places other than within Registry hive files. For example, we may find Registry data within unallocated space from an acquired image, or within the hive file itself (yes, Registry hive files do contain "unallocated space"!). We may also find Registry data and indeed entire hives within a memory dump from a live, running system, or within the Windows pagefile.

Tip

Brendan Dolan-Gavitt has done considerable work with respect to locating and accessing Registry information within Windows memory dumps and has contributed plugins to the Volatility project for accessing this data.

Regardless of where Registry data (keys, values) are found, it is important to understand the binary structure of the Registry, so that we can understand what Registry viewing applications are showing us. Whether we're viewing a Registry hive file via a commercial forensic analysis application or a hive file viewer, understanding the structure of the Registry helps us understand what we're seeing, as well as what we aren't seeing. Remember that the viewer provides a layer of abstraction, representing to the analyst what the data should look like; as such, some data may not be apparent or easily read and understood, due to shortcomings in the viewer, the nature of the data, etc.

REGISTRY HIVES AND SEARCHES

When performing PCI data breach investigations, one of the things I needed to do was search across the entire hard drive for what could be credit card data, including both the numbers themselves, as well as track data. In one particular instance, my search revealed a number of hits within Registry hive files, specifically an NTUSER.DAT hive in one user profile, and within the Software hive file. Viewing the data around the search hits within the hive files, I did not see anything that resembled a Registry key or value; likewise, opening the hive files in a viewer and searching for the search hits provided no indications that the hits were key or value names, or in Registry data. As it turned out, the search hits were actually located in file slack, something that we were able to determine through an understanding of the binary structure of the Registry.

Thankfully, the binary structure of the Registry itself has remained fairly consistent across the various versions of the Windows operating system, from Windows NT all the way through to Windows 7. This means that a viewer application that understands the structure of the Registry will, for the most part, work equally well on all versions. What's changed, however, are the names and locations of various keys and values...where data is stored and what format it is in will differ between versions of the Windows operating system. Windows XP, for example, maintained information about WAPs that had been connected to (connections that were managed by Windows, rather than a third-party utility) in a binary data structure within values beneath a specific Registry key. Vista and Windows 7 employ an entirely different format for similar information and add some additional information…all of which is located beneath a different Registry key.

A great place to start in developing an understanding of the hive file structure is Mark Russinovich's "Inside the Registry" article in Windows NT Magazine (available online at http://technet.microsoft.com/en-us/library/cc750583.aspx). This article provides an excellent overview of the structure of the Registry, identifying the various cell types (key, value, subkey list, value list, etc.), bins, and the cell map relationships between them.

When I initially began looking into the structure of the Registry from a programming perspective, I relied heavily on Peter Nordahl's work with his offline NT Password and Registry Editor (found online at http://pogostick.net/~pnh/ntpasswd) in order to understand the binary structures that comprise a Registry hive file. Peter's utility allows you to boot a Windows system (originally from a diskette, there's now a version that runs on a boot CD) and, for one, modify any password. When you reboot the system, you can then log into the system using the user account you select and the new password you created. I used an early version of this utility to access Windows XP systems turned in by departing users in a corporate environment, and I have used the boot CD version more recently when booting an acquired image through VMWare. While the utility itself has been extremely useful, what I was looking for was the source code, which Peter provides. Within the source distribution archive is a file called "ntreg.h," which contains constant values and definitions for various structures within the Registry. Within the source archive you will also find a file named "WinReg.txt," which has a bit of a summary of what's in the ntreg.h file, including descriptions of some of the structures without as much detail as the header file. Using this information, along with a hex editor, I was able to start writing my own binary Registry hive file parser in Perl, allowing me access the information stored within the files and obtain as much detail as I wanted. As I began developing this hive file parser, I ran across the Parse::Win32Registry Perl module (available online at https://code.google.com/p/parse-win32registry/) written by James Macfarlane. This module provides an easy-to-use object-oriented (OO) interface for accessing various structures within the hive files. I should point out that this is an entirely different module from the Win32::TieRegistry module that ships with ActiveState's Perl distribution, in that the Win32::TieRegistry module allows a Perl programmer to interact with a *live* Registry (on a running system, as may be the case during incident response), not directly with the hive files, as is the case with James' module.

In the spring of 2008, Jolanta Thomassen asked me if I would act as her sponsor for her graduate thesis, which involved understanding the structure of the Windows Registry with a specific focus on locating deleted keys and values within the hive file itself. This topic had intrigued me for quite some time (as a reference for her, I provided a link to a UseNet post I'd made in 2001 asking about unallocated space in hive files), and Jolanta did a fantastic job not only in understanding what deleted keys and values "look like" but also how to recover them and present them in an easy to understand format. The result of her work is a utility called "regslack," the Windows portable executable (PE) version of which I use quite regularly, and I have to say, effectively.

In February 2009, Peter Norris posted his master's thesis regarding *The Internal Structure of the Windows Registry* online at http://amnesia.gtisc.gatech.edu/~moyix/suzibandit.ltd.uk/MSc/. Peter's work goes into considerable detail regarding the binary structure of the Windows Registry and also referenced Jolanta's work. It is beyond the scope and focus of this book to review Peter's work in detail, and such a review is left as an exercise to the reader.

Mark Russinovich's "Inside the Registry" article, mentioned earlier in this chapter, describes a number of Registry cell or "record" types. Of those, we are primarily interested in and will be focusing on the key and value cells/records, as these provide the vast majority of information of interest to forensic analysts. Other cell types (subkey list, value list, etc.), while significant, are beyond the scope of this book, and a detailed examination of those cell types is left as an exercise to the reader. These cell types are simply pointers to lists of subkeys or values, and are not key or value structures themselves.

Note

In January 2015, FBI Special Agent Eric Zimmerman began his own blog called "Binary Foray," describing it as a "blog about programming, digital forensics, and other such things." Eric had already developed several tools, two of which are specifically designed to assist analysts in engaging in Registry analysis: ShellBag Explorer and Registry Explorer. Both of the tools will be discussed at greater length in the subsequent chapters of this book. Eric has put a great deal of effort into developing a detailed understanding of the structure of the Windows Registry, including developing not only an extremely detailed understanding of various cell types within the Registry, but also developing tools that expose those structures to analysts. At the time of this writing, I would definitely consider his blog posts on the various Registry structures to be required reading for anyone interested in developing more than the most basic understanding of the Windows Registry.

Registry hive files are made up of 4-KB sections or "bins." These bins are meant to make allocation of new space (as the hive file grows), as well as the maintenance of the hive file itself, easier. The first 4 bytes of a normal hive file starts with "regf" (or 0x66676572). From there, as you traverse through the hive file on a binary level, as with a hex editor, every 4096 bytes you should see "hbin" (0x6E696268). Per Peter Norris' thesis work, various cells within the hive files do not cross hbin sections; that is, a key cell will not be split between two adjacent hbin sections, overlapping the border between them. As such, the hbin sections can be considered self-contained.

Tip

As with other types of files, allocation of new space for hive files, as the Registry grows, can pose something interesting challenges for a forensic analyst. When a new hbin section is required, that 4-KB section is, in many cases, allocated from previously used space within the file system, space that at one time may have contained valid data. During one examination in particular, I ran a search for credit card numbers and received several hits "in" Registry hive files. Closer examination of the data indicated that the discovered credit card numbers were not part of the "live" Registry (not contained in key or value names, nor in value data), and that the most likely explanation was that the numbers had resided in sectors that had previously comprised another file (possibly a database) which had been deleted.

The first hbin marker is very important, as this is the base location for offset values listed with the key and value cells throughout the rest of the hive file. What this means is that when you're reading values within a key cell structure (which we'll be looking at shortly) and you read an offset, that value is the offset from the first hbin marker. For example, as we'll see shortly, each key cell contains a value for the offset to its parent key, which essentially points back to that key. That offset, in bytes, is measured from the beginning of the first hbin marker, which itself is 4096 bytes from the beginning of the hive file. On the surface of this, you may be wondering how this information is useful. Several open source tools that assist the analyst with locating and extracting (ie, "carving") data from unallocated space within an image allow the analyst to designate a header and footer for locating data or to designate a header or marker (also known as a "magic number") and then read in a set number of bytes. These data carving tools can be used to search unallocated space or similar unstructured data such as the Windows pagefile or a hibernation file for Registry "hbin" sections.

Registry Key Cells

The Registry "hbin" sections are made up of several types of cells, but for our purposes, we're going to focus on the key and value cells. Key cells (or "keys") are very important to forensic analysts as they contain time-based information within their structure, in the form of their LastWrite time. The LastWrite time is a 64-bit FILETIME structure, marking the number of 100 ns intervals since midnight of January 1, 1601 (a description of the FILETIME structure can be found online at http://support.microsoft.com/kb/188768). A key cell (without the name) is 80 bytes long and starts with a 4-byte (in Microsoft parlance, a "DWORD") value indicating its size, followed by the node identifier, node type, the offset to the key's parent, the number of subkeys, the offset to the subkey list, the number of values, the offset to the value list, the offset to the security identifier, and the length of the key name (begins immediately after the key structure). Note that this is not a comprehensive list of the values within the key cell structure but rather an overview of the values that are of greatest interest. Fig. 1.5 illustrates the binary structure of a Registry key (viewed in a hex editor) with the node identifier (ID) and LastWrite time values of the structure highlighted.

As illustrated in Fig. 1.5, the node ID is "6E 6B" (0x6B6E in little endian format), or "nk," and is followed by the node type of 0x2C, which indicates a root node (0x20 indicates a "normal" key node). Immediately following the node type is the LastWrite time, which is a 64-bit FILETIME object.

Warning

It was once thought that a key LastWrite time was only updated when some action was taken through the API: a key was created, or a subkey or value was added or deleted, for example. In 2012, Joakim Schicht created a small utility named "SetRegTime" that allows a user to modify key LastWrite times to arbitrary values through the API. The utility was first available on Google Code (found online at https://code.google.com/p/mft2csv/wiki/SetRegTime), which includes some explanation of the utility as well as examples of how to use it. The utility was later found on GitHub (found online at https://github.com/jschicht/SetRegTime), which includes a link back to the Google Code page.

Table 1.1 lists the key cell structure details, illustrating the elements of that structure that are of primary interest to forensic analysts.

Table 1.1 should not be considered all-inclusive, as it details those structure elements that are most important to forensic analysts. Again, the size of the structure detailed in Table 1.1 is 80 bytes, and the first 4 bytes of the structure contain the size of the

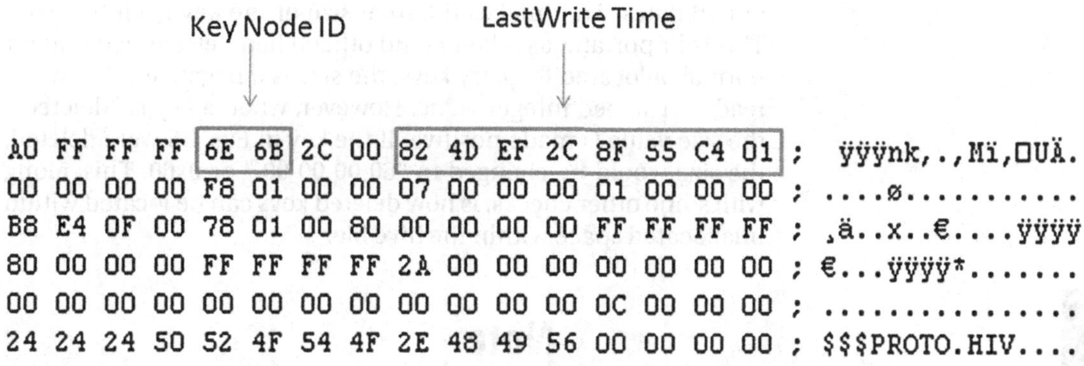

Key Node ID   LastWrite Time

```
A0 FF FF FF  6E 6B  2C 00  82 4D EF 2C 8F 55 C4 01 ;  ÿÿÿnk,.,Mï,☐UÄ.
00 00 00 00  F8 01 00 00  07 00 00 00 01 00 00 00 ;  ....ø..........
B8 E4 0F 00  78 01 00 80  00 00 00 00 FF FF FF FF ;  ‚ä..x..€....ÿÿÿÿ
80 00 00 00  FF FF FF FF  2A 00 00 00 00 00 00 00 ;  €...ÿÿÿÿ*.......
00 00 00 00  00 00 00 00  00 00 00 00 0C 00 00 00 ;  ................
24 24 24 50  52 4F 54 4F  2E 48 49 56 00 00 00 00 ;  $$$PROTO.HIV....
```

Figure 1.5 Registry key structure with node ID and LastWrite time.

Table 1.1 Registry Key Cell Structure Details

Offset (bytes)	Size (bytes)	Description
0	4	Size
4	2	Node ID ("nk," or 0x6B6E)
6	2	Node type (0x2C or 0x20)
8	8	LastWrite time
20	4	Offset to this key's parent
24	4	Number of subkeys
32	4	Offset to the list of subkey records
36	4	Number of values
44	4	Offset to the value list
48	4	Offset to security identifier record
76	2	Length of the key name

key cell, which includes the key name and any necessary padding. Therefore, the total size of a Registry key is the 80 byte header, the name, and padding; for the key illustrated in Fig. 1.5, that is 96 bytes.

The size value (the first 4 bytes or "DWORD") is an important aspect of the key structure of which to take notice. When read as an unsigned integer, the size is "4294967200," and we know that a single key would not usually be expected to be on the order of 4 GB in size. However, when read as a signed integer value, those 4 bytes equal "-96." Again, the key "header" itself is 80 bytes, and the actual name of the key begins immediately after the key structure. The name of the key illustrated in Fig. 1.5, "$$$PROTO.HIV," is 12 bytes and there are an additional 4 bytes of padding, rounding out 16 bytes. That makes the total size of the key itself 96 bytes. This is important, as Jolanta (and others) had determined that for normal, allocated Registry keys, the size is a negative value when read as a signed integer value. However, when a key is "deleted," the size value is made positive. If the key in Fig. 1.5 were deleted, the size would be changed to "60 00 00 00," or 0x60. This, along with some other checks, is how deleted keys can be located within unallocated space within the hive file.

Note

Time-based information is maintained in the Registry (and on Windows systems, in general) in a number of formats. There are values whose data consists of (in part or entirely) a 32-bit Unix epoch time format, while the LastWrite times of keys, as well as data of some values, consist of 64-bit FILETIME objects. Still other time-based data is maintained as 128-bit SYSTEMTIME objects (a description of the SYSTEMTIME structure can be found online at https://msdn.microsoft.com/en-us/library/ms724950(VA.85).aspx) and others are simply maintained as strings (for example, the Skype application has a value named "LastUpdatedDate" in the user's NTUSER.DAT file with string data of "01/10/2009").

Registry Value Cells

The other type of cell that we want to take a close look at is the value cell. Remember, Registry keys can "contain" subkeys and values; actually, as we've seen, a key doesn't actually contain this information, as it instead has offsets to pointers to subkey and value lists. Value cells, on the other hand, are much simpler, as they don't contain pointers to any other cells. They are important as they do contain value names and point to the data that, in many cases, we're interested in knowing and understanding. Fig. 1.6 illustrates the binary structure of a value cell, with the value node identifier and value type highlighted.

Table 1.2 provides the relevant value cell structure details. As with the key cell, the first 4 bytes of a value cell (as illustrated in Fig. 1.6) contain the size of the cell.

Value Node ID   Value Type

```
D8 FF FF FF  76 6B  0B 00  12 00 00 00 68 03 00 00 ; Øÿÿÿvk......h...
01 00 00 00  01 00  3D E1 43 75 72 72 65 6E 74 55 ; ......=áCurrentU
73 65 72 00  00 00 00 00 00 E8 FF FF FF 55 00 53 00 ; ser.....èÿÿÿU.S.
45 00 52 00 4E 00 41 00 4D 00 45 00 00 00 3D E1 ; E.R.N.A.M.E...=á
```

Figure 1.6 Registry value structure with node ID and value type.

Table 1.2 Registry Value Cell Structure Details

Offset (bytes)	Size (bytes)	Description
0	4	Size (as a negative number)
4	2	Node ID ("vk," or 0x6B76)
6	2	Value name length
8	4	Data length
12	4	Offset to data
16	4	Value type

Notice that while value cells contain some specific information, something that they do not contain is a FILETIME object, nor any other reference to a time stamp of any kind. Again, as with the key cell, not all of the value cell structure elements are listed, and Table 1.2 should not be viewed as all-inclusive. For example, immediately after the "value type" element is a 2-byte element called "Flags," and as of this writing, I have not been able to locate an available description of this element, nor of its use.

DATA STRUCTURES FOR THE WIN!

Most analysts will probably look at this information on the structure of Registry keys and values, and wonder to themselves, "when would I ever use something like this?" I'll tell you, I use this information *all* the time. Seriously. The first edition of this book was published in 2011, and even in the early months of 2014, I was using this information to great effect on several examinations. In one particular case, I used the binary structure information for Registry values to identify the use of a Unicode character in the value name that effectively hid the presence of malware from the user, as well as analysts, based on how graphical Registry viewer tools handle the Unicode character. In short, the Unicode character "\xA0" was used in a value name, as well as within the data (a file system path), and that character appeared as a space in viewer tools, so that the value and data appeared to point to a legitimate Microsoft application. Using this information, a hex editor, and some coding skills, I was able to see past this technique and locate the malware.

Registry values can point to data of a variety of types. Table 1.3 lists the available Registry value types, along with their names and descriptions. This information is also available from Microsoft website at http://msdn.microsoft.com/en-us/library/ms724884.aspx.

After walking through all of this information on the structure of individual key and value structures, and even though we haven't

Table 1.3 Registry Value Types

Type	Name	Description
0	REG_NONE	No value type
1	REG_SZ	Unicode null-terminated string; can be Unicode or ASCII
2	REG_EXPAND_SZ	Unicode null-terminated string with environment variables/references
3	REG_BINARY	Binary data (no set length or structure)
4	REG_DWORD	32-bit number
5	REG_DWORD_BIG_ENDIAN	32-bit number
6	REG_LINK	Unicode symbolic link
7	REG_MULTI_SZ	Multiple Unicode strings, each "\00" terminated
8	REG_RESOURCE_LIST	Resource list (resource map)
9	REG_FULL_RESOURCE_DESCRIPTOR	Resource list (hardware description)
10	REG_RESOURCE_REQUIREMENTS _LIST	A series of nested arrays that store information about device drivers
11	REG_QWORD	64-bit number

really gone into how the keys and values are linked together, it should be evident at this point that each hive file is essentially something of a small file system. There's a root key that points to other keys (subkeys) and values. Keys can "contain" or point to other keys and values, and values point to data. The links do not go the other way; however, values do not point back to keys nor do values "contain" keys. So in a way, the keys can be considered to be analogous to folders, with only last modification (LastWrite) time stamps, and values can be considered analogous to files. The Registry hive file can have unallocated space, and keys and values that are deleted become part of the unallocated space within the hive file and can be extracted until they are overwritten (much like files within the file system). It's also possible for value data to contain slack space; if the space allocated for a value data is more than what is actually being used (sound familiar?), then there may be slack space containing data that can be extracted.

Summary

In this chapter, we've taken a look at what the Windows Registry is, on a variety of levels. By now, you should have a basic understanding of not only what the Registry is and its purpose but also where the Registry "lives" on disk and where to look for Registry files within an acquired image. This is extremely important from a forensic analysis perspective, as it allows the analyst to understand issues that may develop through the use of commercial forensic analysis applications. Also, we've addressed more detailed information, going so far as to outline the binary structure of key and value cells. This information allows the analyst to search for and recognize these structures, not only within Registry hive files but also within other data sources, such as the Windows pagefile, memory dumps, and hibernation files, as well as unallocated space on disk.

2

PROCESSES AND TOOLS

INFORMATION IN THIS CHAPTER

- Forensic Analysis

Introduction

When I sat down to address and update/rewrite this chapter for the second edition of the book, I wanted to do two things. First, I removed the "Live Analysis" section of the chapter. The reason for this was that for digital forensic analysis, we're not accessing live systems; access to live systems most often occurs during enterprise incident response, and many organizations already have a capability for accessing the Windows Registry on live systems during such incidents, at an enterprise level. As such, our assumed means for interacting with the Windows Registry throughout the rest of this chapter will be through postmortem or "dead box" analysis. After all, this is the "use case" many of us encounter during day-to-day analysis operations; like many, I either access images acquired from systems or I'll be asked to take a look at specific Registry files that were extracted from images.

I should also point out that F-Response (more information on F-Response is available online at http://www.f-response.com) provides remote access to live systems, but does so in manner such that tools mentioned in this chapter can be used very effectively in conjunction with F-Response to achieve the desired analysis.

Second, I wanted to focus more on analysis processes than tools, focusing on the process but understanding that tools can play an important role in analysis, and that analysis processes are often implemented through the use of tools. Over the years, I've been asked time and again what tools I use for Registry analysis, and what it really comes down to is that the analysis process I'm using defines which tools I use. There are a number of tools available for "Registry analysis" but the tool used depends directly on the analysis process being employed.

Analysts faced with extracting and analyzing data from the Windows Registry may be required to do so in a number of different scenarios. During troubleshooting or incident response scenarios, administrators may want to query multiple systems for Registry data, or an analyst may want to examine Registry hives extracted from an acquired image for indications of an intrusion or violations of acceptable use policies. Regardless of the data to be extracted and reviewed, an analyst is going to use some sort of tool to collect that data, and to some extent analyze it. In this chapter, we'll address some of the options that an analyst has available and present some tools that may be used in those situations. With this foundation, my hope is that analysts will then be able to make decisions on the best option to use for their particular situation.

In this chapter we will be focusing on the use of open source and freely available tools. There are a couple of reasons for this, the first being that such tools are generally accessible to a much wider audience than commercial forensic analysis applications. Second, I feel that it's important for analysts to understand the mechanics of what they're trying to achieve, to understand what's going on "under the hood" before using the commercial forensic analysis applications. Third, there are a number of open source and freely available tools available that provide functionality, either in and of themselves or as part of a process, that commercial forensic analysis applications do not provide. Finally, as an author, I simply cannot afford to purchase all of the forensic analysis applications, and while writing this book, had access to only one of the commercial forensic analysis applications available on the market (ie, ProDiscover).

The processes and tools presented and discussed in this chapter should not be considered an exhaustive list. These are simply the tools I have used or encountered (mostly used) myself and do not indicate a preference either way. Are there other, better tools? Possibly. However, the point I'm trying to make isn't which is the best tool, but to demonstrate what we're trying to accomplish so that you, the reader, will be able to make a decision as to which is the best tool for you. There may be tools available for Linux or Mac platforms, but I will be sticking to the Windows platform; the tools discussed all run on Windows systems. Some of the tools discussed in the chapter will, in fact, work on platforms other than Windows, which does not restrict an analyst to a particular analysis platform.

KNOW YOUR TOOLS

I took a question once from an analyst who was preparing to go to court over an issue with a former employee having been terminated. The tool this analyst was using to parse the Registry, and specifically the user's TypedURLs key, had produced some confusing output; the tool had listed all of the values with the key's LastWrite time, but without each value's name. The question was, how could all of the values have the same time? After all, the defense would make the claim that no person could type over a dozen URLs into the browser's address bar at the same time.

I explained the nature of most recently used values, key versus value structures, how the time stamps applied, and hoped that the explanation helped the analyst with their issue. The fact is that if you're going to use a tool, it's important to be aware of what data it's collecting and how it's displaying that data.

Forensic Analysis

The tool you use for a task depends upon the task itself, doesn't it? When you have a task in front of you, there is a process to completing that task, and for the task or perhaps for various steps within that process, there is a tool that will help you complete that task. Some processes may require a single tool; for some laptop systems, the entire process for disassembling and then reassembling the laptop requires a single screwdriver. Other more complicated processes (building a house) may require a completely different tool—a saw, a hammer, etc.—for various steps of the overall process.

Warning

Tools are fine, processes are great, but one of the biggest issues I've seen when it comes to the analysis of data is analysts understanding what they're looking at and correctly interpreting the data. Tools and processes provide an analyst with a means for extracting and displaying various data from the Registry, be it keys, values, or value data, but it's still incumbent upon the analyst to correctly understand and interpret the meaning and context of that data. Particularly in chapters "Analyzing the System Hives and Case Studies: User Hives" of this book, we will address some of the data that are often misinterpreted, as this can have a significant negative impact on the analyst's findings.

Viewing Registry Hives

One of the first things an analyst may want to do is simply view a Registry hive file; that is, load it into a tool that is capable of interpreting the format and displaying the data within the hive in an easy-to-understand manner. Even with the information about key and value cell formats from chapter "Registry Analysis," most analysts are unlikely to open a hive file in a hex editor to view the contents of the file and will most often use a viewer written to display hive files.

Tip

Opening a hive file in a hex editor is not always a bad thing. In fact, it can be a very valuable troubleshooting step. For example, if you're using any of the tools described in this chapter and not getting the information back that you were expecting to see, or any information at all, it's usually a good idea to try opening the hive file in a hex editor to see if it's really a hive file, or if perhaps something went awry in the extraction process. Take a look at the first 4 bytes of the file; do you see "regf"? Then go 4 KB into the file (4096 bytes, or offset 0x1000 in hexadecimal format); do you see "hbin"? There have been instances when analysts have been unable to extract information from Registry hive files, only to finally open the file in a hex editor and see that it's full of zeros. Jamie Levy has seen this same thing time and again when assisting Volatility users who have reported that various plugins don't work when run against a memory dump... sometimes part of the process goes wrong and you don't get the data that you were expecting. Before reaching out to get assistance, take a moment to check the data itself, as invariably, that's one of the questions that someone attempting to assist you is going to ask.

RegEdit

Perhaps the commonly available tool for viewing the contents of the Windows Registry is the Registry Editor (aka RegEdit). Many administrators and analysts are likely familiar with interacting with the Windows Registry via the RegEdit tool, as illustrated in Fig. 2.1, which is a tool native to Windows systems.

You can load a Registry hive exported from an image by clicking on the HKEY_LOCAL_MACHINE hive in the RegEdit user interface, then selecting File from the menu bar, and choosing "Load Hive." When the "Load Hive" dialog appears, give the hive you're loading a unique name (such as "Software_Test") and click "Ok." The hive will be added to RegEdit, as illustrated in Fig. 2.2.

Once analysis is complete, simply unload the hive. Select the hive, as illustrated in Fig. 2.2, click File in the menu bar, choose "Unload Hive." Click "Yes" on the "Confirm Unload Hive" dialog that appears, and you're done.

RegEdit offers some limited search functionality but doesn't provide an easy means for looking at key LastWrite times and doesn't offer any functionality for translating binary data into something useful to the analyst. After all, RegEdit is a tool that Microsoft developed for administrators to access the Registry, not specifically for forensic examiners and incident responders. However, this application can be useful in providing an analyst with an initial look at a hive file.

Tip

An artifact of the use of RegEdit is that when the application is closed, the last key that was in focus at the time is recorded in a value in the user's NTUSER.DAT hive file. We'll go into this in more detail in chapter Case Studies: User Hives, but suffice to say at this point that this has been an extremely valuable forensic resource on more than one occasion.

Windows Registry Recovery

The Windows Registry Recovery (WRR) from MiTeC is a tool that I like to use if I simply want to view the contents of a Registry hive file. One of the things I like about WRR is that the interface is very similar to that of RegEdit, and as such, it's nice to be able to operate in a familiar environment.

When you first launch WRR and open a hive file, you'll be presented with an interface similar to what is shown in Fig. 2.3.

On the left-most side of Fig. 2.3, you'll notice that there are several "Explorer Tasks" available, which can be very useful

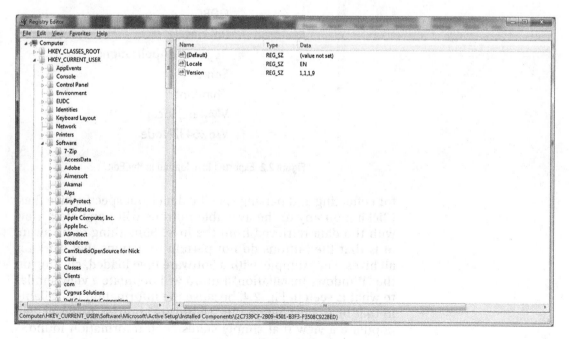

Figure 2.1 The Windows Registry Editor.

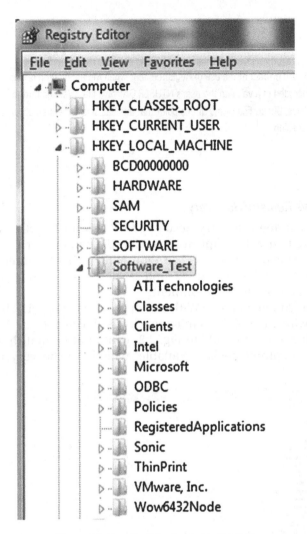

Figure 2.2 Exported hive loaded in RegEdit.

for collecting and parsing specific data from specific hive files. Clicking on any of the available buttons will populate a view with the data retrieved from the hive. Something to be aware of is that the buttons do not pertain to actions that work for all hives. For example, with a Software hive loaded, clicking on the "Windows Installation" button will populate a view similar to what is seen in Fig. 2.4, because the information is available in that hive. Clicking on the "Hardware" button, however, will populate a view that simply states "<no information found>" because the necessary information is found in the System hive, not the Software hive.

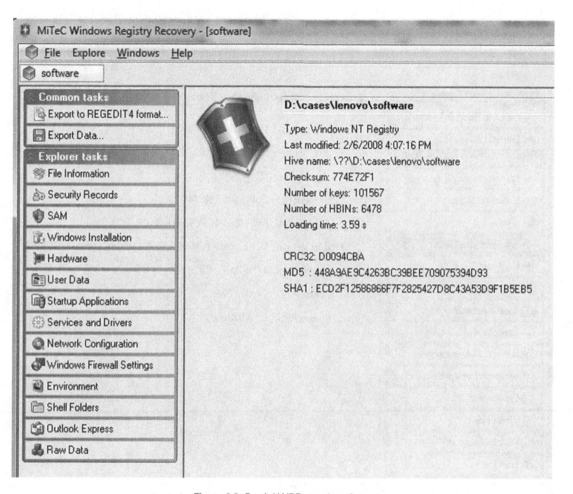

Figure 2.3 Partial WRR user interface.

The Explorer Task functions act as parsers (discussed later in this chapter), albeit without any specific indicators as to the hives to which they apply. Even so, these functions can still be very revealing to an analyst, providing insight into components and information available from various hive files. The information these functions can retrieve is not extensive but it can be informative.

WRR also has a pretty good search capability, or "Find" function that can be very useful when looking for indications of specific artifacts or indicators within a hive file. With a hive opened in WRR, and the "Raw Data" view opened, click on the button with the magnifying glass icon to open the Find dialog, as illustrated in Fig. 2.5.

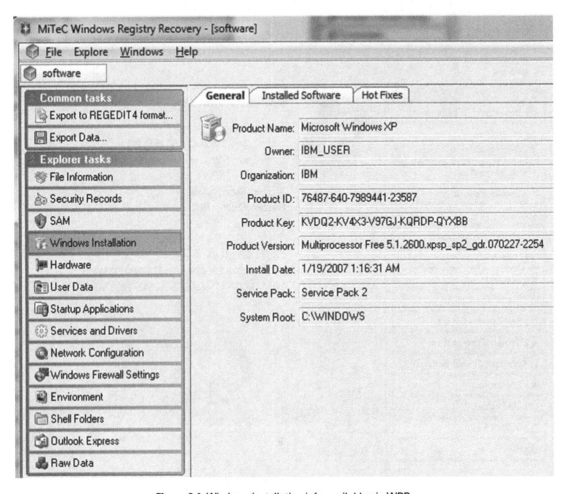

Figure 2.4 Windows installation info available via WRR.

Once the dialog is open, enter your search term, select what structures you want searched (keys, values, data), and click "Find Next". Depending upon how large the hive file is, the search can take several minutes. When the search is complete, any hits will be displayed in the bottom-most pane in the WRR user interface, and double-clicking on any of the hits will cause that location to be opened for viewing. I've used this search functionality to look for globally unique identifiers (GUIDs), key and value names, as well as portions of text that may occur within value data.

Something else that's very useful about WRR is that with the "Raw Data" view open, you can right-click on a key, choose "Properties," and view information about the key, such as the index, the relative offset of the key structure within the hive file, and the Last-Write (or "Date Modified") time.

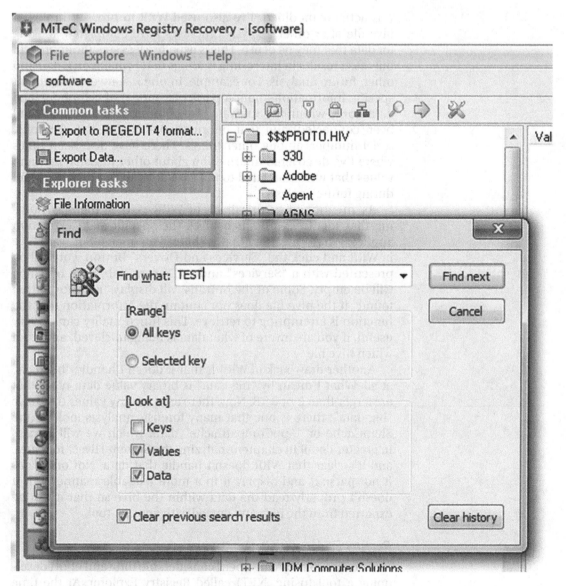

Figure 2.5 "Find" dialog in WRR.

Perhaps my most prevalent use of WRR is to use it in conjunction with other analysis processes, such as to view the values and data within a specific key of interest during timeline analysis (more information regarding timeline analysis will be presented later in the chapter). Knowing that a key was modified at a specific time is very helpful, but it can be even more helpful to understand either what values and data are beneath that key, or what was actually modified. I've also used WRR to browse through a hive file after other analysis processes have completed, looking for data that may be of use. This is usually a less specific approach, but often results in interesting findings that I can incorporate into other, future analysis. For example, in one instance, I found that specific information about a particular model of cell phone had data stored within the Software hive of the system to which it had been connected, and that information included the electronic serial number, among other things. There have also been times where I've discovered information about other Registry keys and values that were unrelated to the case at hand but may be useful during future analysis.

As mentioned, a drawback of WRR is that there is nothing that identifies to which hives the specific data extraction applies. What I mean by that is that if you open a Software hive in WRR and click the "Services and Drivers" button, you will be presented with a "Services" and a "Drivers" tab, both of which will be empty. Some of the buttons will display "no information found" if the hive file does not contain the information that the function is attempting to retrieve. This functionality can be very useful, if you are aware of what data is being retrieved, and from which hive file.

Another drawback of WRR is that it doesn't handle "big data" at all. What I mean by "big data" is binary value data types that are larger than 2 or 3 KB. Now, there aren't many values that have "big data"; there is one that many forensic analysts look to (the ShimCache or "AppCompatCache" data, which we will discuss in greater detail in chapter Analyzing the System Hives) for clues, and it's clear that WRR doesn't handle that data. Not only does it not parse it and display it in a more readable manner, but it doesn't properly read the data within the hive so that it can be exported from the hive and parsed with another tool.

Registry Explorer

Eric Zimmerman has spent considerable time and effort developing a tool (using .NET) called Registry Explorer. At the time of this writing, Eric has graciously made version 0.7.1.0 of Registry Viewer available. A portion of the Registry Viewer interface appears in Fig. 2.6.

From just the portion of the interface available in Fig. 2.6, which illustrates a Software hive loaded into the view, you can already see that it has some pretty interesting features. For example, when the hive is loaded, you can see the "live" hive, or the keys and values within the hive that you would be able to see in the Registry Editor. You can also see deleted keys and values,

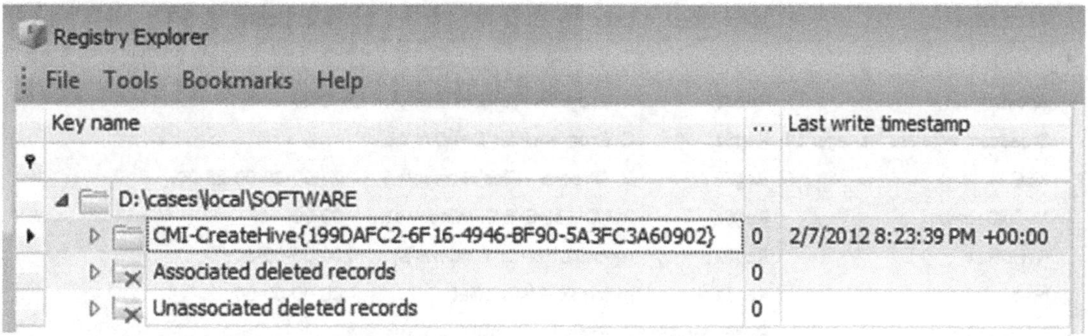

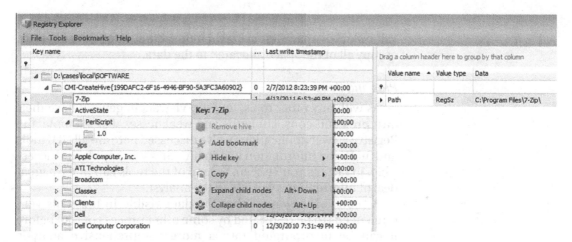

Figure 2.6 Portion of the Registry Viewer interface.

Figure 2.7 Registry Explorer user interface.

which have been broken out into "associated" and "unassociated" deleted records. The "associated" deleted records are those that can be traced all the way back to the root key of the hive, much like a file path that is traced all the way back to the root of the volume, such as "C:\". As such, the "unassociated" deleted records are those that are free standing and cannot be traced back to the root key of the hive.

Fig. 2.7 illustrates a Software hive opened in Registry Explorer.

As you can see in Fig. 2.7, the left-hand pane of the user interface displays Registry keys in the familiar folder view, with the key LastWrite times visible just to the right of the key. Right-clicking on a key brings up a context menu. Values beneath the key are displayed in the right-hand pane.

Something that isn't shown in Fig. 2.7 is that the Registry Explorer will display value slack, which is illustrated in Fig. 2.8.

Value name		Value type	Data	Value slack
?				
Apoint		RegSz	C:\Program Files\DellTPad\A...	00-00
Broadcom Wireless Manager UI		RegSz	C:\Program Files\Dell\DW WL...	
MSC		RegSz	"C:\Program Files\Microsoft S...	73-00-20-00-28-00
NvCplDaemon		RegSz	RUNDLL32.EXE C:\Windows\...	00-00
NVHotkey		RegSz	rundll32.exe C:\Windows\sy...	00-00-00-00
nwiz		RegSz	nwiz.exe /installquiet	00-00-00-00
▶ SysTrayApp		RegExpandSz	C:\Program Files\IDT\WDM\s...	

Figure 2.8 Registry Viewer displaying value slack.

Value slack is space left over when the actual value data does not occupy all of the space allocated to the data.

Pros and Cons

As with any other tools, Registry viewers in general have their own pros and cons, strengths and weaknesses. For example, the Registry viewer applications we've discussed here are all GUI tools and make the information within hive files very visible and accessible. In fact, as you've seen, several of the tools can make a great deal of information available to the analyst.

A "con" of viewers is that the data visible in the tools very often needs to be translated by some other process or tool before it can be incorporated into a more comprehensive analysis process, such as timeline analysis. While several of the viewer applications give you access to the key LastWrite times, if this information is to be incorporated into timeline analysis, it must be entered manually into the timeline. This is not a big deal for a single key, but quickly becomes an issue, as this manual process does not scale well. Also, not all of the GUI tools provide the means to parse and translate the binary data values that are often of interest to an investigator.

That being said, please do not misunderstand me...viewers do have a place in analysis processes. Viewers are excellent when you need to develop some awareness of the type of hive file that you're dealing with, or if you want to browse around the various data within the hive file. When I first encountered one of the new hive files available on Windows 8 systems (more about that in chapter Analyzing the System Hives), I opened the hive file in a viewer just to see what it contained. As the hive file followed the same structure used by other hive files, it was easily opened for viewing.

Tip

Registry viewers are great not only for exploring hive files you've extracted from images for new information but also for exploring hives from other systems. A few friends have shared hive files extracted from Windows Phone 8 smart phones and other systems to which they have had access, and because those hives follow the same structural format as most of the hive files we're familiar with, they've opened for easy viewing and exploration.

Parsers

Tools that parse specific Registry data are different from viewers in that parsers allow analysts to retrieve and decode very specific data sources from within the Registry itself, rather than simply opening the entire Registry for viewing. As we've seen so far, viewers can be very useful, offering the analyst search functionality and providing some capacity for parsing data (albeit limited).

Parsers are also very useful, in that most viewers do not allow for parsing of specific data, and there is a good deal of data within the Registry that requires some sort of parsing or decoding in order for it to be of value to the forensic analyst. In order to get to specific data via a viewer application, analysts need to remember paths and traverse entire structures, which can be very cumbersome, particularly if you're dealing with multiple hives or multiple values within a hive file. Further, a viewer isn't the best tool to use when you're trying to correlate data from multiple keys or values, even within the same hive file, or if you need to parse binary value data that includes things like time stamps, flags and other data within the structure. Many of the available parsers tend to be much better suited to this sort of thing, with the only shortcoming being that it can be difficult to incorporate the output of different parsing applications into other analysis processes (without some sort of transition to and from an intermediate format, that is).

Note

A very useful parsing tool is Microsoft's own Autoruns (found online at https://technet.microsoft.com/en-us/sysinternals/bb963902) application, which includes both a GUI and command line version (autorunsc.exe). This tool is advertised as being able to "analyze offline systems," which I have taken to mean an acquired image mounted as a (read-only) volume. However, when attempting to do so using Autoruns version 13 on several mounted (Windows XP, Windows 7) images, the application would crash. I have found several locations online where the use of this application has been discussed and successfully used, and I have tried using similar parameters but as yet have been unable to get the application to work. However, the application does provide quite a comprehensive listing of locations within the Registry from where applications (including malware) can be automatically started.

There are a number of parsing tools available, and the one (or ones) you may choose to use depends upon which data sources within the Registry you'd like to parse. In this section, I'll present several of the available tools, and this should not be considered to be an exhaustive list, as I am sure that there are tools available that I haven't seen yet. As such, this list should be viewed as simply an example of what is available.

Didier Stevens has a tool named simply "UserAssist" (found online at http://blog.didierstevens.com/programs/userassist/) which parses the UserAssist data from within a user's NTUSER. DAT hive file for versions of Windows ranging from Windows 2000 to Windows 8. This tool can help an analyst get a view as to what applications had been run on a system; in the case of the UserAssist data, the tool provides information about applications a user executed, most often by interacting with the system via the Windows Explorer interface. For example, information recorded in the UserAssist subkeys indicates applications that the user launched by double-clicking an icon on the Desktop, or one that was visible in a folder opened in Windows Explorer, or by traversing the Program Menu on the Taskbar.

The folks at Mandiant (now part of FireEye) released the Python-based ShimCacheParser (found online at https://github.com/mandiant/ShimCacheParser) for parsing the AppCompat-Cache value data from Windows systems up through Windows 8. According to research conducted by the Mandiant team, this data is part of the Application Compatibility functionality within Windows and can provide indications of applications executed on a system. For a more detailed explanation of their findings, see the *Leveraging the Application Compatibility Cache in Forensic Investigations* white paper found online at https://dl.mandiant.com/EE/library/Whitepaper_ShimCacheParser.pdf. I've used the information from this value data to great effect in my analysis, as it has indicated the use of various applications well after those applications have been removed from the system. This value data will be discussed in greater detail in chapter Analyzing the System Hives.

Tip

Something I really appreciate about a lot of the Registry keys and values during investigations involving intrusions and/or malware is that many of them are not created directly by the intruder or the malware, but instead by the intruder or malware's interaction with the "ecosystem." A valuable side effect of this is that efforts to remove indications of malicious activity often leave these indicators behind, and they tend to persist well beyond these "antiforensics" efforts.

In December 2014, Eric Zimmerman released version 0.5.0.4 of his ShellBag Explorer tool (at the time of this writing, found online at https://www.dropbox.com/s/lw9d0zrzqcrccy4/ShellBags Explorer.zip?dl=0), a GUI tool for parsing a user's shellbag entries in an Explorer-style format. Shellbags are an artifact associated with folders accessed by a user through the Windows Explorer interface (or "shell"). I've used the "shellbag" artifacts to develop an understanding of resources accessed by the user, particularly during incident response involving targeted threat actors (commonly referred to as "advanced persistent threats" or "APT") that have foregone the use of malware and have started accessing the compromised infrastructure through Terminal Services. These artifacts will be discussed in greater detail in chapter Case Studies: User Hives.

Eric also provides other parser tools for download via the web page found online at http://binaryforay.blogspot.com/p/software.html.

In January 2015, Willi Ballenthin released his amcache.py Python script (found online at https://gist.github.com/williballenthin/ee512eacb672320f2df5) for parsing the AmCache.hve Registry hive file introduced in Windows 8. Research conducted by Yogesh Khatri, and provided through his blog (found online at http://www.swiftforensics.com/2013/12/amcachehve-in-windows-8-goldmine-for.html), indicates that this file, while not specifically part of what we tend to think of as the "Windows Registry," is formatted in the same manner as Registry hive files and contains information about recently executed applications. As with other data, this file can assist analysts in finding indications of application executed on the system.

Tip

During January 2015, I downloaded the Windows 10 Technical Preview and installed it into a virtual machine running in Virtual Box. After interacting with it a bit, I checked and saw that Windows 10 also has an AmCache.hve file. Later, after updating my Windows 7 host system and guest virtual machines (within Virtual Box), I found that these system also now have an AmCache.hve file. So while the big question from forensic analysts when a new Windows operating system is developed is, "what's new?", it appears that what was once "new" (as of Windows 8) is not only included in Windows 10 ("new–new"), but Windows 7 has also been "retrofitted" with this functionality.

This list of parsing tools is simply an example and should not be considered to be all-inclusive. There are other tools available that will retrieve specific data from Registry hive files and display that data in a manner that is perhaps more meaningful for the analyst. All of the listed tools, as well as many of those that aren't listed here, are excellent tools that an analyst can use to gain insight into various data sources available within the Registry, and further their investigation.

Pros and Cons

While parsers are very useful tools and can quickly provide an analyst with insight into specific keys and values, the one drawback is that with many of them, it's not terribly easy to incorporate the retrieve data into other, more comprehensive analysis processes. So, while an analyst may not need to memorize Registry key paths and spend a great deal of time traversing tree structures in a viewer, they may need to utilize an intermediate data format and some sort of "glue" application (maybe a Perl or Python script) to incorporate that data into other analysis processes.

RegRipper

RegRipper started out as a series of separate scripts I'd written to parse out specific Registry keys, values and data, and after a while, I had more scripts than I could reasonably keep track of and maintain separately. Also, I found that over time, I was running the scripts over and over again, in the same (or similar) sequence. So I sat down and looked at what was common across not only the scripts, and also how I was using them, and from there I created a framework where I could easily reuse what was common and repetitive and focus just on writing the code to parse and translate various keys, values, and value data. I guess you could say that as a whole, RegRipper is something of a "superparser"; rather than parsing one specific subset of data from a hive, such as a user's UserAssist data or the AppCompatCache data, RegRipper allows an analyst to parse a wide range of data from hives, even combining and correlating data from within a hive file.

One of the things I find most useful about RegRipper (and yes, I am more than a little biased, I admit) is its flexibility, and how quickly a plugin can be developed, modified, and deployed. Several years ago, I was working on my own incident response case when another analyst on our team said that he'd found portable executable files stored in Registry values in the case he was working on. Within a few minutes, I wrote a plugin that iterated through the Registry values in a hive file, looked for binary data types that were 1024 bytes or greater in size, and then looked for any that started with "MZ" (the first 2 bytes of a Windows portable executable file). More recently, when I became aware that the right-to-left override (RLO) Unicode control character was being used in both the file system and the Registry to "hide" the existence of malware, I wrote a plugin to detect the use of this character in Registry key and value names within hive files.

Tip

The use of the RLO character to obfuscate the existence of malware on a system was discussed in the "How to Hide Malware in Unicode" article on the Dell SecureWorks Research blog, found online at http://www.secureworks.com/resources/blog/how-to-hide-malware-in-unicode/.

When the Poweliks malware was identified and seemed to be blasting its way across the Internet in the latter half of 2014, I was able to quickly write and utilize a plugin to help determine if a system was infected with the malware. The design of RegRipper, as a framework, makes it easy to update without having to recompile and redistribute significant code bases; all that is required is that a plugin be written, tested, and distributed. As the plugins are really nothing more than text files, they can be quickly and easily shared, and even reviewed and modified just as quickly. RegRipper will be covered in greater detail in chapter "RegRipper" of this book. We will also discuss in that chapter how analysts can derive greater use from RegRipper.

Timeline Analysis

Timeline analysis is an extremely powerful analysis process, as it not only allows an analyst to see when various events occurred, but it also allows them to see when those events occurred within the context of other events. Creating a timeline of system activity from multiple data sources found on Windows systems is covered in detail in Chapter 7 of *Windows Forensic Analysis*, which can be found on Amazon at http://www.amazon.com/Windows-Forensic-Analysis-Toolkit-Edition/dp/0124171575.

From chapter Registry Analysis, we know that Registry keys contain metadata within their structure that is called the Last-Write time, which is analogous to the last modification time of that key. This time can pertain to when the key was created, or when a value or subkey was added or deleted. In short, the time pertains to when the key was modified in some way. We also know that the structure of a Registry value does not contain similar metadata;

there is no element of the structure that records when the value was last modified. Something we will see more in the remaining chapters of this book is that there are a number of values throughout the Registry whose data (be it binary or string data) contain time stamps that can be used in timeline analysis. So, in short, there is a great deal of potentially valuable data in the Registry that can be added to a timeline, and much of this we will discuss in much more depth in the subsequent chapters of this book. However, when creating a timeline, one of the first data sources I tend to add to a timeline is the key LastWrite times from applicable hive files, very often starting with (but not stopping with) the Software and System hives. The tool I use to this is regtime.exe, available online as both a Windows .exe file and a Perl script from https://github.com/keydet89/Tools. Using the tool is fairly straightforward; simply type a command similar to the following at the command prompt:

```
C:\tools>regtime -m HKLM/Software/ -r d:\cases\test\
software >>
      d:\cases\test\events.txt
```

The regtime.exe tool runs through the hive file (in this case, a Software hive), extracting the key names and paths, and LastWrite times, prepending "HKLM/Software/" to the key path, and printing this information to the console (ie, STDOUT) in the appropriate format. As the output is sent to the console, we want to be sure to redirect it to the appropriate file; in this case, we've opted to append it (rather than creating an entirely new file) to the events file that will be the basis for our timeline.

Tip

I tend to have the tools I write send their output to the console so that they're more flexible. For example, let's say you're only really interested in Registry keys beneath the Classes subkey, because you suspect that one of the subkeys may have been added or modified as a malware persistence mechanism. Rather than incorporating all of the keys within the Software hive into your timeline (or using them all to create a nanotimeline of just the Registry key LastWrite times), you can pipe the output of the tool through a "find" command in a manner similar to the following:

```
C:\tools>regtime -m HKLM/Software/ -r d:\cases\test\software| find
"Classes" /i >> d:\cases\test\events.txt
```

The above command will only redirect those key paths that include the word "Classes" (the "/i" switch means that case is irrelevant) to the output file.

The use of regtime.exe is pretty flexible and doesn't lock you into just one analysis process or mechanism. For example, if you have a regular, consistent process that you use, you can easily automate this process. If one of the steps in your analysis process is to extract the hive files of interest from an acquired image or to mount the acquired image as a read-only volume, it can be easy to automate the use of this tool using a batch file.

The current version of RegRipper (version 2.8, available online from https://github.com/keydet89/RegRipper2.8) available as of this writing includes a number of plugins that end in "_tln". These plugins provide output in the five-field TLN format, similar to regtime.exe, but tend to primarily focus on extracting time-stamped information from various Registry value data rather than key LastWrite times. As such, it's often advantageous to run both regtime.exe and various RegRipper plugins (depending upon the nature of your investigation) as this approach may provide indications of Registry keys that were modified, which may then become pivot points in your analysis. I've done this time and again; in fact, not long ago, this technique provided indications of a Registry artifact associated with specific malware that seems to provide indications not only that the malware is/was installed on the system but also provides a possible indication of the version of the malware. Additional analysis and research is required to validate this finding, but this finding may have been missed if a comprehensive, inclusive analysis approach hadn't been employed from the beginning.

Not all RegRipper plugins that produce TLN output focus solely on parsing value data for time stamps. The secrets_tln. pl plugin, for example, retrieves the LastWrite time for the "Policy\Secrets" key within the Security hive. I wrote this plugin because the work that I do involves responding to incidents where intruders have stolen credentials from an organization, and one of the tell-tale indicators of a specific use of the tool gsecdump.exe, as described in *The Art of Memory Forensics* (information about the book can be found online at http://www.memoryanalysis.net/#!amf/cmg5), is that the LastWrite time for this key is modified. Once I heard of this, I wrote the plugin and began incorporating the information in timelines. However, rather than running regtime.exe against the entire Security hive and incorporating a lot of extraneous data in my timeline (the increased volume simply makes the timeline more cumbersome to analyze) I only included the output of the plugin. Over time, I saw the finding shared by the Volatility team validated time and time again.

Warning

When incorporating time-stamped information from any data source to a timeline of system activity, analysts must keep the context of that time stamp in mind at all times. Misunderstanding the context of the time value can lead to significant misinterpretation of the data in the timeline. We'll address this again in much greater detail in chapter Analyzing the System Hives (it's important enough to mention several times) but a great example of this is the time stamps within the ShimCache, or AppCompatCache value, data from the System hive file. For all but one version of Windows, there is only a single time stamp for each entry in the AppCompatCache data, and that time stamp is last modification time from file system metadata (ie, the $STANDARD_INFORMATION attribute for NTFS file systems). This time stamp is often misunderstood to be the last time the listed application was executed, and this misinterpretation has led to analysts misidentifying the window of compromise on the system. This misinterpretation has been seen in conference presentations that have been made publicly available.

Differencing

Determining the difference between two Registry hive files can be a very valuable analysis technique, particularly when conducting malware analysis, or comparing historical data to "current" data and attempting to determine changes that may have occurred between two points in time. Tools such as RegShot (found online at http://sourceforge.net/projects/regshot/) allow malware analysts to create a snapshot of the Registry at one point in time, take some action (infect a system with malware), and then compare a subsequent Registry snapshot to the first one in order to determine what changes may have occurred as a result of the action that had been taken.

"Diffing" Registry hive files is not something that is solely reserved for use by malware analysts. Comparisons of Registry hive files can be very useful during digital forensic analysis, by comparing the currently available hives to those from Volume Shadow Copies (VSCs) or those available within the *C:\Windows\system32\config\RegBack* folder.

Tip

I've used this technique a number of times to determine the nature of Registry data that I was analyzing; specifically, was the data I was looking at newly created, or had it been modified by some action? In most cases, I had found that a Registry key had been modified during a particular time period, and the other artifacts that I observed "near" that time indicated that a malware infection had occurred. By comparing the contents of the hive file to a previous iteration of the hive, either from within the RegBack folder or from a selected VSC, I was able to determine that the key had been created, rather than modified, at that time. This has helped me to identify artifacts that can then be used as indicators to determine if other systems had been infected with the same, or similar malware.

The Perl module on which RegRipper is based, Parse::Win32 Registry, ships with several scripts, one being regdiff.pl. When you install the module (if you need to do so), the script is automatically added to your system in the \Perl\site\bin folder. Using this script is very simple; just type the name of the script and include the two Registry hive files that you want to compare, similar to the following:

```
C:\Perl\site\bin>regdiff.pl d:\cases\test\software d:\
cases\test\regback\software
```

As with other command line tools, the output of the script is displayed in the command prompt window. As and as such, the output can be filtered through a "find" command, or it can be redirected to a file for preservation and later analysis.

There is also a command line tool named regdiff.exe, available online from http://p-nand-q.com/download/regdiff.html, which will allow you to compare two Registry files in much the same way as the regdiff.pl Perl script.

Deleted Keys and Values

In the spring of 2008, Jolanta Thomassen contacted me about providing an idea (and being a sponsor) for her dissertation for work at the University of Liverpool. I pointed her to an old (c.2001) post on the Internet, asking about unallocated space within a Registry hive file. Not long after, Jolanta produced regslack, a Perl script that combs through a hive file and locates deleted keys and unallocated space. If you remember from chapter Registry Analysis, when a key is deleted, the first 4 bytes (DWORD) of the key, which is the length of the key, is changed from a negative value (as a signed integer) to a positive value. For example, if the "live" key had a length of –120 as decimal value, then the deleted key length is 120.

Regslack is a command line tool, and very easy to use. Simply open a command prompt and pass the path to the Registry file in question to the program:

```
C:\tools>regslack.pl d:\cases\test\software
```

Regslack sends its output to the console (ie, STDOUT), so be sure to redirect it to a file (ie, "> file"), as in some cases, there can be quite a lot of information. Regslack has proven quite useful during a number of examinations. For example, if you find indications of a user account being active on a system but can't find that account listed in the SAM hive, try running regslack against the hive file. In one instance, I found indications of a user account with the name "Owner" and an RID of 1003 in the Event Logs on the system, but no indication of such an account within the SAM hive. Running regslack, I found the following:

```
SAM\SAM\Domains\Account\Users\Names\Owner
Offset: 0x3c70 [Fri Jun 18 17:03:22 2004]
SAM\SAM\Domains\Account\Users\000003EB
Offset: 0x3d08 [Fri Jun 18 18:59:27 2004]
```

The second key (Users\000003EB) had two values (F and V) associated with it, just as you'd expect for a local user account. The V value included the name "Owner." Thanks to regslack, I'd found the user account, as well as the time when the account had been deleted, indicated by the time stamp "[Fri Jun 18 17:03:22 2004]." With a little more work, using Perl code that I've already written (as part of RegRipper), I could extract and translate that binary data from those values into something a bit more understandable.

I have also used regslack to great effect to recover deleted keys and values from a user's hive file, in particular after the user had run an application called Window Washer on their system. I researched the version of the application and found that it reportedly did delete certain keys when run. Sure enough, the key was not visible in the allocated (or "live") space within the hive file, but it was fairly easy to recover using regslack. There were indications that Window Washer had been run several times, so I suggested to the customer that we extract the user hive files from the System Restore Points and see if we could find anything of value within them.

Tip

Jolanta's dissertation is available online at the SentinelChicken website at http://sentinelchicken.com/data/Jolanta ThomassenDISSERTATION.pdf.

As of version 0.51, the Parse::Win32Registry module also has the ability to extract deleted keys and values from within a hive file. One of the scripts that James provided with the distribution of the module, regscan.pl, includes code that references checking whether or not a found entry is allocated (ie, $entry->is_allocated). Modifying the code slightly to skip over and not display allocated entries allows us to see just the deleted keys and values. The documentation that James has provided for the module includes a section on lower level methods for processing hive files and refers to the entry object methods that allow for a lower level of access to entries within the hive file. This can allow us to walk through a hive file and locate deleted keys and values.

As we've already discussed earlier in this chapter, there are a number of other tools that will also retrieve deleted Registry keys and values as well as display unallocated space within the hive file. As of this writing, Eric Zimmerman has put a great deal of effort into ensuring that his tool, Registry Explorer, correctly locates and displays information about deleted keys and values.

Memory

I know I said that this chapter focused specifically on "dead box" analysis and that remains true...even though we're now going to discuss accessing Registry information in memory. The fact is that I've conducted analysis of a good number of images acquired from laptops where the hibernation file has proved to be extremely valuable. In one particular instance, I was able to determine that a particular remote access Trojan (RAT) was running on a system when the hibernation file was created, allowing me to see that it was running at one point. This was important, because analysis of the rest of the acquired image indicated that not only had the user installed the RAT from a thumb drive, but that same user had also removed the RAT files and its persistence mechanism as well.

There are a number of Volatility plugins available for parsing memory dumps for Registry data. The command reference for those plugins can be found online at https://code.google.com/p/volatility/wiki/CommandReference#Registry. Using these plugins, you can list available hives, dump individual hives, print the contents of arbitrary keys, or dump a user's UserAssist key entries (the UserAssist key entries will be discussed in more detail in chapter Case Studies: User Hives). Even if there isn't a plugin available to pull specific information that you're interested in from within a memory dump or hibernation file, you can always extract the hive file (or files) you're interested in and use other tools to view the file or parse out specific keys, values, or data. On September 25, 2012, the Volatility team posted an article on their blog that described, in part, a shellbag Volatlity plugin that would parse shellbag entries from memory, comparing that to the output of the printkey plugin. That blog post can be found online at http://volatility-labs. blogspot.com/2012/09/movp-32-shellbags-in-memory-setregtime. html. This topic is also covered on pages 299 and 300 of the book, *The Art of Memory Forensics* (information about the book can be found online at http://www.memoryanalysis.net/#!amf/cmg5).

Summary

There are a number of very useful tools and techniques available for extracting data from Registry hive files, during both "live" (interacting with a live system) and "forensic" (interacting with hive files extracted from a system or acquired image) analysis. The tools or techniques you employ depend on how you engage and interact with the Registry, as well as the goals of your interaction and analysis. You can opt to use a viewer application, something like RegRipper that extracts and parses specific keys and values based on plugins or like regslack which parses unallocated space within a hive file. In my opinion, tools such as those discussed in this chapter have the advantages of not only being freely available, but the open source tools I've written and provided were written by someone actively involved in a wide range of analysis; I've not only been engaged in data breach investigations (most commonly associated with the theft or exposure of credit card data), but I've analyzed malware outbreaks, intrusions (including those associated with the APT), and I've assisted law enforcement in dealing with potential "Trojan defense" issues. As I mentioned in this chapter, the RegRipper suite of tools (which includes rip.pl and the Plugin Browser) was developed to meet and service my needs and the needs of my analysis. These tools were not developed in a manner that resulted in my having to modify my analysis to meet the needs or limitations of the tools. Ultimately, the goal has always been to provide my customers with timely, accurate results, and the tools discussed in this chapter have helped me deliver on this.

Regardless of which approach is taken, as described in chapter Registry Analysis, your actions and analysis should be thoroughly documented in a clear, concise manner.

3

ANALYZING THE SYSTEM HIVES

Introduction

While I was working on the second edition of this book, I read through the introduction of this chapter, and realized that, for the most part, nothing about the content really changed. Most of what I'd written in the first edition has remained, for the most part, true and valid. This time, however, I wanted to present the information in a different manner, one that I hope would eventually make sense to the reader. You see, I'd found that just presenting lists of Registry keys and values wasn't terribly useful; most volumes that attempt to do so are far too long to be any real use, and most analysts don't read them, and for those who attempt to do so tend to not remember a great deal of what they've read. As such, my thought was to present the material in "artifact categories," so that analysts who've decided upon their analysis goals could then go to the section that describes the particular category of artifact that they're interested in and begin there.

As with the previous edition, this chapter (and the one after it) will not be a comprehensive list of all possible Registry keys and values that would be of interest to an analyst, mapped into artifact categories. I don't think that something like that is possible, and in the time it takes for a book to be published, the information will likely have been extended, as research into the topic of Registry analysis is continual. My hope is to present a process for conducting analysis while focusing specifically on the Windows Registry, a process that can be used and carried forward to the entire operating system, as well as to other platforms. Throughout this chapter, I will attempt to provide use cases and examples, hopefully to illustrate how the artifacts (ie, keys and values) have been found to be valuable during an investigation. Ultimately, what I'd like to see is more analysts investigating artifacts within the Registry.

Artifact Categories

An approach I wanted to take in this edition was to present various Registry keys and values, as well as use cases and analysis processes, in terms of "artifact categories." No one seems to find any value in a long list (or a spreadsheet) of Registry keys and values, particularly if that list does not include any sort of context as to the specific value associated with each of the items listed. An alternative to such lists is to provide context around the value that a Registry key or value may have to an analyst by grouping them into categories that correlate to areas of interest during analysis. For example, one category is "auto-start," which comprises locations within the Registry that allow applications to start automatically when the system is booted or when a user logs in. As discussed in chapter "Processes and Tools," Microsoft's own "Autoruns" tool (found online at https://technet.microsoft.com/en-us/sysinternals/bb963902) is an excellent tool for locating artifacts within the "auto-start" category (both in the Registry and within the file system) on live systems.

Another category is "program execution," and this category comprises artifacts that indicate that programs and applications were launched on a system.

As you can see, categories can overlap. For example, "auto-start" locations are those locations within the Registry that permit applications to be started automatically when the system starts or when a user logs in. As such, when associated with a system boot or a user logging in, these artifacts can also be indicators of program execution. The "program execution" category also applies to indications of programs being launched in other ways, such as through user interaction.

Artifacts within a category can vary depending upon the version of Windows being examined. As many analysts are aware, earlier versions of Windows, such as [Windows2000] and XP, were not nearly as prolific as later versions. As the versions of Windows has progressed, analysts have become aware of more and more locations, particularly within the Registry, that seem to record a variety of artifacts. In some cases, the locations have persisted, changing slightly in the structure of the stored data, and therefore how it is parsed. Two examples of this include the *AppCompatCache* data (discussed later in this chapter) and the *UserAssist* data (discussed in chapter: Case Studies: User Hives).

As functionality has been added to Windows as the versions have progressed, this functionality has been associated with more and more artifacts being available to for digital forensic analysis. More information has been recorded regarding the system state and configuration, as well as both system and user activity (files accessed, images viewed, etc.).

Where do these categories come from? The categories appeared, in part, from the 2012 SANS DFIR poster (found online at http://digital-forensics.sans.org/blog/2012/06/18/sans-digital-forensics-and-incident-response-poster-released), as well as the work done by Corey Harrell; go to his blog at http://journeyintoir.blogspot.com and search for the term "artifact categories." I've also described artifact categories at considerable length on my blog, found at http://windowsir.blogspot.com. During July of 2013, I posted 14 articles to the blog, several of which were directly related to enumerating artifacts within specific categories. In some ways, these artifacts may seem to be completely arbitrary; however, the fact is that analysts such as Corey and I have looked back over the type of examinations we've conducted and incidents we've responded to and compiled lists of categories that apply broadly across the spectrum. That is not to say the categories discussed within this and the following chapter are the only categories that exist; they are simply exemplar categories used by some analysts. Each analyst is free, and even encouraged, to create their own artifact categories.

Security Hive

As with the other Registry hives we will be looking at in this chapter, the Security hive is one of the Registry hives within Windows that contains information that is specific and pertinent to the running and operations of the system itself; that is to say, the information available in this and other hives tends to pertain to the system, rather than to specific users on that system. That being said, the Security hive contains some useful information regarding the system configuration and settings, but there's also one particular place we can look for an artifact that falls within the "program execution" category.

As strange as it may seem, the Security hive also contains some interesting data that pertains to the "program execution" artifact category. This particular indicator comes from the authors of *The Art of Memory Forensics* (which can be found online at http://www.memoryanalysis.net/#!amf/cmg5) and is associated with the use of the tool GSecDump, a credential theft tool that is available online from http://www.truesec.se. However, a public link is no longer available, reportedly due to the fact that "various social media have decided to classify them as dangerous"; you need to submit through the site's contact page in order to receive a link to the tool.

Anyone experienced with working on incident response engagements where a dedicated adversary has targeted an organization has likely seen systems on which GSecDump has been used. Around the time *The Art of Memory Forensics* became available, Jamie Levy shared with me that when the tool is used to dump the LSA secrets from a system, the LastWrite time of the *Policy/ Secrets* key within the Security hive is modified. This is also listed on pages 552 and 553 of the *Memory Forensics* book. As soon as she shared this, I wrote the *secrets.pl* and *secrets_tln.pl* plugins, so that I could check the LastWrite time of the key or include the time stamp in a timeline, respectively. The following output from the *secrets.pl* plugin illustrates what the data looks like when extracted from the Security hive of a Windows 7 system:

```
Launching secrets v.20140730
secrets v.20140730
(Security) Get the last write time for the Policy\Secrets key
Policy\Secrets
LastWrite Time Thu Dec 30 21:42:38 2010 (UTC)
```

What this output shows is that the key was last modified on December 30, 2010. This can be very useful information, particularly when combined with other data sources that can illustrate what else occurred "around" that time, and provide additional context to the event itself. For example, while there may be legitimate reasons for this key being updated at the time in question, including additional data sources in your analysis may illustrated that the GSecDump tool had been run, which led to the key being modified.

Since incorporating this artifact into my analysis process, I've found that this "temporal fingerprint" has been a very reliable indicator of the fact that GSecDump had been executed on the system (with specific arguments, of course). As with other Registry artifacts, this one is most valuable when combined with other indicators, such as AppCompatCache data (discussed later in this chapter) and application prefetch files. However, this artifact has proved to be reliable even in the absence of application prefetch files.

At the time of this writing, I am aware of little data within the Security hive that might be relevant to an examination that has been discussed or shared publicly; however, there are a few keys and values that are of interest. One Registry key that can be found on the Wikipedia page for "security identifiers" (SIDs) (found online *at* http://en.wikipedia.org/wiki/Security_Identifier) is the PolAcDms key. The "Default" value within this key contains the SID for the system and is a unique identifier for that system. As we will address later in this chapter, this information can be used to determine which users on a system are local users, and which are domain users, which is something that can be very useful with respect to a domain-connected (as opposed to stand-alone) system, and in particular a system with multiple domain trusts. Parsing the SID from the binary data is not an arduous task and is included in the RegRipper polacdms.pl plugin, the output of which (when run against a Security hive extracted from a Vista system) is shown below:

```
Launching polacdms v.20100531
PolAcDmS
Policy\PolAcDmS
LastWrite Time Fri Aug 31 15:14:53 2007 (UTC)
Machine SID: S-1-5-21-3831915772-716441274-3601324335
PolPrDmS
Policy\PolPrDmS
LastWrite Time Thu Nov 2 12:48:01 2006 (UTC)
Primary Domain SID: S-1-5-
```

Not only does this plugin extract and parse the machine SID from the PolAcDmS key, but it also extracts and parses the domain SID (for the domain to which the system was connected) from the PolPrDmS key. In this example, the Security hive was extracted from a stand-alone system used by a home user. In instances where the system was connected to a domain, the primary domain SID can be parsed from the "Default" value of that key and will be visible following "Primary Domain SID:". Later in this chapter we'll discuss local user accounts found in the SAM hive, as well as the ProfileList key from the Software hive, and see how an analyst can use this information.

Another key that is of use and interest to analysts from the Security hive is the "PolAdtEv" key. Parsing the binary data retrieved from this value is not a trivial task. However, our understanding of how this data can be parsed and understood can be helped along with Microsoft (MS) Knowledge Base (KB) article 246120 (found online *at* http://support.microsoft.com/en-us/kb/246120). As stated, this article applies to Windows NT 4.0, and there are only seven areas of auditing listed in the article. However, Windows XP has nine areas of auditing, as illustrated in Fig. 3.1.

In order to view the information illustrated in Fig. 3.1, all we need to do is open the Administrative Tools Control Panel applet and select the Local Security Policy shortcut. Another

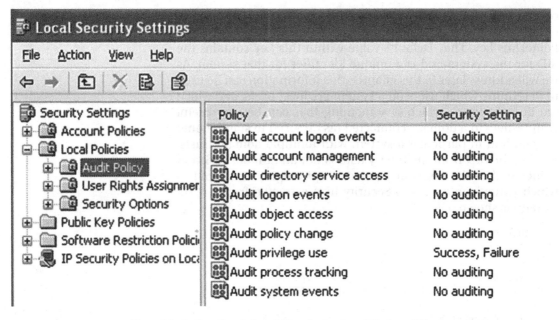

Figure 3.1 Audit policy via Local Security Settings (Windows XP).

way to view this information on Windows XP systems (one that is useful during live response, as it can be added to a batch file) is to run auditpol.exe; running it on that same live system, we see:

```
D:\tools>auditpol
Running ...
(X) Audit Enabled
System = No
Logon = No
Object Access = No
Privilege Use = Success and Failure
Process Tracking = No
Policy Change = No
Account Management = No
Directory Service Access = No
Account Logon = No
```

For Windows 7 and beyond systems, using auditpol.exe is a bit more involved, as the information being audited by default is much more extensive than on previous versions of Windows (specifically, Windows XP and 2003). An in-depth discussion of the various command line arguments for this tool is beyond the scope of this book, but an extensive list of the available options can be found online at https://technet.microsoft.com/en-us/library/cc731451.aspx.

We know how to extract the audit policy information from a live system, but what about from an acquired image? Using MS KB article 246120 as a basis and toggling various settings on and off, we can see what modifications affect which areas of the data and develop an extrapolation of the data to our Windows XP system. Or, the RegRipper plugin *auditpol.pl* can be used to extract and parse the necessary information from Windows XP and 2003 systems, as illustrated below:

```
Launching auditpol v.20080327
auditpol
Policy\PolAdtEv
LastWrite Time Mon Jul 12 18:09:46 2010 (UTC)
Auditing is enabled.
  Audit System Events = N
  Audit Logon Events = N
  Audit Object Access = N
  Audit Privilege Use = S/F
  Audit Process Tracking = N
  Audit Policy Change = N
  Audit Account Management = N
  Audit Dir Service Access = N
  Audit Account Logon Events = N
```

This information can be very valuable, as it tells us a lot about the state of auditing on the system at the time that an image was acquired. First, the LastWrite time of the key lets us know when the settings were last modified (the time is listed in Universal Coordinated Time, or UTC). This can be very helpful in understanding why we see, or don't see, certain events in the Event Log, as well as provide an indication of when the audit policy was changed. There've been a number of examinations where I've created a timeline and seen clearly when the incident occurred, and seen that as a result of response and remediation actions taken by local IT staff, antivirus scans have been run and the audit policy has been updated, just prior to an image being acquired from the system.

Next, we see whether or not auditing is enabled on Windows XP and 2003 systems, and if so, which events are audited. This will also provide us with some indication of what we can expect to see in the Event Log. For example, if auditing of successful logon events isn't enabled, then we wouldn't expect to be able to see when someone logged into the system using a user account, either legitimately or as a result of compromised credentials. I have used this information during examinations quite extensively; during one instance, I used the fact that auditing for both successful logins and failed login attempts was enabled, but there were no indications of remote logins via the remote desktop protocol (RDP) to further illustrate that a particular user account had been accessed locally and used to view illegal images.

Tip

If successful use of privilege events are being audited (ie, Audit Privilege Use = S) on a Windows XP system, and a user modifies the system time via the "Date and Time" Control Panel applet (this can also be done by right-clicking on the time display on the Task Bar and choosing "Adjust Date/Time"), an event ID 577 appears in the Security Event Log, indicating the use of the "SeSystemtimePrivilege" privilege.

It is important to note that while this key and value exist on Windows Vista and higher systems, there has yet to be extensive testing of parsing the value on these systems. Fig. 3.2 illustrates the audit policy on a Windows 7 Ultimate system.

As you can see from Fig. 3.2, there are 9 areas of auditing listed, just as there are with Windows XP. In fact, the audit policies in Figs. 3.1 and 3.2 look very similar. However, the "Default" value for the PolAdtEv key on Windows XP contains data that is 44 bytes long, whereas on Windows Vista and 2008 systems that I've had access to, the data is 136 bytes long, and 138 bytes on some Windows 7 systems. In early December 2015, I ran across a reference to a document that outlined the structure of the value data for Vista and above systems, through Windows 10. The document even listed default values for the workstation and server operating systems at each level. I happened to have two systems, one

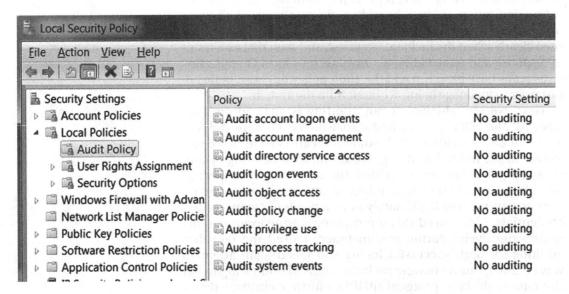

Figure 3.2 Audit policy on a Windows 7 Ultimate system.

Windows 7 and one Windows 10, so I ran the following command on each system and saved the output:

```
auditpol /get /category:*
```

I then used FTK Imager to export the Security hive off of each system and was able to write a RegRipper plugin that correctly parsed the data to display the effective audit policy from each hive file. Once this was done, I renamed the plugin that parses the data from Windows XP systems to *auditpol_xp.pl*, and named the new plugin *auditpol.pl*, and added both to the GitHub repository. But again, this plugin is based on an extremely limited sample set, and considerable testing needs to be performed in order to ensure that plugin that works correctly and is updated for other systems.

SAM Hive

Most administrators and analysts are aware that information about local users on a system is maintained in the SAM "database" or hive file. In corporate environments, the SAM hive may not have a great deal of useful information (that information may be found on a domain controller, for example), but for environments where the users will access systems using local accounts (home users, laptops, etc.), this hive file can provide a great deal of valuable data. However, this does not mean that the SAM hive is useless during incident response engagements within a corporate infrastructure, as there have been a number of times when I've seen an intruder create a local administrator account on a system, as opposed to a domain administrator account. We'll also see later in this chapter how the SAM hive can be used in other ways.

Tip

While information about user accounts local to the system is maintained in the SAM hive, the Software hive contains the ProfileList key (the full key path is *HKLM\Software\Microsoft\Windows NT\CurrentVersion\ProfileList*) which is a list of all the profiles on the system. This can show you remote or domain users who have logged into the system. We will discuss the ProfileList key later in this chapter.

The *samparse.pl* plugin extracts both user and group information from the SAM hive. Most of the information specific to each user is available beneath the *SAM\Domains\Account\Users\RID* key for each user, where *RID* is four zeros followed by the user's relative identifier (RID) in hexadecimal format. For example, the

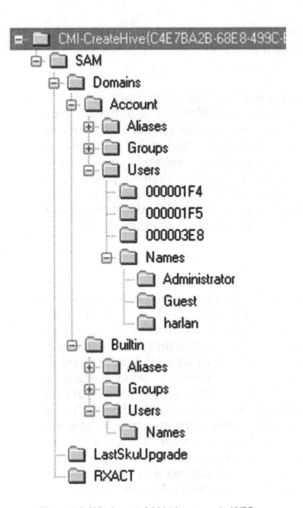

Figure 3.3 Windows 7 SAM hive, open in WRR.

Administrator account has an RID of 500, which would appear as 000001F4 in the SAM, as illustrated in Fig. 3.3.

The key for each user contains at least two values, F (contains several time stamps, etc.) and V (contains username, comment, etc.), which are binary data types and contain information about the user account. I have relied heavily on the source code for Peter Nordahl-Hagen's ntpasswd utility (found online at http://www. pogostick.net/~pnh/ntpasswd) to understand and decode this data into something usable. Sometimes within the user's key you will also find a value name "UserPasswordHint", which contains a string value if a user has entered a password hint. Many Windows systems (including Windows XP and Windows 7) allow the option to add a password hint to the user account, as illustrated in Fig. 3.4.

Harlan
Administrator
Password protected

Current password

New password

Confirm new password

If your password contains capital letters, they must be typed the same way every time you log on.
How to create a strong password

Type a password hint

The password hint will be visible to everyone who uses this computer.

Figure 3.4 Add a password hint to a Windows 7 user account.

Tip

I was once examining an image and found an odd entry in the UserPasswordHint value within the SAM hive for a user. I used LiveView (found online at http://liveview.sourceforge.net) to create a virtual machine from the image and booted it. Once the login screen came up, I tried the string from the UserPasswordHint value and was able to log into the virtual machine. Be sure to NOT enter your password as the password hint!

An excerpt of the user information extracted from the F and V values in the SAM hive by the RegRipper *samparse.pl* plugin appears as follows:

```
User Information
-------------------------
Username         : Administrator [500]
Full Name        :
User Comment     : Built-in account for administering the
computer/domain
  Account Created : Tue Sep 11 14:26:13 2007 Z
  Last Login Date : Fri Aug 31 15:52:42 2007 Z
  Pwd Reset Date  : Thu Nov 2 13:09:52 2006 Z
  Pwd Fail Date   : Never
  Login Count     : 4
  --> Password does not expire
  --> Account Disabled
  --> Normal user account
```

```
Username              : Guest [501]
Full Name             :
User Comment          : Built-in account for guest access to
the computer/domain
Account Created       : Tue Sep 11 14:26:13 2007 Z
Last Login Date       : Never
Pwd Reset Date        : Never
Pwd Fail Date         : Never
Login Count           : 0
 --> Password does not expire
 --> Account Disabled
 --> Password not required
 --> Normal user account
Username              : Harlan [1000]
Full Name             :
User Comment          :
Account Created       : Tue Sep 11 14:26:01 2007 Z
Password Hint         : usual plus a bit more
Last Login Date       : Mon Jan 12 12:41:35 2009 Z
Pwd Reset Date        : Tue Sep 11 14:26:02 2007 Z
Pwd Fail Date         : Fri Jul 11 19:54:07 2008 Z
Login Count           : 16
 --> Password does not expire
 --> Password not required
 --> Normal user account
```

As you can see, a great deal of information is available in the user's keys within the SAM. This information can be used to demonstrate activity on the system (ie, Last Login Date, Login Count values) for a specific user account, as well as tell you a number of other things, such as if the Guest account has been enabled and used. You can also use the samparse_tln.pl RegRipper plugin to incorporate the time stamped information associated with the user accounts into a timeline in order to provide additional context to your investigation.

PASSWORD NOT REQUIRED

Of particular note in the output of the samparse.pl plugin is the entry for "Password not required". In some cases, analysts have taken this flag value to mean that the account does not have a password, and that is not the case. Rather, it means that password policies (length, complexity, etc.) applied to the user accounts on the system do not apply to those accounts for which the "Password not required" flag is set. I had posed the question to someone knowledgeable in this area and had been informed, "That specifies that the password-length and complexity policy settings do not apply to this user. If you do not set a password then you should be able to enable the account and logon with just the user account. If you set a password for the account, then you will need to provide that password at logon. Setting this flag on an existing account with

PASSWORD NOT REQUIRED—Cont'd

a password does not allow you to logon to the account without the password." This is somewhat corroborated by MS KB article 305144 (found online at http://support.microsoft.com/kb/305144), which indicates that enabling the flag means that a password is not required.

So, again…having the "Password Not Required" flag set on a user account does not mean that it does not have a password; instead, it means that any policies set regarding passwords will not apply to that account.

THE CASE OF THE DISAPPEARING USER ACCOUNT

I was examining an image sent to me, looking for indications of malicious activity. As is often the case, I didn't have a really good idea of the specific activity of interest, nor of the time frame in question. I had created a timeline of activity on the system, using the file system metadata, Prefetch file metadata, Event Log record data, etc., as sources and had started to see some unusual activity. In one instance, I found that a particular user account had logged in about a year prior to the image being acquired, but I didn't find any indication of that user account in the SAM. I used regslack.exe to extract deleted keys and values, and unallocated space from the SAM hive, and found an account with the same RID as the account I was interested in, but in the deleted data, the key had a different username associated with it. I also noted that the LastWrite time on the deleted key was very close to the time that the image of the system had been acquired. As it turned out, a system administrator had logged into the system, changed the name on the account when they heard that "someone was coming to acquire the system," and then deleted the account. This was confirmed by that same system administrator.

The *samparse.pl* plugin will also extract information about groups local to the system from the SAM hive, including the group name, comment, and the SIDs for the users in the group. An excerpt of this output from a Windows 10 Technical Preview system, installed as a virtual machine, is illustrated below:

```
Group Name : Administrators [2]
LastWrite : Tue Jan 20 16:17:15 2015 Z
Group Comment : Administrators have complete and
unrestricted access to the computer/domain
Users :
  S-1-5-21-3106756646-2393192417-535628121-500
  S-1-5-21-3106756646-2393192417-535628121-1000
Group Name : Power Users [0]
LastWrite : Tue Jan 20 19:08:25 2015 Z
Group Comment : Power Users are included for backwards
compatibility and possess limited administrative powers
Users : None
Group Name : Cryptographic Operators [0]
```

```
LastWrite : Tue Jan 20 19:08:25 2015 Z
Group Comment : Members are authorized to perform
cryptographic operations.
Users : None
```

As you can see from the sample output from the samparse.pl plugin, the samparse.pl plugin works on Windows systems up to Windows 10 Technical Preview (what was available at the time of this writing). The information derived from the plugin can be very helpful in determining the level of access that a particular user account had on a system at the time that system was acquired, in order to determine what actions that user could take on the system, such as submit Scheduled Tasks (which is one way that a user could obtain elevated privileges), etc.

Also, the *samparse.pl* plugin is very convenient as it allows you to obtain and view a great deal of local user and group information from a system, all in one easy-to-reference location.

Cracking User Passwords

There are a number of times during investigations where you would want to determine a user's password. For example, in a number of examinations, law enforcement officials have wanted to know if the user account had a password at all. In most instances, I have seen this sort of query associated with cases where something suspicious (or illegal) is associated with the user account of another family member, and law enforcement officials want to determine if the suspect had free access to that account; an account with no password is extremely vulnerable. In other cases, the "Password not required" flag in the user account settings (mentioned previously in this chapter) can be very confusing to some analysts, and determining if the user account had a password at all, and attempting to determine what that password is, is paramount to the investigation. Finally, there may be a time during an investigation where, after you've acquired an image of the system, you may want to boot the system, either the original system or the acquired image, which can be "booted" in a virtual environment via LiveView (found online at http://liveview. sourceforge.net) in order to "see" what the user saw or had access to while logged into the system.

There are a number of free, GUI-based password cracking tools available, such as Cain & Abel (available online at http://www. oxid.it/cain.html), OphCrack (found online at http://ophcrack. sourceforge.net), and John the Ripper (found online at http://www. openwall.com/john). Going into detail about how to use each of these tools is beyond the scope of the book, but don't worry, the programs are very easy and straightforward to use. While you can use these tools to crack passwords, keep in mind that they can also be used to do a quick check to see if a user account *has* a password (as opposed to being blank).

Again, a detailed discussion of password cracking attacks or of the Cain or OphCrack applications is beyond the scope of this book. My purpose in mentioning the tools in this chapter has been to point to freeware tools that can be used to derive (and validate) information from Registry hive files; in this case, to illustrate information about user accounts extracted from the SAM database and to validate whether or not a user account actually has a password associated with it that needs to be typed in by a user. As I mentioned previously, simply determining whether or not an account has a password can be very valuable to an investigation.

System Hive

So far in our discussion in this chapter, we've touched a very little bit on how the System hive can be useful during an examination, with some references to information found in the hive. The System hive contains a great deal of configuration information about the system and devices that were included in and have been attached to it, so let's take a look at how to derive and interpret some of that data.

Throughout this section, as well as the rest of this chapter, I'm going to be presenting and discussing Registry keys and values that are most often seen, viewed, and accessed during incidents, and subsequently, during analysis. Neither this chapter nor this book is intended to be an all-inclusive listing of Registry keys, as that would be impossible and quite boring. Rather, I'd like to offer up some insight into specific keys and values, and how what you find (or, in some cases, don't find) can be used to further your examination.

Finding the "Current" ControlSet

From chapter "Registry Analysis," we know that there are portions of the Registry that are volatile, in that they only exist when the system is running. One such portion is the Current-ControlSet key in the System hive. Microsoft states in MS KB article 100010 (found online at http://support.microsoft.com/kb/100010) that a ControlSet, "contains system configuration information, such as device drivers and services." When we access the Registry on a live system, we may see two (or more) ControlSet keys (as illustrated in Fig. 3.5), in addition to the CurrentControlSet key.

Figure 3.5 SYSTEM hive via RegEdit, showing the CurrentControlSet.

Name	Type	Data
(Default)	REG_SZ	(value not set)
Current	REG_DWORD	0x00000001 (1)
Default	REG_DWORD	0x00000001 (1)
Failed	REG_DWORD	0x00000000 (0)
LastKnownGood	REG_DWORD	0x00000003 (3)

Figure 3.6 Contents of Select key in the System hive.

During a postmortem examination, we may need to determine which ControlSet was loaded as the CurrentControlSet when the system was running. In order to do so, all we need to do is view the values within the Select key in the System hive, as illustrated in Fig. 3.6.

Within the Select key, the Current value tells us which Control-Set was loaded as the CurrentControlSet when the system was running. This helps us understand a bit about the system state when it was running; for example, each ControlSet contains a list of Services installed on the system and how they are set to run (ie, automatically at boot, disabled, etc.), among other settings.

Note

All of the current RegRipper plugins that access the System hive will first check the "Current" value within the Select key and then extract information from the appropriate ControlSet based on the value data. This is simply a matter of preference and not a hard-and-fast requirement; plugins can be written to access all of the available ControlSets (I have seen System hives with three ControlSets listed) and search for/extract the desired information from each one. This may be useful for comparison, particularly if the LastWrite times on the keys themselves differ.

System Configuration Information

The System hive maintains a great deal of information that pertains to the configuration of the system, configuration settings that can have an impact on your investigation.

System Name

One of the first pieces of information I generally tend to look for within the System hive is the system name. I tend to do this in order to include the information in my case notes and documentation and to keep track of the systems I'm looking at, particularly if there are several systems involved in a particular case. Many times, this information can be helpful when correlating systems during a large breach, particularly ones that involved a great deal of lateral movement by the adversary. While we generally look for system IP address in logs, when looking at other artifacts such as the RunMRU or shellbags (both will be discussed in chapter: Case Studies: User Hives), we will often be able to track a user's movements using the system name.

IS THIS THE RIGHT SYSTEM?

Having the system name as part of your case documentation can be very important, as I've actually received the wrong system before. That's right…I've been asked to analyze a web server for signs of an intrusion and was provided the system name during the initial conversations, and the same system name was included on the chain of custody documentation. However, when I began my examination of the provided image, the system name was not correct. It turned out that the wrong image had been sent.

I've also heard of incidents where the right hard drive was sent to an analyst, but it was the wrong system. It turned out that between when the incident was identified and action was taken, an administrator had wiped the hard drive and completely reinstalled the operating system and applications and then copied the data back over. As such, the correct hard drive was provided to the analyst, but the actual system that needed to be analyzed was no longer available.

ClearPagefileAtShutdown

Some of the systems configuration settings on a Windows system may have a significant impact on an analyst's investigation; one such setting is the ClearPagefileAtShutdown value setting. This value is found within the *HKLM\System\CurrentControlSet\ Control\Session Manager\Memory Management* key (see the section earlier in this chapter where we discussed how to determine the CurrentControlSet for a System hive extracted from the system image). If the value exists and is set to "1", then the page file will be cleared when the system is shut down. This can impact an investigation, as the page file can be combed for strings and even carved for a variety of data that may prove to be valuable to the analyst.

Tip

More modern versions of Windows are capable of maintaining multiple paging files. Within the *Memory Management* key on Windows 7 and 10 systems, you will find values named "ExistingPageFiles" and "PagingFiles" that can contain a list of page files.

Network Interfaces

Much like other devices, information about the network interfaces available on the system is maintained in the System hive. The main path for information about the network interfaces available on a system is the *ControlSet00n\Services\Tcpip\Parameters\Interfaces* ("ControlSet00n" refers to the ControlSet marked as "Current" when the system is offline) key. Beneath this key, you'll find a number of subkeys whose names are globally unique identifiers (or GUIDs, pronounced *goo-idz*). Each of these subkeys refers to a specific interface, and the GUID names can be mapped to more easily readable names for the interfaces (see the "Network Cards" subsection later in this chapter).

The interface subkeys contain information about IP addresses assigned (static assignments or via DHCP), gateways, domains, as well as when DHCP leases were assigned, and when they terminate. This information can be extremely helpful during a wide variety of examinations, particularly when attempting to tie a particular system to entries found in router or web/FTP server logs. An excerpt of what this information looks like in the Registry is illustrated in Fig. 3.7.

The RegRipper plugin *nic2.pl* does a really good job of extracting this information and even goes so far as to translate some of the 32-bit time stamp values (LeaseObtainedTime, LeaseTerminatesTime, etc.) into something a bit more human readable.

Routes

One of the tricks that malware authors have used to "protect" their tools is to add entries to the hosts file so that critical assets (update sites for the operating system, applications, antivirus, etc.) cannot be reached. By forcing the query for a host or domain to resolve to a specific IP address, malware authors can inhibit the

[ab] DhcpDefaultGateway	REG_MULTI...	192.168.1.1
[ab] DhcpDomain	REG_SZ	chvlva.adelphia.net
[ab] DhcpIPAddress	REG_SZ	192.168.1.10
[ab] DhcpNameServer	REG_SZ	192.168.0.1
[011] DhcpRetryStatus	REG_DWORD	0x00000000 (0)
[011] DhcpRetryTime	REG_DWORD	0x0000a8bd (43197)
[ab] DhcpServer	REG_SZ	192.168.1.1
[ab] DhcpSubnetMask	REG_SZ	255.255.255.0
[ab] DhcpSubnetMaskOpt	REG_MULTI...	255.255.255.0
[ab] Domain	REG_SZ	
[011] EnableDeadGWDetect	REG_DWORD	0x00000001 (1)
[011] EnableDHCP	REG_DWORD	0x00000001 (1)
[ab] IPAddress	REG_MULTI...	0.0.0.0
[ab] IPAutoconfigurationAddress	REG_SZ	0.0.0.0
[ab] IPAutoconfigurationMask	REG_SZ	255.255.0.0
[011] IPAutoconfigurationSeed	REG_DWORD	0x00000000 (0)
[011] IsServerNapAware	REG_DWORD	0x00000000 (0)
[011] Lease	REG_DWORD	0x00015180 (86400)
[011] LeaseObtainedTime	REG_DWORD	0x4c739caa (1282645162)
[011] LeaseTerminatesTime	REG_DWORD	0x4c74ee2a (1282731562)

Figure 3.7 Excerpt of network interface values (Windows XP).

functionality. After all, you wouldn't want the installed antimalware product to update itself and then detect the presence of your malware, would you?

This is also something that can be used legitimately. According to the MS KB article on name resolution order (found online at https://support.microsoft.com/en-us/kb/172218), after checking to see if a name is its own, a Windows system will then check the hosts file. System administrators can add entries that redirect traffic to specific sites, and even some antimalware and anti-spyware applications will modify this file to force known-bad hosts/domains to resolve to the local host (ie, 127.0.0.1). Parents can also do this with Facebook and MySpace!

Another technique that can be used is to modify persistent routes on the system. One command that many incident responders run when collecting information is *route print*, which displays the current routing table for TCP/IP communications on the system. This facility also has the ability to add persistent routes that will remain in place between reboots through the *route add* command (more information about this command can be found online at https://technet.microsoft.com/en-us/library/cc757323(v=ws.10).aspx). If an added route is designated as "persistent" through the use of the "-p" switch, the command adds the routes to a Registry key within the System hive (which can be extracted using the *routes.pl* RegRipper plugin). Interestingly enough, malware such as Backdoor.Rohimafo (a description of this malware is available at the Symantec website) appears to add persistent routes to the system in order to prevent the system from accessing sites that may result in updates that allow the malware to be detected.

File System Settings

The System hive also maintains information about the configuration of the file system beneath the *ControlSet00n\Control\FileSystem* key, and there are several settings that may affect your analysis. For example, there is a value named "NtfsDisableLastAccessUpdate" (a description of the value can be found online at https://technet.microsoft.com/en-us/library/cc959914.aspx) which, back in the early days of Windows XP and 2003, was intended as a setting that could be used to enhance the performance of the system. The intention was that on high-volume file servers, disabling the updating of last access times on files would improve overall performance; however, this was an optional setting at the time, as the value did not exist by default.

Interestingly enough, one of the surprises with the release of Windows Vista was that not only did this value exist, but updating of last access times on files was disabled by default! Consider for a moment the effect that had on a lot of traditional computer forensic methodologies. Actually, I'd say that this has been very helpful, as it has forced us to look for alternative methods of demonstrating that a user accessed a file, and this search has proven to be extremely fruitful.

Beneath the same key is a value named "NtfsDisable8dot3NameCreation"; if this value is set to 1 (and the file system is NTFS), then the creation of short file names will be disabled. This may be an issue if you expect to see file names on the system similar to "PORTER~!.PPT" rather than "porter's latest widgets sales presentation.ppt". Enabling this functionality tells the file system to not create the shorter file names.

Prefetch Settings

All Windows systems, beginning with Windows XP, have had the ability to perform both boot and application prefetching. The intent of this capability is to speed up the boot or application loading process, and the result of application prefetching for forensic investigators has been valuable information that illustrates that an application was executed.

Now, I said that Windows systems have the ability to perform both boot and application prefetching, but not all do. By default, only workstation versions of Windows (XP, Windows 7, and Windows 8/8.1/10) perform application prefetching. Server versions (Windows 2008 R2, Windows 2012) do not perform application prefetching by default.

A Windows system's ability to perform boot or application prefetching, or neither, or both, is controlled by a single value within the Registry; specifically, the "EnablePrefetcher" value beneath the *ControlSet00n\Control\Session Manager\Memory Management\PrefetchParameters* key. The RegRipper *prefetch.pl* plugin will extract the Prefetch configuration setting from the System hive and display it in a human-readable format.

AutoStart

Autostart settings are those that allow applications and programs to start with no interaction from the user beyond booting the system or simply logging in. Registry keys and values within this category are most often associated with malware, as the intention of the authors is to get their malware onto a system and to get it to start automatically when the system is started, with no interaction or notice from the user.

Windows Services

Perhaps the most referenced and analyzed pieces of information in the System hive, particularly during incident response activities, are the Windows services. Windows services are programs that run automatically when the system is booted and are started by the system and with no interaction from the user (however, users with the appropriate privileges can install, start, and stop services). Windows services can be very useful; web and FTP servers, as well as DNS and DHCP servers, are all Windows services. However, the nature of Windows services (run automatically with no user interaction, as well as with elevated privileges) makes them a target for malware authors as well, and a great number of bits of malware install as Windows services.

Services on Windows systems can be extremely powerful; they generally run with elevated privileges and start without any interaction from the user beyond booting the system. Is there any wonder why services are targeted so often by malware authors and intruders? Not so much to exploit a vulnerability (yes, that does happen), but instead to use Windows services as a persistence mechanism, ensuring that the malware or backdoor or remote access Trojan (RAT) is started each time the system is booted.

Warning

Creating services (and other actions, such as submitting Scheduled Tasks) on Windows systems requires Administrator-level privileges; as such, the fact that new services are created tells you something about the level of access that the malware or the intruder had on the system. Analysts often see partial infections by malware, where the infection process was hindered by the fact that user context that was involved did not have Administrator privileges on the system. So while limiting user privileges can prevent or hamper the effects of a compromise, the flip side is that the artifacts of a compromise that you do find can tell you a lot about what may have happened.

In many cases, experienced incident responders will be able to look at a system Registry and "magically" pick out the obscure or malicious services. Some malware creates services with random names (either the service name itself, or the DisplayName value), so a quick look at the Registry is all it takes to find the offending service. Other techniques that can be used by incident responders and analysts are to look for services that have odd paths to the executable images (that is, point to executables in the Program-Data folder, within a user's profile folder, etc.) or do not have a *Description* value; many legitimate services have descriptions, and some of them can be long, depending on the vendor. The bad guys learned from these techniques and began using services names that looked a bit more legitimate and began filling in the various values to make the service itself look more legitimate, at least when the values were seen via a Registry viewer. For instance, there have been Description values that appear legitimate, and I have seen others that have had some misspellings (ie, "down load" spelled as two words) which was enough for me to take a closer look.

Another value beneath a service key that can provide a good deal of context and perspective to an examination is the Start value. A description of the various Start values can be found in MS KB article 103000 (found online at https://support.microsoft.com/en-us/kb/103000). In most instances, you'd expect a Start value of "0x02", indicating that the service is autoloaded or run automatically. Every now and again, I see malware services that have a Start value of 0x03, which indicates that they're set to start manually, meaning that a user must do something, take some action, for the service to be started. This can be critical when attempting to determine the "window of compromise" for a customer. Basically, if the malware service was installed with a Start value of 0x03, started and run, and then the system shut down, when the system was started again, the service would not start automatically. This may play a significant role in your examination.

RegRipper includes a number of plugins for extracting service key information from the System hive, and to be honest, because RegRipper is open source, there's really no limit to how you parse and display the information. Most of the plugins will start off by locating the ControlSet00n marked "Current" in the Select key of the System hive; however, this is not a hard-and-fast requirement. Plugins can be written that will display the same key/value information from all of the available ControlSets, or you can write a plugin to display the information from both ControlSets if the information itself is not the same in both (or all...I've seen hives with more than two ControlSets) locations.

Warning

I was performing emergency incident response for an organization that had some issues with malware. The malware wasn't widespread and didn't seem to be infecting systems; in fact, all indications were that the malware was isolated to just a few systems, and the organization simply wanted it gone. Using regedit.exe, I found a service that appeared to be suspicious, deleted it and rebooted the system...but the malware wasn't gone. In this case, the malware used *two* services for persistence...one that was the malware, and the other that checked for the existence of the malware, and if it didn't find it, installed it.

During another incident response engagement, we had located a malicious service that had a Start value of 0x02, and would dump the virtual memory from credit card back office processing software and collect track data from the

Continued

Warning—Cont'd

memory dump. Using some commercial tools, we found that the code within the executable for the service included a *sleep()* function; it used this because when the system is first started, there is no credit card data in memory. Instead, it would read the contents of a register, shift the value to the right four times, and then *sleep()* that number of seconds; based on other artifacts, it appeared at one point to *sleep()* for several days. Under the circumstances, understanding the interaction of the malware on the system, taking all factors into account, helped us provide the customer with a more accurate window of compromise.

In another instance, the first real indicator I'd seen of malicious services was an Event Log record. The source was "Service Control Manager" and the event ID was 7035, indicating that a service had started...even though our findings indicated that the system had been running for quite some time. Further examination indicated that the service was set to start when the system was booted. All other information about the service appeared to be legitimate, even down to the executable file appearing to be a legitimate Windows file.

The point is that it's not always easy to locate a suspicious service or process, particularly when the bad guy is trying really hard to not be discovered.

Not long ago, the bad guys were found to be employing an even trickier technique to hide and maintain the persistence of their malware or backdoors. Instead of creating a service with an ImagePath value that pointed directly to the malware executable file, what they were doing was creating a service that was loaded by the venerable svchost.exe process. Per MS KB article 314056 (found online at http://support.microsoft.com/kb/314056), the Svchost.exe process is essentially a "service host," in that multiple copies of svchost.exe can be running, each "hosting" multiple services running from DLLs. When the svchost.exe process starts, it reads through the Registry to see which services it needs to be running, under which instances. Services that run under svchost.exe have ImagePath values that contain references to svchost.exe itself, such as:

```
%SystemRoot%\system32\svchost.exe -k netsvcs
```

Then, beneath the service key, there will be a "Parameters" subkey that contains a value named "ServiceDll", which points to the DLL from which the service is run. Conficker is an example of a worm that used this technique for persistence. By creating a service in this manner, it makes the malware a bit harder to find, but not impossible. All we have to do is drop down to the Parameters subkey beneath the malicious service, and the ServiceDll value will point us to the offending malware. Some of the things we'd want to look for with respect to the listed DLL are unusual paths (ie, the path name includes "temp", etc.), odd looking or apparently names for the DLL itself, etc. Looking at the referenced DLL itself, misspelled or missing file version information, evidence of the use of a packer to obfuscate the executable code, etc., are indicators of possibly malicious files.

Note

The *Microsoft\Windows NT\CurrentVersion\SvcHost* key within the Software hive can also provide information about services that should be running "under" svchost.exe.

The RegRipper *svcdll.pl* plugin combs through the services keys within the System hive and displays all of those that are loaded by svchost.exe, sorting them based on their key LastWrite times. The *svchost.pl* plugin extracts the values and data from the SvcHost key within the Software hive. Because RegRipper and its plugins are open source, anyone with a modicum of Perl programming skill (or even the ability to use copy-paste) can easily create new plugins that perform different functions or display the output in a more meaningful manner. See chapter "RegRipper" of this book for more information regarding writing RegRipper plugins.

A side effect of the use of services as a persistence mechanism for malware is that the Windows XP and 2003 operating systems (similar activity has not been widely observed on Vista systems and above, including Windows 7, etc.) tend to record information that can make an analyst's task of locating the malware, or the initial date that the system was compromised, a bit easier. In particular, when a service or device driver is actually "run," in many cases, an entry beneath the *System\CurrentControlSet\Enum\Root* key appears; specifically, a subkey whose name is "LEGACY_<*service name*>", as illustrated in Fig. 3.8.

Figure 3.8 Enum\Root\LEGACY_* keys (Windows XP).

Again, these keys appear to be created relatively close to the time that the service is first run. During multiple malware and intrusion examinations involving the creation of services (particularly those that are loaded and run via svchost.exe), there appears to be a correlation between when the file was first created on the system, an Event Log entry indicating that the service was started, and the LastWrite time on the LEGACY_* subkey related to the service. This information can be very valuable when attempting to determine and/or validate the time frame of the initial compromise, or an overall window of compromise. In my experience, this information applies primarily to Windows XP and 2003 systems, as I haven't seen a similar correlation, to a great extent, on Windows 7 systems.

Beneath each of these LEGACY_* keys you will often find a subkey named "0000", which also appears to be created and modified in some way when a service is launched. Therefore, the LastWrite time on the LEGACY_*\0000 key for a particular service should closely approximate the last time the service was run. For example, on a Windows XP Service Pack 3 system I was examining, the Browser service was configured to start automatically when the system booted. The LastWrite time on the Browser service key was August 11, 2010, at approximately 08:10:28 UTC, and the LastWrite time on the *LEGACY_BROWSER\0000* key was 08:11:23 UTC on the same day. As it turned out, the system had last been booted at approximately 08:08 UTC on August 11, 2010. The LastWrite time on the *LEGACY_BROWSER* key was May 9, 2008 at approximately 01:56:17 UTC, which approximates to the time that the system was installed. This same sort of analysis applies to services that are started manually and should be carefully considered as part of your analysis, including correlating this information with other artifacts from the image, such as Event Log entries, etc.

During an examination I was working on some time ago, I found what turned out to be a service installed within the time frame of an incident. I say "an incident" because, as is sometimes the case, when examining a system to determine the root cause of one incident, I run across indications of a previous or multiple incidents. In some instances, I've found indications of multiple different bits of malware, as well as one or more intrusions. In this case, I found a service that had been installed, and the file system metadata (ie, time stamps) for the executable file indicated that it had been created on the system in February 2009, which was 15 months prior to the incident I had been asked to look into. The LastWrite time on both the *LEGACY_** and *LEGACY_*\0000* subkeys for the service indicated that it had been first launched shortly after the executable file had been created on the system, and that was the only time that the service had been launched.

Further analysis determined that the service was not configured to start automatically when the system was booted, but instead was set to be started manually.

Note

The *legacy.pl* plugin extracts the names of the *LEGACY_** subkeys from the *Enum\Root* key and displays them sorted based on their LastWrite times. Correlating this information with the output from other plugins (or any others that extract information about services) can prove to be very beneficial in locating malware, as well as establishing at time frame for the initial intrusion.

Another way that the LastWrite time for the *LEGACY_** key can be useful in determining the time frame of an incident or intrusion is when the executable file (.exe or .dll file) itself is subject to "time stomping." That is, there is malware that, when it is installed, the executable file MAC times are modified so that it remains hidden from rudimentary detection techniques, such as searching for new files on a system based on creation dates or creating a time-line of system activity for analysis. In this case, an anomaly may be detected if the creation date for the executable file were some-time in 2004, but the LastWrite time for the service's *LEGACY_** key were, say, in 2009.

Warning

Similar to what has been observed with respect to modifying file MAC times (ie, *SetFileTime()*) to arbitrary times (referred to as "time stomping"), the tool SetRegTime (found online at https://code.google.com/p/mft2csv/wiki/SetRegTime) can be used to modify key LastWrite times.

I, and others, have used this technique to great effect. There have been a number of examinations during which I have found a suspicious file, or an unusual service referenced in the Event Log, and locating the *LEGACY_** entry has led me to other interesting information in my timeline. In most cases, I've seen file creations "nearby" in the timeline that provide me with a clear indication of the initial indicators of the incident.

Program Execution

Program execution artifacts are those artifacts that demon-strate that a program was actually executed or launched at some point. There are times during an examination where you may find an executable program file on a system, but the existence of the file isn't as important as determining if the program had been executed. There are other artifacts that we can look to for indications that the program may have been executed. As you might think, program execution artifacts may be a subset of autostart artifacts, particularly if the condition of the autostart mechanism (system booting, user logging in, etc.) has been met. Again, we're focusing in this book on those artifacts found in the Windows Registry.

AppCompatCache

In 2012, members of the consulting firm Mandiant (now part of FireEye) published an article to their company blog (found online at https://www.mandiant.com/blog/leveraging-application-compatibility-cache-forensic-investigations) describing their findings regarding the Windows "Application Compatibility Cache," or shim cache.

Tip

I should note that the Mandiant analysts also authored a five-page white paper that explains their findings. It's an easy read and does a very good job of describing what led them to the data and what they were able to determine from the data.

One aspect of the AppCompatCache, or Shim Cache, data to be aware of is that very often the time stamp that is included in the data is misinterpreted. So far, the data from all versions of Windows (except 32-bit versions of Windows XP) have a single time stamp associated with the individual file path entries in the data. In all of these cases, this time stamp has been determined to be the last modified time for the file, from the file system metadata (specifically, the $STANDARD_INFORMATION attribute within the master file table). I've seen many times during presentations and in reports that this time stamp is misinterpreted and misunderstood to be when the file was last executed.

Timeline Tip

When creating a timeline of system activity, it can be very beneficial to include AppCompatCache data entries in the timeline. If the file still exists within the file system, you will see that time stamp in the AppCompatCache data will line up with the file system last modified time for the file.

As of this writing, the RegRipper *appcompatcache.pl* plugin can parse the AppCompatCache value from Windows XP through Windows 10 and Windows [Server2012] systems, and the *appcompatcache_tln.pl* plugin will output the data in a format suitable for inclusion in a timeline.

Malware

I generally reserve the "malware" artifact category for indicators of malware that do not fall into other categories, such as "auto-start" or "program execution." There are malware variants, and even some families, which leave artifacts within the Windows Registry that have nothing to do with the persistence of the malware, and by looking for the artifacts specifically, we may be able to detect the malware, where other mechanisms failed to do so. Some examples of RegRipper plugins that can be useful in this artifact category include *fileless.pl, rlo.pl, routes.pl,* and *sizes.pl.*

I originally wrote the *fileless.pl* plugin as a means of detecting the Poweliks malware; this malware was referred to as "fileless" because it didn't persist by writing a file to the file system. Instead, this particular malware persists via what amounts to a script in an autostart Registry value, and when that script is launched, it reads a Registry value with encoded data that performs the functions of malware. While early versions of this malware were found in the user's USRCLASS.DAT hive and within the Software hive, once the malware was found installed as a Windows service, I adapted the plugin to be much more general.

The *rlo.pl* plugin resulted from some research involving the Unicode "right-to-left override" (RLO) control character, which essentially reverses the characters that follow the Unicode control character, a technique that has been used to hide malware on systems. From the perspective of a user or investigator looking at a Registry hive file in a viewer, a key or value name would appear normal, so much so that it might even appear to be a legitimate name. However, from the computer's perspective, the sequence of bytes that comprise the name are markedly different and, as such, searching for a specific key or value name without taking the RLO character into account would fail. As such, I wrote a plugin that would run through a Registry hive and identify any key or value names that included this specific character. The issue of the RLO character being used was discussed in the "How to Hide Malware in Unicode" article published to the Dell Secureworks Security and Compliance Blog on Oct 1, 2013. That article can be found online at http://www.secureworks.com/resources/blog/how-to-hide-malware-in-unicode.

I wrote the *sizes.pl* plugin originally as a testing plugin; I wanted to see how many values that contain binary data were larger than a specific size (the AppCompatCache data can be "large," on the order of tens or even hundreds of kilobytes) within hive files. I had read online about a particular malware variant that had been modified from maintaining its configuration data in a file to keeping it in a value with binary data. Knowing that key paths and value names can (and do) change, I wanted a way to look for all values with binary data of specific minimum size or larger. This plugin was instrumental in my testing process and essentially allows a user to create a whitelist of Registry values with "large" data within their environment. As this data was specific to the malware configuration and not related to its persistence, I included it in the "malware" artifact category.

The *routes.pl* plugin is, at the time of this writing, 5 years old, originally written in August 2010. The "route" command is often used in batch scripts that provide for automated volatile data collection during incident response activities, as the command "route print" outputs the network routing tables for the system in question. During my career as an incident responder, I have seen systems with specific persistent routes that had been set up for a legitimate business purpose; information about persistent routes is maintained in the Registry. Interestingly, the *routes.pl* plugin was featured in recipe 10.8 of the *Malware Analyst's Cookbook*, which was published in 2011.

I should note that, with the exception of the *routes.pl* plugin, these plugins are not specific to the System hive but can be run across all hives, including those found within the user profile.

USB Devices

Another item of interest to analysts will often be the devices (particularly USB devices) that had been attached to the system. Research into this area has been going on for some time; Cory Altheide and I published some of our joint research in this area in 2005, and some more recent analysis findings have been documented by Rob Lee on the SANS Forensic Blog (found online at http://blogs.sans.org/computer-forensics) on September 9, 2009. In short, the System hive maintains a great deal of information about the devices and when they were attached to the system. Additional information regarding user-specific artifacts of USB devices will be covered in chapter "Case Studies: User Hives" of this book.

In short, when a USB device is connected to a Windows system, the Plug-and-Play (PnP) manager receives the notification and queries the device. Information about the device, extracted from the device descriptor (which is *not* part of the memory area of the device),

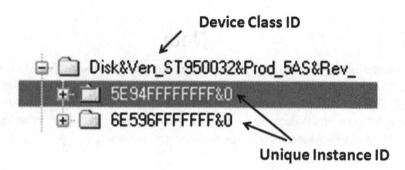

Figure 3.9 USB device in the Enum\USBStor key.

is then stored in the System hive beneath the *ControlSet00n\Enum\USBStor* and ...\USB subkeys. The storage device is then (most often) recognized as a disk device and mounted as a drive letter or volume on the system. As such, additional information related to the device is recorded in the *MountedDevices* key within the System hive, as well as two subkeys beneath the *Control\DeviceClasses* key.

Let's take a look at what this looks like in the System hive. First, beneath the *Enum\USBStor* key, we can see where devices are listed, first by a key known as a device class identifier (ID), and by a subkey beneath the device ID known as the unique instance ID, as illustrated in Fig. 3.9.

As you can see in Fig. 3.9, the device class ID tells us a little bit about the device itself (in this case, the device is a 500 GB Seagate "wallet" drive). Beneath the device class ID, we see two unique instance IDs, which are the device serial numbers extracted from the device descriptor of each device. In each case, the unique instance ID key contains information about the devices within Registry values, including the device "FriendlyName" (in both cases, "ST950032 5A2 USB Drive").

Now, not every USB device has a serial number in its device descriptor. In such cases, Windows will assign a unique instance ID to the device. In order to tell when this is the case, take a look at the unique instance ID for the device, and if the second character (*not* the second to last character, but the second character in the string) is an "&" (as illustrated in Fig. 3.10), then the unique instance ID was created and assigned by the operating system, rather than extracted from the device descriptor of the device.

Figure 3.10 Unique instance ID assigned by Windows.

Note

The *usbstor.pl* RegRipper plugin extracts information from the *Enum\USBStor* key; specifically, for each device class ID, it lists the FriendlyName value (and on Windows XP and 2003 systems, the ParentIdPrefix value) for each unique instance ID (listed as "S/N" for "serial number" in the plugin output). The *Enum\USB* key contains information about all USB devices that had been connected to the system (quite naturally, on some systems, I have entries for "Tableau USB-to-SATA" device), and the *usbdevices.pl* plugin will extract this information.

Mapping Devices to Drive Letters

Once we have information about the USB devices attached to the system, we can attempt to map that device to a drive letter. This may not always be possible, particularly if multiple devices had been connected to the system successively. For example, I've connected a thumb drive to my system that has been mounted as the drive letter F:\. Later, I disconnect the device and then at some point connect another device, which is also mounted as the F:\ drive.

Before continuing, we need to understand that Windows treats external USB drives (hard drives in enclosures, such as "wallet" drives) and thumb drives or USB keys differently. Specifically, thumb drives contain a value within their unique instance ID key called the *ParentIdPrefix*; external drives do not contain this value. I have also seen where neither the storage component of my Motorola MB300 BackFlip smartphone nor a Garmin Nuvi (both the SD card and the flash device) will have a *ParentIdPrefix* value populated beneath the unique instance ID key. The usbstor. pl RegRipper plugin will display the *ParentIdPrefix* value for those devices that have the value, as illustrated as follows:

```
Disk&Ven_Generic-&Prod_Multi-Card&Rev_1.00 [Sat Jan 2
12:56:01 2010]
  S/N: 20071114173400000&0 [Sun Aug 1 10:06:03 2010]
   FriendlyName : Generic- Multi-Card USB Device
   ParentIdPrefix: 7&24e8d74f&0
```

However, as indicated, external drives (usually, those in enclosures, produced by Maxtor, Western Digital, etc.) will not have *ParentIdPrefix* values, as illustrated as follows:

```
Disk&Ven_Maxtor&Prod_OneTouch&Rev_0125 [Thu Mar 4 15:50:13
2010]
  S/N: 2HAPT6R0____&0 [Wed Jun 30 01:27:21 2010]
   FriendlyName : Maxtor OneTouch USB Device
  S/N: 2HAPT6VY____&0 [Thu Jul 8 00:34:48 2010]
   FriendlyName : Maxtor OneTouch USB Device
```

\??\Volume{d99297b2-0b5d-11df...	REG_BINARY	D9 60 41 F7 00 7E 00 00 00 00 00 00
\??\Volume{daca9310-8f32-11df-...	REG_BINARY	71 75 43 51 00 7E 00 00 00 00 00 00
\??\Volume{e26e3ff7-f948-11de-...	REG_BINARY	5C 00 3F 00 3F 00 5C 00 53 00 54 00 4F 00
\??\Volume{fec5eece-f71f-11de-...	REG_BINARY	00 00 00 D0 00 7E 00 00 00 00 00 00
\DosDevices\C:	REG_BINARY	00 00 00 D0 00 7E 00 00 00 00 00 00
\DosDevices\D:	REG_BINARY	00 00 00 D0 00 84 12 4C 1D 00 00 00
\DosDevices\E:	REG_BINARY	5C 00 3F 00 3F 00 5C 00 49 00 44 00 45 00
\DosDevices\F:	REG_BINARY	71 75 43 51 00 7E 00 00 00 00 00 00
\DosDevices\G:	REG_BINARY	23 48 3D D4 00 7E 00 00 00 00 00 00
\DosDevices\H:	REG_BINARY	5C 00 3F 00 3F 00 5C 00 53 00 54 00 4F 00
\DosDevices\I:	REG_BINARY	2A 24 56 20 00 00 90 0C 00 00 00 00

Figure 3.11 Excerpt of values from MountedDevices key.

This is important because we may be able to use this information to map a thumb drive or key to a drive letter. I say "may be able to," because it really depends on how soon after the device being connected to the system that an image (or just the System hive) is acquired from the system. As I mentioned previously, drive letters will very often be reused, so disconnecting one device and connecting another may result in both devices being assigned the same drive letter.

All of the values within the MountedDevices key have binary data. However, different data can mean different things. For instance, Fig. 3.11 illustrates an excerpt of values from the MountedDevices key of a System hive file.

As you can see from Fig. 3.11, there are two basic types of value names; those that begin with "\DosDevices\" and refer to a drive or volume letter, and those that begin with "\??\Volume" and refer to volumes. These values have data of different lengths; some are 12 bytes long, others are longer. Many of the longer ones are actually Unicode strings that refer to devices, strings that we can read by double-clicking the value. The contents of the data for "\DosDevices\H:" (highlighted in Fig. 3.11) is illustrated in Fig. 3.12.

```
\.?.?.\.S.T.O.R.
A.G.E.#.R.e.m.o.
v.a.b.l.e.M.e.d.
i.a.#.7.&.2.4.e.
8.d.7.4.f.&.0.&.
R.M.#.{.5.3.f.5.
6.3.0.d.-.b.6.b.
f.-.1.1.d.0.-.9.
4.f.2.-.0.0.a.0.
c.9.1.e.f.b.8.b.
}.
```

Figure 3.12 MountedDevices key value data showing ParentIdPrefix.

The Unicode string in Fig. 3.12 refers to a removable storage device ("\??\Storage#RemovableMedia#", in this case, a USB device), and the highlighted substring "7&24e8d74f&0" is the *ParentIdPrefix* value for one of the USB devices that had been connected to the system. Therefore, we can use the *ParentIdPrefix* value to map a USB thumb drive from the *Enum\USBStor* key to a volume identifier within the MountedDevices key, and possibly even to a drive letter. An important factor to keep in mind, however, is that if you plug in one device that is mapped to drive H:\, disconnect it, and then connect another device that is mapped to drive H:\, the previous data for "\DosDevices\H:" is replaced.

GETTING HISTORICAL INFORMATION

Historical information about drive mappings in the hive files can be found in Windows XP System Restore Points, as well as within hive files from Volume Shadow Copies on Vista and above systems.

Using the *usbstor.pl* RegRipper plugin, we can obtain information about USB removable storage devices attached to the system (note that the key LastWrite times are displayed but are irrelevant to this example), an excerpt of which is illustrated as follows:

```
Disk&Ven_Generic-&Prod_Multi-Card&Rev_1.00 [Sat Jan 2
12:56:01 2010]
   S/N: 20071114173400000&0 [Sun Aug 1 10:06:03 2010]
      FriendlyName : Generic- Multi-Card USB Device
      ParentIdPrefix: 7&24e8d74f&0
```

From the mountdev.pl plugin, we can get information about the values listed in the MountedDevices key, which appears as follows:

```
Device: \??\STORAGE#RemovableMedia#7&24e8d74f&0&RM#{53f563
0d-b6bf-11d0-94f2-00a0c91efb8b}
   \??\Volume{47042c43-f725-11de-a8a5-806d6172696f}
   \DosDevices\H:
```

So now, we're able to map a USB thumb drive to a drive letter. But what about the USB external drives, such as those in enclosures (ie, "wallet" drives, etc.)? If you remember from Fig. 3.11, several of the values have data that is only 12 bytes long. These are volume identifiers and drive letters that refer to the external drives. In these cases, the first 4 bytes (DWORD) are the drive signature (also known as a volume ID) from the hard drive itself. This signature is written to a hard drive, beginning at offset 0x1b8 (440 in decimal) within the master boot record (MBR) when Windows formats the drive. You can view this value by opening the first 512 bytes of the

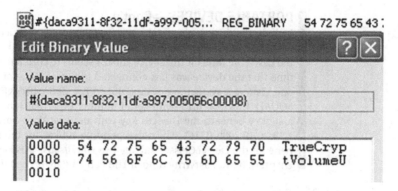

Figure 3.13 TrueCrypt volume listed in the MountedDevices key.

hard drive (MBR) in a hex editor and navigating to offset 0x1b8. The remaining 8 bytes of the data are the partition or volume offset. In Fig. 3.11, we see two drive letters (\DosDevices\C: and \DosDevices\F:) with partition offsets of 0x7e00, which is 32256 in decimal; dividing by 512 byte sectors, this means that the partitions or volumes start at sector 63 on their respective hard drives (note that \DosDevices\C: refers to the hard drive installed in the system and is used as an example).

What this means is that there is not a direct method for mapping a USB external hard drive listed in the *Enum\USBStor* key to a drive letter listed in the MountedDevices key.

While not specifically recognized as a device, per se, the MountedDevices key also maintains information about TrueCrypt volumes (may still be in use) that had been mounted on the system, as illustrated in Fig. 3.13.

As you can see, the value name is a bit different from other entries within the MountedDevices key, and the binary data is 16 bytes long and spells out "TrueCryptVolumeU". I have seen other similar values where the data spells out "TrueCryptVolumeT" or "TrueCryptVolumeS". While this will give you an indication of a user accessing TrueCrypt volumes, it does not explicitly tell you where those volumes exist.

PORTABLE DEVICES

On Windows versions beyond Vista (including Windows 7 and 10) even more information about attached (portable) devices is maintained in the Registry, albeit in the Software hive. Beneath the *Microsoft\Windows Portable Devices\Devices* key, you will see a number of subkeys that refer to devices. The subkey names can be parsed to get the name of the device and, if available, the device serial number. These subkeys also contain a value named "FriendlyName", which in many instances will

Continued

PORTABLE DEVICES—Cont'd

include the drive letter to which it was mounted, such as "Removable Disk (F:)". Further testing is required, but in some limited sample cases, the LastWrite time for the device subkey seems to correlate closely to the time that the device was last connected to the system. For example, on one Vista test system, a device (DISK&VEN_BEST_BUY&PROD_GEEK_SQUAD_U3&REV_6.15, with serial number 0C90195032E36889&0) had a subkey beneath the Devices key with the LastWrite time of Thu Feb 7 13:26:19 2008 (UTC). The corresponding subkey for the same device, beneath the DeviceClasses subkey (we will discuss this key later in the chapter), had a LastWrite time of Thu Feb 7 13:26:02 2008 (UTC).

When a USB device is first plugged into a Windows system, the PnP manager queries the device to determine information about the device in order to figure out which drivers to load for that device. On Windows XP and 2003 systems, this information is maintained in the setupapi.log file (for Vista systems and beyond, the file is setupapi.dev.log). Once the device is loaded, two additional keys are created for the device beneath the DeviceClasses key within the System hive. Both of these keys are GUIDs; one refers to disks, and the other refers to volumes, as shown below:

```
Disk GUID - {53f56307-b6bf-11d0-94f2-00a0c91efb8b}
Volume GUID - {53f5630d-b6bf-11d0-94f2-00a0c91efb8b}
```

Both of these GUIDs are defined in the ntddstor.h header file used in Windows. The first GUID, which begins with "53f56307", is defined as GUID_DEVINTERFACE_DISK, or DiskClassGUID, and refers to disk devices. An example of what the DiskClassGUID subkeys look like is illustrated in Fig. 3.14.

As illustrated in Fig. 3.14, we see keys whose names begin with "##?#USBSTOR#"; these keys go on to contain device names that look very much like the device descriptor names from the USBStor key mentioned previously in the chapter. The key name also contains the unique device descriptor or serial number for the device. According to research conducted and published by Rob Lee (of Mandiant and

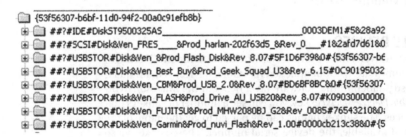

Figure 3.14 DiskClassGUID keys in Windows XP System hive.

Figure 3.15 VolumeClassGUID keys in Windows XP System hive.

SANS fame), the LastWrite time for this key indicates the first time that the device was last connected to the system during the most recent boot session. What this means is that if the system was booted at 8:30 am and the device connected to the system at 9:00 am, disconnected, and then reconnected later that day, the LastWrite time of the device's subkey beneath the DiskClassGUID key will be 9:00 am. This should remain consistent regardless of the number of times the device is disconnected and reconnected to the system.

Tip

According to Rob Lee's research, the time that a USB device was last connected to a Vista system can be correlated to the LastWrite time of the *ControlSet00n\Enum\USB* key for the device. For Windows 7 systems, the LastWrite time of the *ControlSet00n\Enum\USBStor* key for the device will tell you when it was last connected to the system.

The other GUID is defined as GUID_DEVINTERFACE_VOLUME, or VolumeClassGUID, and refers to volumes. The subkeys beneath this key are associated with volumes that are mounted on the system, as illustrated in Fig. 3.15.

As illustrated in Fig. 3.15, the device's key name contains the ParentIdPrefix value for the device, mentioned earlier in this chapter.

USB DEVICES

According to research conducted and presented by Rob Lee, additional information regarding determining the last time that a USB device was connected to a system is available in the user's NTUSER.DAT hive, specifically beneath the MountPoints2 key. This will be discussed in greater detail in chapter "Case Studies: User Hives," but this provides an analyst with two important pieces of information; one is, of course, the

Continued

> **USB DEVICES—Cont'd**
>
> last time that the device was connected to the system. The other is that by the presence of the key within the user's hive, there is now an association with a specific user. While a device may have been connected to a system, the analyst will be able to determine the time frame that it was last connected, which may be important when developing a timeline of activity on the system, as well as which user account was logged in when the device was connected.

Finally, to close out this discussion of USB devices, I wanted to include a caveat. You'll notice that throughout the discussion of USB device artifacts, I used terminology that referred to someone else's research; I did so because that's the state of the art at the moment. A great deal of the research that has gone into developing a method for tracking USB devices on (and across) Windows systems has been thorough, but short-lived. What I mean by that is that much of the research has been conducted within a short time frame, such as a few minutes, or maybe up to a few days. Very often what happens then is that we get a lot of questions from real world investigations, where analysts have run across anomalies to what has been revealed through the research. In particular, one question I see time and again has to do with time stamps (Registry key LastWrite times or values whose data contains a time stamp) not being what they "should be," or are expected to be, based on what the analyst knows about the case. Very often, these exams occur months after the device had been connected to the system, and in the interim, drivers may have been updated, patches to the operating system installed, etc. As such, my recommendation to you, dear reader, is that particularly with the number of different artifacts that you have available for something like tracking USB devices, carefully consider what you're seeing in the data. Do not just think, "...well, Harlan said in his book..." and go about your analysis. Consider what you're seeing in the data, as there is always more research to be done, and that needs to be done, especially as new versions of Windows operating systems and applications become available.

Software Hive

The Software hive maintains a great deal of configuration information for the overall system as well as applications and can provide indications to a knowledgeable analyst of how the system and installed applications may have appeared, behaved, and responded when the system was running. Understanding the role that these keys and values play in configuration of applications and the operating system can provide the analyst with a great deal of insight into a variety of different types of examinations. Throughout this section, we will discuss various keys and values from the Software hive that play a significant role in the overall configuration of the system and applications. Keep in mind, though, that we cannot cover every possible key and value because, quite simply, I need to finish this book at some point and send it to the printer! Also, there are constantly new applications being developed, as well as current applications (and the operating system) being updated to include new keys and values. What I hope to do is provide you with insight into some of the keys and values that you can expect to find on a wide range of systems, including Windows XP all the way up through Windows 7, with some information regarding Windows 8 and Windows 10.

REDIRECTION

In order to handle some differences between 64- and 32-bit systems, Windows system use Registry redirection in order to maintain different logical "views" of the Registry, as different versions of software may use different Registry keys and values. In short, the major difference (from the perspective of Registry analysis) is that 32-bit applications run in WOW64 mode will access and write to keys and values beneath the Wow6432Node key within the Software hive. As such, rather than the usual key path that appears as follows:

```
HKEY_LOCAL_MACHINE\Software\Microsoft\Windows\
CurrentVersion
```

...you would then see the key path as appears below:

```
HKEY_LOCAL_MACHINE\Software\WOW6432Node\Microsoft\
Windows\CurrentVersion
```

However, not all Registry keys are redirected on a 64-bit system; some are shared by both 32- and 64-bit versions of the operating system. Microsoft maintains a list of redirected and shared keys in the article "Registry Keys Affected by WOW64" (found online at https://msdn.microsoft.com/en-us/library/aa384253(VS.85).aspx). What this means is that when analyzing the Registry from 64-bit systems, you'll need to be cognizant of the updated key path and how it applies when viewing hives via a Registry viewer, or be sure to modify your RegRipper plugins to take this into account. Many of the RegRipper plugins that access keys and values that can be found beneath the "Wow6432Node" key have already been modified; however, as versions of the Windows operating system progress from Windows 7 through Windows 10 and beyond, it's important to continue researching and keep up with any new keys that appear, as well as new keys that may appear beneath the Wow6432Node key.

System Configuration Information

There are a number of configuration settings that could affect your analysis, and ultimately, your case; in previous books, I have referred to these as "time bombs," because at the time, they weren't something that I (or others) had seen on a regular basis. We've already mentioned some of these settings in the System hive section of this chapter, and we'll be discussing some of the settings in the Software hive here in this section.

Windows Version

Perhaps the most important values that you can extract from the Software hive is the version of the operating system. Why does this matter? This information alone can have a profound impact on the direction of your examination, as it sets our expectations as to what we *should* see on the system, and the truth is that not all versions of Windows are the same. For example, when someone wants to know what forensic artifacts they should be looking at in order to achieve the goals of their exam, that list is going to be significantly different between Windows XP and Windows 7. There is an abundance of artifacts available on Windows 7 systems that are simply nonexistent on Windows XP systems (which, to some extent, is what I've been trying to illustrate throughout this book, and other books as well).

The values we're interested in are found beneath the *Microsoft\Windows NT\CurrentVersion* key; specific values include "CurrentVersion", "ProductName", and "CSDVersion" (that last one tells us which service pack is installed). These values will tell us what version of Windows we're dealing with and provide information that we can use to guide our investigation.

The RegRipper *winver.pl* plugin extracts information from the Software hive that will tell you exactly which version of Windows you're working with; this is one of the first plugins that I run when I first start each examination, as I have seen instances where the paperwork accompanying an acquired image incorrectly stated the version of the operating system.

Tip

There are a number of Registry keys that exist in both the Software hive as well as within the user's NTUSER.DAT hive and have identical paths. One example is the Run key. The precedence of these entries will depend upon the key itself and what is specified in vendor documentation. Just as with the key in the Software hive, the Run key in the user's NTUSER.DAT hive is also used as a persistence mechanism for malware. In some cases, the key paths are the same, but very different information is maintained within the keys. For example, with the Software hive, the key may maintain

Tip—Cont'd

configuration information, while within the NTUSER.DAT hive, the key will contain settings, most recently used (MRU) lists, etc. The Internet Settings values described in MS KB article 323308, for example, allow the system administrator to set the described functionality on a system-wide basis via the Software hive or on a per-user basis by applying those settings to the appropriate user profile.

ProfileList

The Software hive maintains a list of the various profiles that are resident on the system, which includes both local and domain users. Now, let's be clear about this…this is not a list of accounts on the system, it's a list of user profiles. The SAM hive maintains a list of the user accounts on the system, but the ProfileList key maintains a list of profiles on the system, which can include both local and domain users.

When a user logs into a Windows system, the system first checks to see if that user account has a profile on the system. This is located in the *Software\Microsoft\Windows NT\CurrentVersion\ProfileList* key, as illustrated in Fig. 3.16.

Each subkey beneath the ProfileList key is an SID, and you can find a list of well-known SIDs in MS KB article 243330 (found online at https://support.microsoft.com/en-us/kb/243330). Each of the keys visible in the ProfileList key contains information about the user profile, as illustrated in Fig. 3.17.

Some of the information visible in Fig. 3.17 can be very useful for, well, some pretty obvious reasons. For example, the ProfileImagePath value tells us where the user profile and all of its associated files (NTUSER.DAT, for example) and subdirectories are located. On [Windows2000], XP, and 2003 systems, the default or usual path where we expect to see user profiles is in the path, "C:\Documents and Settings"; for Vista and above systems (including

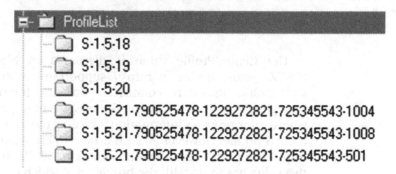

Figure 3.16 Example ProfileList key contents.

Value	Type	Data
ProfileImagePath	REG_EXPA...	%SystemDrive%\Documents and Settings\Paul
Sid	REG_BINARY	01 05 00 00 00 00 00 05 15 00 00 00 26 76 1E
Flags	REG_DWORD	0x00000000
State	REG_DWORD	0x00000100
CentralProfile	REG_SZ	
ProfileLoadTimeLow	REG_DWORD	0xFA2BF50E
ProfileLoadTimeHigh	REG_DWORD	0x01C714E9
RefCount	REG_DWORD	0x00000001
RunLogonScriptSync	REG_DWORD	0x00000000
OptimizedLogonStatus	REG_DWORD	0x00000005
NextLogonCacheable	REG_DWORD	0x00000001

Figure 3.17 Contents of a ProfileList subkey.

Windows 7 through 10), it's "C:\Users". This value, in combination with the key name (ie, the user's SID), provides a quick and easy means for associating the long SID to a username. This also allows us to quickly see if the system was at one time part of a domain (refer section Security Hive), because if it was and domain users logged into the system, some of the SID key names would be different (as opposed to just the last set of numbers...the RID...being different). Further, if the ProfileImagePath value points to some path other than what is expected, then that would tell us a couple of things, the first of which would be where to look for that user profile. The second thing it would tell us is that someone took steps to modify the default behavior of the operating system, possibly in an attempt to hide certain user activity.

Tip

It's important to remember that a user profile is not created until the account is used to log into the system. This is true not only for local accounts found in the SAM database but also for domain accounts and domain-connected systems. This may prove to be important during incident response activities, as an intruder may create local accounts on systems that they can then access at a later date, if they need to for any reason.

The CentralProfile value is discussed in MS KB article 958736 (found online at https://support.microsoft.com/en-us/kb/958736). Research conducted on the Internet (okay... "Googling") indicates that the State value may be a bit mask, whose value provides information regarding the state of the locally cached profile. However, MS KB article 150919 (found online at https://support.microsoft.com/en-us/kb/150919) indicates that this value has to do with the profile type, which can be changed via the System Control Panel applet, by going to the Advanced tab

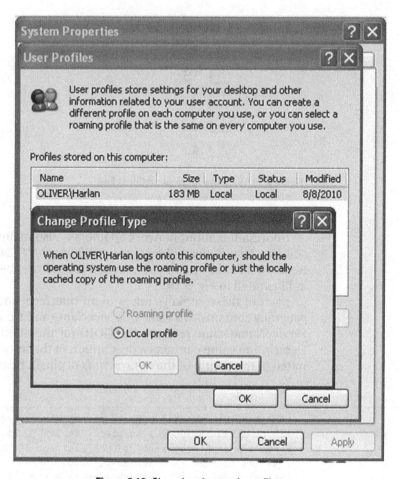

Figure 3.18 Changing the user's profile type.

and clicking the Settings button in the User Profiles section, as illustrated in Fig. 3.18.

CHANGING USERNAMES

I've seen questions posted to forums where someone has asked how to determine when a user account name was changed. I've been fortunate in the past and examined systems where auditing for "User Account Management" was enabled and found a record in the Event Log that indicated when the change was made. However, this isn't always the case. Another way to determine when this may have occurred would be to compare the LastWrite time for the user's key in the SAM (the one with the user RID in hexadecimal; for the Administrator, 000001F4 = 500) beneath the *SAM\Domains\Account\Users* key to the LastWrite time on the user's ProfileList key. Changing the username will cause the appropriate value in the SAM hive to be modified, and the key's LastWrite time will be updated.

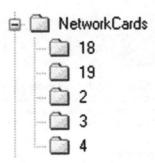

Figure 3.19 Windows XP NetworkCards key.

Network Cards

Information about network adapters is also maintained in the Software hive. Beneath the *Microsoft\Windows NT\CurrentVersion\ NetworkCards* key path, you may see several numbered subkeys, as illustrated in Fig. 3.19.

Each of these subkeys refers to an interface, and the subkey generally contains two values, ServiceName and Description. The ServiceName value refers to the GUID for the interface, and the Description value contains a description of the interface, as illustrated in the output of the *networcards.pl* plugin below:

```
Launching networkcards v.20080325
NetworkCards
Microsoft\Windows NT\CurrentVersion\NetworkCards
ADMtek AN983 10/100 PCI Adapter [Mon Sep 30 21:01:28 2002]
Siemens SpeedStream Wireless USB [Sat Apr 22 08:17:30 2006]
1394 Net Adapter [Mon Sep 30 21:02:04 2002]
Instant Wireless USB Network Adapter ver.2.5 [Fri Jan 20
07:30:12 2006]
```

The output of the plugin provides an indication of the various interfaces on the system; in this case, we can see a PCI adapter and two wireless adapters (one of which is USB). This information can provide an analyst with clues as to where to look for additional information, as the information from the Software hive supports that information about network interfaces available in the System hive (discussed earlier in this chapter).

Wireless Connections

The Windows operating system maintains information about wireless access points (WAPs) to which the system has been connected. On Windows XP, this information is visible in the Preferred Networks box in the Wireless Network Connection Properties as illustrated in Fig. 3.20.

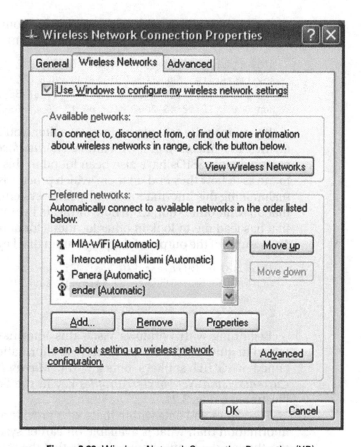

Figure 3.20 Wireless Network Connection Properties (XP).

How and where this information is maintained and visible depends on which process or application manages the wireless network connections. For example, some systems will use the Dell Wireless WLAN Card utility, and other systems may have their wireless connections and setting managed by an Intel application.

Information about wireless connections managed by Windows, such as those illustrated in Fig. 3.20, can be found in the *Microsoft\ WZCSVC\Parameters\Interfaces* key. Beneath this key, you will find a subkey with the GUID for the wireless interface, and beneath that key you'll find several values that start with "Static#00xx", where "xx" is the number of the connection. Each of these values contains binary data that appears to be a structure that is very similar to the WZC_WLAN_CONFIG structure. The *ssid.pl* plugin for RegRipper parses this structure and displays the SSID of the WAP, its MAC address, and the date that the system last connected to the WAP, as illustrated below (extracted from a Windows XP Software hive using the *ssid.pl* RegRipper plugin):

```
NIC: 11a/b/g Wireless LAN Mini PCI Express Adapter
Key LastWrite: Thu Feb 7 10:38:43 2008 UTC
Wed Oct 3 16:44:25 2007 MAC: 00-19-07-5B-36-92 tmobile
Mon Oct 8 10:12:46 2007 MAC: 00-16-B6-2F-5B-16 ender
```

If you open the ssid.pl plugin in an editor, you'll see that it also queries the *Microsoft\EAPOL\Parameters\Interfaces* key. In some cases, wireless SSIDs have also been found in this key. It's unclear to me as to how they end up there, which process is responsible for maintaining this information, or why some systems have the information while others don't, but now and again I've found information that has lead me to look in other locations for additional artifacts. An example of the output of the plugin from that key appears below:

```
NIC: 11a/b/g Wireless LAN Mini PCI Express Adapter
LastWrite time: Thu Sep 27 14:59:16 2007 UTC
1 ender
2 tmobile
```

Beginning with Windows Vista, this information was maintained in quite a different manner. This information is now maintained in GUID subkeys beneath the *Microsoft\Windows NT\ CurrentVersion\NetworkList\Profiles* key in the Software hive, as illustrated in Fig. 3.21.

The values and data within these keys provide a good deal more information than what is available on earlier systems. For example, there is the profile name, the date that the profile was created (the first time that the system connected to the WAP), and the last

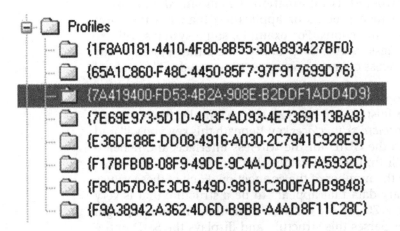

Figure 3.21 Wireless interface profile keys.

Value	Type	Data
ProfileName	REG_SZ	ender2
Description	REG_SZ	ender2
Managed	REG_DWORD	0x00000000
Category	REG_DWORD	0x00000000
DateCreated	REG_BINARY	D7 07 09 00 01 00 18 00 16 00 10 00 0A 00 52 00
NameType	REG_DWORD	0x00000047
DateLastConnected	REG_BINARY	D8 07 08 00 06 00 10 00 0A 00 35 00 10 00 AD 03

Figure 3.22 Wireless interface values.

Value	Type	Data
ProfileGuid	REG_SZ	{7A419400-FD53-4B2A-908E-B2DDF1ADD4D9}
Description	REG_SZ	ender2
Source	REG_DWORD	0x00000008
DnsSuffix	REG_SZ	<none>
FirstNetwork	REG_SZ	ender2
DefaultGatewayMac	REG_BINARY	00 15 E9 EA 39 D2 00 00

Figure 3.23 Values from *Signature\Unmanaged* subkeys.

time that the system was connected to the WAP. These values, and others, are illustrated in Fig. 3.22.

You'll notice that the data within the DateCreated and DateLastConnected values are a bit bigger than we'd expect for Unix time (32-bit) or FILETIME (64-bit) objects. The data within these values is actually 128-bit SYSTEMTIME objects. This is important as it's yet another time stamp format we have to be prepared to handle when analyzing Windows systems.

One piece of data that we don't see in these values is the WAP MAC address. If we go back to the Software hive and locate the *Microsoft\Windows NT\CurrentVersion\NetworkList\Signatures* key, we'll see *Managed* and *Unmanaged* subkeys. As the data for the Managed value illustrated in Fig. 3.22 is 0, we go to the *Unmanaged* key, and we'll see a number of subkeys whose names are long strings. Within each of these keys we find additional data that we can correlate to the data from the Profile key, using the ProfileGuid value, as illustrated in Fig. 3.23.

I wrote the RegRipper *networklist.pl* plugin to access a Vista or Windows 7 Software hive and extract and correlate the above information, an excerpt of which (run against a Vista system Software hive) is shown below:

```
Launching networklist v.20090811
Microsoft\Windows NT\CurrentVersion\NetworkList\Profiles
linksys
  Key LastWrite : Mon Feb 18 16:02:48 2008 UTC
  DateLastConnected: Mon Feb 18 11:02:48 2008
  DateCreated: Sat Feb 16 12:02:15 2008
  DefaultGatewayMac: 00-0F-66-58-41-ED
ender
  Key LastWrite : Mon Dec 22 04:09:17 2008 UTC
  DateLastConnected: Sun Dec 21 23:09:17 2008
  DateCreated: Tue Sep 11 10:33:39 2007
  DefaultGatewayMac: 00-16-B6-2F-5B-14
ender2
  Key LastWrite : Sat Aug 16 14:53:18 2008 UTC
  DateLastConnected: Sat Aug 16 10:53:16 2008
  DateCreated: Mon Sep 24 22:16:10 2007
  DefaultGatewayMac: 00-15-E9-EA-39-D2
ender2 2
  Key LastWrite : Mon Jan 12 12:42:49 2009 UTC
  DateLastConnected: Mon Jan 12 07:42:49 2009
  DateCreated: Mon Aug 25 19:19:39 2008
  DefaultGatewayMac: 00-21-29-77-D0-2D
```

The above excerpt from the networklist.pl plugin output provides an interesting view into activities on the system with respect to recording and managing the wireless connections. First, take a look at the "Key LastWrite" and "DateLastConnected" values for each profile listed; depending upon the time of year, and the time zone settings (time zone, if daylight savings is enabled), these times are exactly either 4 or 5 hours off. Remember, Registry key Last-Write times are 64-bit FILETIME objects based on GMT/UTC, and the DateLastConnected values are 128-bit SYSTEMTIME objects. What this tells us is that when the dates and times are recorded for DateCreated and DateLastConnected values, the time zone and daylight savings settings are included in the computation. This is a very important piece of information for analysts, as assuming that these values are actually UTC will be incorrect and can make a mess of your analysis, a timeline, etc.

Second, in the above excerpt we see two profiles that include the name "ender2", and the second one has an additional "2" as well as a different MAC address. In this case, I know what happened...the original WAP with the SSID "ender2" had "died" and was replaced. Rather than replacing the original information,

Windows (in this case, Vista) created a second profile and left the original profile information intact. Understanding or just being aware of this can be very helpful to an analyst.

AutoStart

Much like the System hive, the Software hive contains a number (albeit a limited one) of locations from which applications and programs can be started with little to no interaction from the user beyond simply booting the system and logging in. Many of these locations are used by application authors for completely legitimate purposes; unfortunately, as we've mentioned with respect to Browser Helper Objects (BHOs), they're also used by malware authors.

The Run Key

Perhaps the most well known of all of the autostart locations is the ubiquitous "Run" key (*Microsoft\Windows\CurrentVersion\Run*) described in MS KB article 314866 (found online at https://support.microsoft.com/en-us/kb/314866). This key has long been used by both malware and legitimate applications alike as a refuge for persistence, and continues to be used, even today. I regularly see malware that creates a value beneath this key, whether I'm performing analysis during a breach response or researching new malware via such sites as the Microsoft Malware Protection Center (MMPC, found online at https://www.microsoft.com/security/portal/threat/threats.aspx). Further, I've seen systems infected by one variant of malware that were later infected by another variant of the same malware (as determined by reviewing the write-ups on the malware), so the Run key contained multiple values that pointed to the malware variants.

I'm not sure what it is about this particular key, but a good deal of malware persists via this location. And what's really interesting about this is that often times, the malware that persists via this key goes undetected for weeks or months when conventional, antivirus techniques (file examination) are used.

In October 2015, I ran across a description of malware that had been dubbed "Moker"; the write-up on this malware is available from the EnSilo website, found online at http://blog.ensilo.com/moker-a-new-apt-discovered-within-a-sensitive-network. The description of the malware went into significant detail regarding techniques the author(s) had used to ensure that the malware would avoid detection, and if found, be difficult to analyze. However, as determined later in the comments section of the write-up, the persistence mechanism turned out to be the Run key (the particular hive…Software or NTUSER.DAT…is dependent upon the privileges of the infected user, as is often the case); at that point, I had difficulty understanding how this malware was difficult to detect.

Note

Many times, malware write-ups get an important aspect of persistence incorrect. Specifically, if malware infects a system via a user account with normal user privileges, very often that malware will persist by creating a value beneath the user's Run key, in the "HKCU" hive for the currently logged in user. In such instances, the malware will not start again once the system reboots; rather, it won't start until the infected user logs in.

If the infected user account has Administrator-level privileges, the malware will often create a value beneath the Run key within the Software hive, which will allow the malware to start once the system has been rebooted, and without requiring any user to log into the system.

The *soft_run.pl* RegRipper plugin collects values from the Run key within the Software hive, as well as a number of other similar autostart keys. For example, the *Microsoft\Windows\Current Version\Policies\Explorer\Run* key can be used by group policies to specify autostart programs (as described online *at* https://technet.microsoft.com/en-us/magazine/ee851671.aspx). The plugin will also check for redirected keys on 64-bit systems (if you remember the discussion of the Wow6432Node key earlier in this chapter).

The Notify Key

Another location of interest within the Software hive is the *Microsoft\Windows NT\CurrentVersion\Winlogon\Notify* key. Entries beneath this key define packages (most often DLLs) that are to receive notifications from the WinLogon process. These notifications can include when the user logs in and the shell (ie, Windows Explorer) loads, when the screensaver starts, when the workstation is locked or unlocked, when the user logs out, etc. All of these actions cause an event to be generated, and packages can be designated to take some action when this occurs. Examples of malware that makes use of this key include Virtumonde (aka Vundu) and Contravirus, and a backdoor identified at the ThreatExpert site as "Eterok.C" actually deletes entries from the *Winlogon\Notify* key.

When I say "location of interest," I know that sounds kind of hoity-toity, but one of the things I've found time and again over the years, especially with respect to autostart locations in the Registry, is that once you stop looking at the ones you know about, and you stop looking for new ones, they start being used more often. Over the years, I've heard malware authors say that some autostart locations are no longer of use (the same has been said of NTFS alternate data streams but that's outside the scope of this book) but the fact of the matter is that there are a great deal of system administrators out there (as well as forensic analysts) who simply aren't aware of these locations and how they can be used. Add to that instances where antivirus applications do not detect the malware that's actually loaded (or the antivirus applications are disabled during the malware installation process) from these locations, and what ends up happening is that systems get and remain infected for a considerable period of time.

Tip

Different malware families will employ different persistence mechanisms using the Registry. For example, one of the hallmarks of a ZBot infection is the presence of a reference to the malware within the UserInit value in the *Microsoft\Windows NT\CurrentVersion\Winlogon* key within the Software hive.

Other malware will leave various artifacts within the Registry; while not used to maintain persistence, these artifacts can be used as indicators to determine if (and possibly when) the system was infected. For example, some variants of Ilomo/Clampi have been found to create the Microsoft\9593275321 key within the Software hive. Virut is a file infector, but some variants have been found to add a value named "UpdateHost" to the *Microsoft\Windows\CurrentVersion\Explorer* key in the Software hive, as well as adding an exception for themselves to the firewall policy.

Image File Execution Options

Yet another autostart location (I told you there were a lot of these!) can be found in the *Image File Execution Options* key. Now, Microsoft provides documentation (found online at http://support.microsoft.com/kb/824344) on the use of this key, which is intended to provide debugging capability and can also be used to turn off the Windows Update feature in Windows XP (found online at http://support.microsoft.com/kb/892894). Like many other tools and techniques that are useful to administrators, this technique can also be used for malicious purposes, and malware authors have been seen using this technique to maintain persistence of their applications. In fact, the Microsoft Threat Encyclopedia discusses the malware known as Win32/Bebloh.A (found online at https://www.microsoft.com/security/portal/threat/encyclopedia/entry.aspx?Name=TrojanSpy:Win32/Bebloh.A#tab=2), which uses this functionality to force Internet Explorer to be launched whenever any other browser (Opera,

Safari, Firefox, etc.) is launched. And this is nothing new...Dana Epp wrote a blog post (found online at http://silverstr.ufies.org/blog/archives/000809.html) on this issue in March 2005.

In short, by adding a "Debugger" value to the application sub-keys beneath the *Image File Execution Options* key, you can force a debugger or another application to be loaded instead. You can demonstrate this easily by adding a key called "notepad.exe", and within that key, add a string value named "Debugger." Then, add the string "sol.exe" (or any other application that launches as a GUI) to the value. Now, use any method to launch Notepad. Pretty neat, huh? And this works with any application. If you were running a tool like Process Monitor while launching Notepad and monitoring for Registry accesses, you'd notice that the operating system accesses this key and attempts to locate a subkey for the application being loaded. So, this is functionality that, while included in Registry value, is implemented as a function of how the operating system operates. Interestingly, I have seen this auto-start location during engagements and, as such, wrote the RegRipper *imagefile.pl* plugin to query the *Image File Execution Options* subkeys, looking for and displaying Debugger values.

Note

In August 2010, Microsoft released KB article 2264107 (found online at http://support.microsoft.com/kb/2264107) in order to address issues related to the DLL Search Order vulnerability, specifically as it relates to remote resources (ie, folders) accessible via SMB and WebDAV. Specific applications can be protected by adding the "CWDIllegalInDllSearch" value, with the appropriate data setting, to the Image File Execution Options key. The RegRipper *imagefile.pl* plugin was updated to check for both the Debugger and CWDIllegalInDllSearch values.

To see an example of how this functionality can be used for malicious purposes, consider the "Sticky Keys" accessibility functionality provided by Windows systems, particularly those running Terminal Services. With prior access to the system, an intruder can add the "sethc.exe" subkey to the *Image File Execution Options* key ("utilman.exe" also works) and then add the "Debugger" value, pointing it to the command prompt, cmd.exe. Once a connection is established from a remote system, the command to create the key looks like the following:

```
C:\>reg add "\\192.168.1.110\HKLM\Software\Microsoft\
Windows NT\CurrentVersion\Image File Execution Options\
sethc.exe" /v "Debugger" /t REG_SZ /d "cmd.exe" /f
```

Returning later using the Terminal Services Client (and with network level authentication disabled, which can also be done

Figure 3.24 System-level command prompt, courtesy of "Sticky Keys".

remotely), the intruder does not need to authenticate to the system at all (that is, enter a username and password) but instead just hit the Shift key five times (or the "Win + U" key combination for utilman.exe) to get a System-level command prompt, as illustrated in Fig. 3.24.

Again, this requires no authentication whatsoever, which means that it will still work even if the IT staff has changed passwords throughout the enterprise. With a command prompt with System-level privileges, the intruder can run commands to…well, pretty much anything they want. For example, they can add a user account to the system, modify system settings, etc.

Using the functionality provided by this key is not something limited solely to the bad guys; the good guys can use it as well. Does your organization use *at.exe* to create Scheduled Tasks within the infrastructure, particularly on remote systems? Do your system administrators use *net.exe* to manage (create accounts, etc.) user accounts within the infrastructure? If not, why not create a subkey for the executables and point it to another executable or a batch file that will alert you to its use? That way, the first time an intruder tries to use either of these programs, they will find that they don't work, and you will be alerted. They may try again (and you'll be alerted again), and they may even go to the file itself, see if it exists, and even try to determine if it's the real one. It will take them some time and effort to figure out what's going on. In fact, they'll have to change their approach, perhaps enough so that you're provided some "breathing room" to respond. Regardless, you'll be alerted to the attempted use of the executable.

AppInit_DLLs

The AppInit_DLLs value is interesting, as according to MS KB article 197571 (found online at https://support.microsoft.com/en-us/kb/197571) the DLLs listed in this value (comma or space delimited) are loaded by each "Windows-based application." This means that the value will be read and the DLLs loaded with each GUI application that's launched on the system. Within Windows 7 and [Windows2008] R2, Microsoft modified the infrastructure for this value and its capabilities, as described online at https://msdn.microsoft.com/en-us/library/windows/desktop/dd744762(v=vs.85).aspx.

The value is located beneath the *Microsoft\Windows NT\CurrentVersion\Windows* key; you can use the *appinitdlls.pl* RegRipper plugin to retrieve any data from the value. I will say that in 15+ years (at the time of this writing) of performing incident response and digital forensic analysis, I have rarely seen DLLs listed in this value. Again…rarely. Not "never."

Shell Extensions

Shell extensions can also provide an autostart mechanism. In 2010, our team observed what was an apparently novel approach to persistence based on the use of approved shell extensions. There are a considerable number of articles available at the Microsoft website that address topics such as writing shell extensions and also shell extension security. However, where shell extensions come into play as a persistence mechanism is that they are loaded when the Windows Explorer "shell" loads and provide some sort of functionality extension beyond the basic shell. Many of the approved shell extensions that are loaded by the shell have explicit paths that lead directly to the DLL to be loaded, and in many cases, these are located in the Windows\system32 directory. However, some of the approved shell extensions (in the Software hive, as well as in the user's NTUSER.DAT hive) do not have explicit paths. Therefore, when Explorer.exe attempts to load the shell extension, it must first locate it, and in doing so, it begins searching in its own directory (C:\Windows) first. This DLL search order behavior is documented at the Microsoft website; the documentation can be found online at http://msdn.microsoft.com/en-us/library/ms682586.

During the malware reverse engineering panel at the "SANS What Works In Incident Response and Forensics" conference in July 2010, Nick Harbour (Nick worked at Mandiant at the time) briefly described this persistence mechanism, as well, based on what his team had seen, and how they approached the issue (Nick is well known for his malware reverse engineering skills). Nick's blog post addressed the DLL search order issue from a much wider scope and appeared to refer to DLLs that are loaded based on their presence in an executable file's import table. To read more about how he described the issue, take a look at what Nick had to say about this persistence mechanism in an M-union blog post, found online at http://blog.mandiant.com/archives/1207. Nick also mentions how to use the KnownDLLs (*ControlSet00n\ Control\Session Manager\KnownDLLs*, described at the Microsoft website, at http://support.microsoft.com/kb/102985) key to protect a system from this sort of attack.

From the perspective of the shell extensions, in short, by using the same name as a legitimate approved shell extension (albeit one that was located in the *C:\Windows\system32* directory) and placing that DLL in the *C:\Windows* directory alongside explorer. exe, the malware was able to ensure that it was loaded each time a user logged in; however, this persistence mechanism required NO modifications to any files on the system (outside of the creation of one new one), nor did it require any modifications to the Registry. From the Microsoft site, we can see that the *SafeDllSearchMode* functionality is enabled by default (and can be disabled). However, close examination of the article reveals that regardless of whether the functionality is enabled or disabled, the DLL search order begins in "the directory from which the application loaded." As such, whenever a user logs into the system, the Windows Explorer shell (explorer.exe) is loaded, and then the approved shell extensions are automatically loaded.

In order to assist in investigations where this functionality may have been used as a persistence mechanism, I wrote the *shellext.pl* plugin for RegRipper. This plugin parses through the values of the *Microsoft\Windows\CurrentVersion\Shell Extensions\ Approved* key in the Software hive, collects the names (GUIDs) and data (description of the shell extension) for each value, and then navigates to the *Classes\CLSID* key to map the GUID to a DLL path. An excerpt of the output of this plugin is provided as follows:

```
{6756A641-DE71-11d0-831B-00AA005B4383} MRU AutoComplete
List
   DLL: %SystemRoot%\system32\browseui.dll
   Timestamp: Mon Apr 4 17:43:08 2005 Z
{7BD29E00-76C1-11CF-9DD0-00A0C9034933} Temporary Internet
Files
   DLL: %SystemRoot%\system32\shdocvw.dll
   Timestamp: Mon Apr 4 17:43:09 2005 Z
{f81e9010-6ea4-11ce-a7ff-00aa003ca9f6} Shell extensions
for sharing
   DLL: ntshrui.dll
   Timestamp: Mon Apr 4 18:37:13 2005 Z
```

Due to the amount of data available, this plugin can take several seconds to run; as such, I tend to run it via rip.exe rather than via a profile. However, from the output excerpt, you can see that two approved shell extensions (browseui.dll and shdocvw.dll) have explicit paths, whereas the third (ntshrui.dll) does not. In this case, in order to load the DLL, the Explorer.exe process must search for it in accordance with DLL search order; therefore, the search begins in *C:\Windows*, where Explorer.exe is located.

A very quick way to use this information during an examination is to collect all of the lines of the output that start with "DLL:" to a file, and then to parse the file looking at directory paths. For example, start with a command that appears as follows:

```
C:\tools>rip.exe -r D:\case\software -p shellext | find
"DLL:" >
D:\case\file\shellext.txt
```

The result of the above command will be a file containing only the lines that start with "DLL:", and from there, you can strip out the entries that do not contain path information such as "%SystemRoot%\system32" or something else. Of the remaining files, run a search for those files that appear in the C:\Windows directory. If they only appear in the C:\Windows directory, depending on the DLL in question, that may be expected; however, if files with that name appear in both the C:\Windows and the C:\Windows\system32 directory, you may have found something of value.

Note

The use of approved shell extensions as a persistence mechanism is very insidious, due to its very simplicity. This mechanism requires only that a DLL file of a specific name be created in a specific directory and does NOT require any modifications to the Registry. As long as the "subverted" shell extension does not remove regularly accessed functionality and the capability provided by the shell extension is not missed, then the malware may be run without any complaints from the user.

To protect a system against the sort of attack that takes advantage of the DLL search order, there are two options available. One is to locate all of the shell extensions in the Registry that use implicit paths and give each of them the appropriate explicit path. Another method is to add an entry for the DLL (ntshrui.dll) to the *ControlSet00x\Control\Session Manager\KnownDLLs* Registry key (found online at http://support.microsoft.com/kb/164501).

Overall, however, this is simply one example of a much larger issue that was originally identified as far back as the year 2000, but became more visible in August and September 2010, and was referred to as "DLL hijacking." In short, the use of shell extensions is but one example of a mechanism to get an executable to search for a DLL that it needs to load in order to perform some function. Readers interested in learning more about this issue should search for "DLL hijacking" via Google.

Using this technique, I mounted an acquired image as a read only drive letter on my analysis system and ran the above command. I located a shell extension named "slayerXP.dll", and when running the search, I found instances of the DLL in a ServicePack directory, as well as in the C:\Windows\system32 directory. Both instances had the same size, as well as the same MD5 hash. Further examination of the DLL indicated that it was a legitimate Microsoft file.

Browser Helper Objects

If the web browser in use on a system is Internet Explorer (IE), then another area that can be examined for indications of malware (usually, some sort of adware or a browser toolbar, although not always...) is the BHOs listing, which is found in the following key in the Software hive:

```
Microsoft\Windows\CurrentVersion\Explorer\Browser Helper
Objects
```

BHOs are DLLs that IE can load to provide additional functionality and allow for customization to the browser, much like plugins used for Firefox, or shell extensions for Windows Explorer (discussed in the "Shell Extensions" section later in this chapter). Examples of common BHOs include those for the Adobe Acrobat Reader, and the Google, Alexa, and Ask.com toolbars. Again, these are DLLs that are loaded by IE and not when the system is booted or a user logs into the system. If IE is not launched, the DLLs will not be loaded. However, if IE is used, then the DLLs will be loaded without any interaction by the user.

The use of BHOs to load malicious software is nothing new. In 2002, I was working in a full-time employment (as opposed to consulting) position at a company where someone had found something a bit unusual on their system. It turns out that the employee was in the marketing department, so what she found was indeed concerning. She was viewing the online content for our company website, and she noticed that in each instance where our company name was in the web page, the name was now a hyperlink...which was not the behavior for which the web page was designed. Out of curiosity, she clicked on the hyperlink (yeah, bad idea, I know...) and was taken to a competitor's web page! It turned out that her system had been infected with a BHO that would look for specific words and names in web pages and modify the contents of the web page to create hyperlinks to competitor's websites. I use the RegRipper bho.pl plugin to extract information about BHOs installed on the system for every examination, particularly those that involve malware of some kind.

Scheduled Tasks

Scheduled Tasks are likely not often thought about by most users (or administrators), but they do provide an excellent facility to ensure applications are run on a regular basis. In addition, some Scheduled Tasks can be configured to run based on various triggers, such as when a user logs in or logs out, for example. Scheduled Tasks can be created via a wizard or through the use of command line tools such as *schtasks.exe* or *at.exe*. In fact, dedicated adversaries are known to use Scheduled Tasks for both persistence (providing an autostart mechanism) and lateral movement with a network infrastructure.

Another important point with respect to Scheduled Tasks is that a good number of processes that were installed as Windows services on Windows XP and 2003 systems were moved to Scheduled Tasks as of Windows Vista, and this trend continued with Windows 7 and beyond. Want an easy way to see how many Scheduled Tasks are on a default installation of Windows 7 or even Windows 10? Simply open a command prompt and type "schtasks", and hit enter. If you want an accurate count, pipe the output of the command to a file and start counting.

When a Scheduled Task is created, a number of artifacts are created, including files within the file system, Windows Event Log records, and (to the focus of this book) a Registry key. For example, we can use the following command to create a Scheduled Task:

```
C:\>schtasks /create /sc daily /tn blahblah /tr "C:\program
files\microsoft games\solitaire\solitaire.exe" /st 22:16:00
```

The above code creates a task named "blahblah", which appears in the Registry beneath the *HKLM\Software\Microsoft\Windows NT\Schedule\TaskCache\Tree* key, as illustrated in Fig. 3.25.

Scheduled Tasks created using the *schtasks.exe* command can be set to run at a specific time (as with the above command), when a user logs on, when the system starts, or when the system is idle. If no other changes are made to the Scheduled Task, then the key LastWrite time can be incorporated into a timeline in order to further analysis.

Similar to *schtasks.exe*, using the *at.exe* command to create a Scheduled Task will create a Registry key in the same path; however, the *at.exe* command does not provide an option to name the tasks. Instead, it uses its own naming convention. The first task created is named "At1", the second is named "At2", and so on. The RegRipper *at.pl* plugin will display all Scheduled Tasks created using the *at.exe* command still visible in an extracted Software hive, and the *at_tln.pl* plugin will output the same information in a format suitable for including in a timeline.

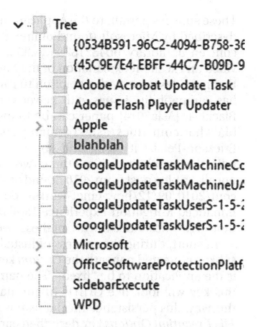

Figure 3.25 Scheduled Tasks viewed via the Registry Editor on Windows 10.

Again, dedicated adversaries use the Scheduled Task facility to great effect to not only remain persistent on systems, but to also move laterally within an infrastructure. Scheduled Tasks can be created on remote systems.

Warning

One aspect that an intruder can rely on is that many live incident response toolkits that I've seen will include commands to run either *schtasks.exe* or *at.exe*. These toolkits are intended to allow an analyst to run a number of commands, usually via a batch file, in order to quickly collect information from a live system. Each of the commands will show only those tasks created with that command; that is to say that commands created with *at.exe* will not appear when the list of Scheduled Tasks is queried using *schtasks.exe*. As such, both commands will need to be used in these toolkits.

AppCompatFlags

The AppCompatFlags key is usually thought of as providing information within the program execution category, but several of the subkeys may provide information within the autostart category; specifically, the *Custom* and *InstalledSDB* subkeys beneath the *Microsoft\Windows NT\CurrentVersion\AppCompatFlags* key.

These subkeys pertain to the Application Compatibility Database, described by Microsoft (found online at https://msdn.microsoft.com/en-us/library/bb432182(v=vs.85).aspx). Jon Erikson provided an excellent explanation of the Microsoft "Fix-It" capability that provides users with a solution to running an application that has compatibility issues with newer versions of Windows (Jon's BlackHat [Asia2014] paper can be found online at https://www.blackhat.com/docs/asia-14/materials/Erickson/WP-Asia-14-Erickson-Persist-It-Using-And-Abusing-Microsofts-Fix-It-Patches.pdf); this capability utilizes these two subkeys as well. And that's not all…a blog post from 2010 (found online at http://0xdabbad00.com/2010/09/12/how-emet-works) describes how Microsoft's Enhanced Mitigation Experience Toolkit (or "EMET") works and thoroughly describes the use of these two subkeys.

In short, during the process of installing a "Fix-It" database, a subkey is created beneath the *Custom* key, and this subkey's name is the application to be "fixed." The names of the values beneath this key will look like GUIDs (there may be more than one). In this way, this persistence mechanism is very similar to the *Image File Execution Options* key described earlier in this chapter. Then, beneath the *InstalledSDB* key, there will be one subkey for each of the value names beneath the *Custom\{AppName}* subkey, and each key will have several values that pertain the particular database file to which the entry refers. One value, named "DatabasePath", points to the specific database (or *.sdb file) on disk; another value, named "DatabaseDescription", gives a short description of the database.

Microsoft uses this capability to provide legitimate "fixes" for applications. For example, a patch for the Microsoft XML Core Services included the installation of an *.sdb file intended to "fix" Internet Explorer (a description can be found online at https://isc.sans.edu/forums/diary/Microsoft+Security+Advisory+2719615+MSXML+CVE20121889/13459). The "DatabaseDescription" value beneath the *InstalledSDB\{GUID}* keys read "CVE-2012-1889", indicating that the patch was intended to address a known vulnerability. This same capability can be (and has been) abused by malware authors who wish to have their application remain persistent, as well. Symantec's write-up on Trojan.Gootkit (found online at http://ae.norton.com/security_response/print_writeup.jsp?docid=2010-051118-0604-99), first published in 2010 and updated in 2015, describes malware that attempted to "patch" a number of applications, including OutLook, a number of different web browsers, and even the Windows Explorer shell.

The *appcompatflags.pl* plugin can be used to extract and correlate information from the *Custom* and *InstalledSDB* keys in order to illustrate the contents of the persistence mechanism to the analyst; however, the caveat is that not all of the entries may be malicious, as some may be completely legitimate.

Program Execution

As stated previously in this chapter, very often the program execution category overlaps a good deal with the autostart category. With respect to locations within the Software hive that indicate program execution beyond those already discussed in the autostart category earlier in this chapter, I can't say that I've found many. You may see some applications recorded beneath that *AppCompatFlags* subkeys, but I tend to find indicators more often within the NTUSER.DAT hive than the Software hive; the RegRipper *appcompatflags.pl* plugin can be run against both hives.

LANDesk

Back in 2009, I was working with Don Weber, and he sent me something interesting from an engagement he was working on; specifically, the client he was working with was using the LANDesk product for software and system management within their infrastructure. What he found was the LANDesk application was recording information about program executions, and this information was being maintained in the following key:

```
LANDesk\ManagementSuite\WinClient\SoftwareMonitoring\
MonitorLog
```

I should note that if the operating system is 64-bit and the application is 32-bit, the path will be prepended with "Wow6432Node".

Beneath the MonitorLog key is a series of subkeys, one for each application executed, and in many cases, the key name contains the full path to executable (ie, "C:/Program Files (x86)/Internet Explorer/iexplore.exe"). Each of these keys has several values that appear to be self-explanatory, including "Current User" (the user account under which the application was most recently run), "First Started", "Last Started", "Total Duration", and "Total Runs". An example of these values, and their data, can be seen in Fig. 3.26.

This information can be extremely valuable to an analyst, providing information not only about when programs were first and most recently executed but also by which user account. From the few systems I've seen that have the LANDesk application installed, this information persists and provides a record of program execution much longer than the AppCompatCache data in the System hive, which we discussed earlier in this chapter.

ab (Default)	REG_SZ	(value not set)
Current Duration	REG_BINARY	00 00 00 00 00 00 00 00
ab Current User	REG_SZ	SYSTEM
First Started	REG_BINARY	c0 3c c1 9d d6 eb d0 01
Last Duration	REG_BINARY	30 ab 6e 01 00 00 00 00
Last Started	REG_BINARY	a0 26 87 2c a8 ec d0 01
Total Duration	REG_BINARY	d0 6f 2a 04 00 00 00 00
Total Runs	REG_DWORD	0x00000004 (4)

Figure 3.26 LANDesk values seen via the Registry Editor.

The *landesk.pl* plugin, last updated in March 2013, can parse and display this information for the analyst, and the *landesk_tln. pl* plugin will retrieve the same information in a format suitable for inclusion in a timeline of system activity.

Malware

There are a number of malware variants that have been seen to create Registry keys or values that are not associated with persistence. In some cases, the entries created are used to maintain configuration information or some value that the malware uses to identify the infected system. Some time ago, I began documenting many of these keys and values in RegRipper plugins; for example, I wrote the *renocide.pl* plugin based on what Microsoft published about the malware in February 2011 (the write-up can be found online at http://www.microsoft.com/security/portal/threat/encyclopedia/ entry.aspx?Name=Win32/Renocide#tab=2). Microsoft's findings indicate that the malware created the *HKLM\Software\Microsoft\ DRM\amty* key and then created a number of values beneath that key that held configuration information for the malware.

More recently, I've started documenting many of the Registry keys and values that I find that are used by malware, but not for persistence, within the *malware.pl* plugin. This particular plugin is broken down into sections, depending upon the hive in question, and all of the keys and values I'm interested in checking for are included in this one plugin. So, yes, it will fail to find something in the Software hive if it's specifically looking for something in the System hive. However, the plugin is designed to keep going and not throw an exemption or do something else to cause RegRipper to have issues. Using it tends to go pretty smooth, and I know I'm going to be really glad when it finds something that I'd forgotten about.

Audio Devices

In November 2014, Brian Baskin posted an article to his blog (found online at http://www.ghettoforensics.com/2014/11/dj-forensics-analysis-of-sound-mixer.html) that discussed analyzing sound mixer settings or artifacts on systems for indications of applications (possibly malware, or more specifically, RATs) that were registered with an audio device. From the article, "Whenever an application requests the use of the Windows audio drivers, Windows will automatically register this application in the registry." In Brian's case, he found a reference to an alternate browser that had been run from a TrueCrypt-encrypted volume.

This is yet another example of artifacts (potentially, indicators of malicious activity) that are left on a system, not due to the direct action of a malicious user or malware (ie, something specifically included in the code of the malware), but rather due to the malware interacting within its ecosystem. As such, as Brian stated in his article, these artifacts tend to persist on a system and survive even an application uninstall.

The RegRipper *audiodev.pl* plugin will enumerate information from the appropriate data sources within the Software hive.

AmCache Hive

The "AmCache" hive is a file that has an identical structure to other Registry files but does not appear to be part of the Registry, at least not as we think of it or view it, such as via the Registry Editor. However, the file can be opened in a hive viewer application (see chapter: Processes and Tools), other tools have been written to parse the information in this file, and I wrote a RegRipper plugin specifically for parsing the file. The file is named "AmCache.hve", and is located in the *C:\Windows\AppCompat\Programs* folder. This file was first seen on Windows 8 and 8.1 systems and then on Windows 10 systems. I'd also seen it on the Windows 10 Technical Preview (by those who downloaded and installed it; I installed it as a virtual machine in Oracle's VirtualBox). In December 2014 and January 2015, folks started noticing that this file was appearing on Windows 7 systems as well, possibly as a result of an update. At the time of this writing, several folks have reported attempting to track down the Windows update that resulted in the creation of the file, but so far, no results have been shared.

Note

While the information within the AmCache.hve file does not appear in the Registry Editor view while the system is running, according to information available on the Microsoft Developer Network (MSDN), the debugger command "!reg hivelist" will result in the AmCache.hve file being listed as part of the response. This information can be found online at https://msdn.microsoft.com/en-us/library/windows/hardware/ff564790(v=vs.85).aspx.

The first time I heard about this file was when I read a blog post from Yogesh Khatri (the post can be found online at http://www.swiftforensics.com/2013/12/amcachehve-in-windows-8-goldmine-for.html) from December 2013. The file appears to be part of the Application Compatibility functionality on Windows systems and reportedly replaces the RecentFileCache.bcf file.

The AmCache.hve file appears to contain two keys that are of primary interest; Files and Programs. Fig. 3.27 illustrates these keys as seen in the AmCache.hve file extracted from a Windows 7 system.

Yogesh addresses and describes the contents of both of these keys (subkeys and values) in his blog post listed previously in this chapter, and in a subsequent blog post, found online at http://www.swiftforensics.com/2013/12/amcachehve-part-2.html.

As you can see in Fig. 3.27, beneath the *File* key are subkeys that Yogesh has identified as volume GUIDs; each of the subkeys identifies a different volume. This volume GUID information can be tracked back to the MountedDevices key in the System hive in order to determine to which drive letter that volume was mounted on the system. As seen in Fig. 3.27, the two volume GUIDs (b75801db-1456-11e0-9309-806e6f6e6963, and b75801dc-1456-11e0-9309-806e6f6e6963) map to the C:\ and D:\ volumes, respectively, on the Windows 7 system.

Beneath each of the volume GUID subkeys, there are additional subkeys, as illustrated in Fig. 3.28.

Yogesh has identified each of these subkeys as the MFT file reference number for a particular file. The first 2 bytes are the sequence number, and the remaining bytes of the key name are the MFT record number.

Let's take a look at an example using the AmCache.hve file first illustrated in Fig. 3.27. Beneath the volume GUID key for the D:\ volume, there is a subkey named "a00001d2", and per Yogesh's research, the key name would indicate that the MFT record number for the file is "1d2" in hex, or 466, in decimal, and the sequence number is "a", or 10 in decimal. Parsing the MFT for the D:\ volume from this system, we see that this is, in fact, the case; the file associated with file record number 466 has a sequence number of 10, or "a" in hex.

Figure 3.27 Windows 7 AmCache.hve file (opened in WRR).

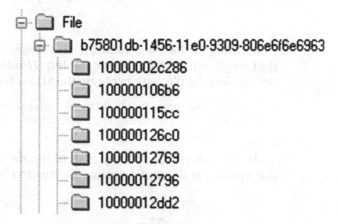

Figure 3.28 Volume GUID key contents (via WRR).

The contents of the "a00001d2" key appear in Fig. 3.29.

As you can see in Fig. 3.29, the key contents refer to a file named "lnk_parser_cmd.exe", which is found on the D:\ volume of this Windows 7 system. Per the MFT from this system, the MFT record in question points to ".\tools\lnk\lnk_parser_cmd.exe".

Yogesh's blog post from December 2013 contains a reference table for the various value names and their data that appear beneath the "file reference" keys. According to that table, value 15 is the full path to the program, value 17 is a last modified time stamp for the

Value	Type	Data
17	REG_QWORD	62 D8 B1 A7 19 6C CE 01
15	REG_SZ	d:\Tools\LNK\lnk_parser_cmd.exe
100	REG_SZ	0000ffea705b14e334ad0ac04e1a8011a00d0000ffff
101	REG_SZ	000063ab2a6d6868ef71c1e79ee295cfd14b8725ad5a

Figure 3.29 "a00001ds" key contents (via WRR).

file, and value 101 is the SHA-1 hash of the file. Yogesh's table (listed in his blog post) contains a greater listing of what various potential values refer to, so be sure to reference the post (in case there are updates), particularly if you need to identify other values.

Tip

The RegRipper plugin *amcache.pl* can be used to parse and display the contents of the AmCache.hve file.

Running a hashing tool (in this case, Jesse Kornblum's sha1deep64.exe, found online at http://md5deep.sourceforge. net) against the file, we can obtain the SHA-1 hash, as follows:

```
D:\Tools>sha1deep64 d:\tools\lnk\lnk_parser_cmd.exe
   63ab2a6d6868ef71c1e79ee295cfd14b8725ad5a d:\tools\lnk\
lnk_parser_cmd.exe
```

As you can see, the SHA-1 hash of the file matches the value that appears in the AmCache.hve file seen in Fig. 3.29.

Tip

Analysts can take advantage of the fact that the SHA-1 hash of a file is maintained in the AmCache.hve file. For example, let's say that you're looking at an AmCache.hve file from a compromised system, and you find a key that refers to a file that no longer exists on the system. The key name for the file is "a00001d2", and the path to the file is suspicious (perhaps something like "C:\Windows\Temp\g.exe"). After parsing the MFT, you determine that the sequence number for the MFT record number 466 ("1d2" in hex) is now 12, or "c" in hex. This supports the finding that the file "C:\Windows\Temp\g.exe" was deleted from the system, and as the MFT record was reused, the sequence number was updated accordingly. However, if you suspect that the file was malware, you can use the SHA-1 hash of the file to search a site like VirusTotal.com to see if a file with that hash had been uploaded to the site and identified as malware.

Value	Type	Data
13	REG_DWORD	0x00000000
0	REG_SZ	Microsoft Security Client
1	REG_SZ	4.6.0305.0
2	REG_SZ	Microsoft Corporation
3	REG_SZ	1033
5	REG_DWORD	0x00000101
6	REG_SZ	AddRemoveProgram
b	REG_QWORD	00 00 00 00 00 00 00 00
a	REG_QWORD	E7 F4 8A 54 00 00 00 00
Files	REG_MULTI_SZ	b75801db-1456-11e0-9309-806e6f6e6963@4000031!
7	REG_MULTI_SZ	HKEY_LOCAL_MACHINE\Software\Microsoft\Windo
11	REG_MULTI_SZ	{23f2c78c-e131-4ca0-8f84-3473fb7728ba}
12	REG_MULTI_SZ	{266F7358-F5CB-4BD1-A279-A6992423A9A4}
f	REG_SZ	{23f2c78c-e131-4ca0-8f84-3473fb7728ba}
10	REG_SZ	{266F7358-F5CB-4BD1-A279-A6992423A9A4}
14	REG_DWORD	0x00000000
15	REG_DWORD	0x00000000
16	REG_BINARY	46 41 44 44 00 00 00 00 00 00 00 00 00 00 01 00 30

Figure 3.30 ProgramID key contents.

According to Yogesh's further research into the AmCache.hve file (his findings can be found online at http://www.swiftforensics.com/2013/12/amcachehve-part-2.html), the Programs key contains references to programs installed on Windows 8 (and Windows 7) systems, specifically information that is similar to what can be found in the "Programs and Features" applet in the Control Panel. Most often, this information appears to refer to programs or applications installed via a Microsoft Installer (MSI) file.

Beneath the Programs key (see Fig. 3.27), the subkeys appear to refer to program identifiers (IDs), which are assigned when an MSI file is compiled. Each of these keys contains information similar to what is illustrated in Fig. 3.30.

As with the contents of the Files key in the AmCache.hve file, Yogesh's blog post contains a table that illustrates what each of values visible in Fig. 3.30 references. For example, value 0 is the

```
b758001db-1456-11e0-9309-806e6f6e6963@4000031561
b758001db-1456-11e0-9309-806e6f6e6963@400003154f
b758001db-1456-11e0-9309-806e6f6e6963@4000031559
b758001db-1456-11e0-9309-806e6f6e6963@400003155b
b758001db-1456-11e0-9309-806e6f6e6963@5d00001a513
b758001db-1456-11e0-9309-806e6f6e6963@417e00001bbe8
b758001db-1456-11e0-9309-806e6f6e6963@400003155d
b758001db-1456-11e0-9309-806e6f6e6963@4000031535
b758001db-1456-11e0-9309-806e6f6e6963@400003155f
b758001db-1456-11e0-9309-806e6f6e6963@4000031545
```

Figure 3.31 Files value data opened in WRR.

program name ("Microsoft Security Client"), and value 1 is the program version ("4.6.0305.0"). Value 6 refers to the Entry Type, or category, under which this program was installed. In many cases, the data for this value appears to be "AddRemoveProgram", but I have seen other data for this value. In this same AmCache.hve file, the ProgramID key that refers to Google Chrome includes a value "6" for which the data is "AddRemoveProgramPerUser".

The "Files" value is interesting, as the data is reportedly a list of files included in the MSI package, but not by file name. Instead the files are listed by volume GUID and the MFT file reference number, separated by the "@" symbol. The data appears as illustrated in Fig. 3.31.

As you can see in Fig. 3.31, the strings listed in the "Files" value point to the volume GUID for the D:\ volume on this system. The portion of each string following the "@" symbol reportedly is the MFT file reference number, but you should not expect to find these beneath the "Files" key within the AmCache.hve file, as these file reference numbers are associated with files that were part of the installer package.

The information beneath the Programs key can be useful to an analyst, depending upon the nature and goals of the investigation. In reviewing the data extracted from the AmCache.hve file from this Windows 7 system, I found that the program "pidgin-otr 4.0.0-1", from "Cypherpunks CA", was installed on the system. Admittedly, malware does not generally get installed on a system through the use of an MSI file, but information such as this can be used to determine programs that were installed on the system and may be useful in demonstrating a violation of corporate acceptable use policies.

Note

I should note that Yogesh's research regarding the AmCache.hve file is based on Windows 8, and the example we used in this chapter validates Yogesh's findings based on Windows 7 systems. However, while the AmCache.hve file has also been found to exist on Windows 10 Technical Preview systems (I have such a system installed as a virtual machine via Oracle's VirtualBox application), this research has yet to be extend to and validated with respect to the Windows 10 platform. This is an important distinction, as Microsoft has a long history of making subtle changes between versions of Windows, changes that can significantly impact research findings from folks like Yogesh.

Summary

In this chapter, we've discussed the Registry hives that pertain to the configuration and operation of the system as a whole and seen how there is a good deal of information available that can be extremely valuable to an analyst during an examination. What I've also tried to do is to break down the various keys and values of interest into artifact categories so that maybe they'd be a bit more manageable.

I've attempted to provide a quick snapshot of information available in the Security, SAM, System, and Software hives, as well as some information regarding a file that uses the same format, but is not part of the Registry; no volume or tome will ever be able to encapsulate every possible key, value, and setting that could potentially be of interest to an analyst. Rather, I've tried to give you, the reader, an overview of what's available, including some of the more common keys and values, and hopefully a few that you haven't seen before, but still said, "wow" when you read about them. I've mentioned some of the Registry keys and values that I, and other analysts, look for most often during examinations; however, that does not mean that these are all the keys and values that contain pertinent information. In fact, this will never be the case; there will always be a new application or new version, or some new malware or technique to compromise a Windows system that leaves a footprint in the Registry. Research into the Windows 7 Registry was still on-going while Windows 8, 8.1, and then 10 were released, and we haven't scratched the surface of what may be "new" in Windows 10. What I hope I have done, and continue to do, is provide you with an appreciation for how powerful a technique Registry analysis can be, particularly when used in combination with other analysis techniques, such as timeline analysis. The Windows Registry truly is a veritable treasure chest of data that can be used effectively by a knowledgeable analyst to add a great deal of context to an examination.

4

CASE STUDIES: USER HIVES

INFORMATION IN THIS CHAPTER

- NTUSER.DAT
- USRCLASS.DAT

Introduction

When first I sat down to write this book, it occurred to me that this chapter...one about tracking user activity...might be the most useful and interesting chapter. Windows does a great job of providing a quality experience to the user, keeping track of documents they had opened, saved, or accessed, how they had set up and configured their favorite Solitaire game, which web browser they used, which application is launched when the user double-clicks on a file in the shell, and even the size and position of various application windows on the desktop. All of this information has to be tracked somehow, and for the most part, a great deal of it is tracked through the user's Registry hive files. The fact that this information is recorded in any manner at all is transparent to the user, but for a knowledgeable analyst, the Registry, and in particular the user's hives, can be veritable treasure trove of forensic data.

In the previous chapter, we discussed several of the Registry hives that pertain most directly to the system; the SAM, Security, System and Software hives. In this chapter, we will be focusing primarily on two hives found within the user profile directory; the NTUSER.DAT hive and the lesser known USRCLASS.DAT hive. These two files, to varying degrees based on the version of Windows being examined, can provide a great deal of data regarding the user's activities on a system. In this chapter, we're going to take a look at the various ways this information can be used, and more importantly, how it can be used effectively to support a number of types of investigations.

As with the previous chapter, this chapter should not be considered a comprehensive and complete list of all possible Registry keys and values that might be considered important or valuable to an analyst. While Windows XP systems are fairly well understood, there is still a lot about Vista systems, and now Windows 7 systems, and even Windows 8 and 10 systems, that require a great deal of research, particularly in the area of Registry analysis. Add to that the proliferation of applications on these systems, and there's an apparent never-ending supply of Registry locations that can be of value, including (but not limited to) used by malware to maintain persistence on the system. Rather than providing a long list of Registry keys and values of interest, it's more important to understand how some keys and values can be used, not only by an intruder or malware author but more so by a forensic analyst in order to paint a more complete picture of an examination. Understanding how the user hives can be used is far more important than maintaining a long list of keys and values that don't have any context or anything to indicate how they're important.

A final thought before we head into this chapter; as with previous chapters, the most important aspect of Registry analysis is to first understand your goals; what are you looking for or trying to prove. Many analysts kick off an examination by loading Registry hives into a viewer, without really understanding what it is they're looking for; this will often result in "no findings" and a great deal of time spent finding this out. If you understand what you're interested in and what you're looking for, you can find it very quickly.

NTUSER.DAT

The main Registry hive for the user is the NTUSER.DAT hive, located in the root of the user's profile folder.

One of the things we'll be addressing in this chapter is referred to as a "most recently used" list, or "MRU." This sort of list usually appears as values beneath a Registry key (and can appear in other artifacts and data sources, such as Jump Lists), and most (if not all) of them are found within the user hives. The idea behind an MRU, from the perspective of a forensic analyst, is that there is some mechanism for differentiating which of the events or actions occurred most recently. An example of an MRU may be several values that point to image files the user accessed via a specific application. The most recently accessed (or "used") file may be identified by having a specific value name or by reviewing a separate value named "MRUList" or "MRUListEx". What having an MRUList means is that there is some sort of ordered numbering scheme that is used to track the entries, and in the case of some values, there may also be another value named MRUList or MRUListEx that will tell you the order of the MRU values. In some cases the values are given numbers as names ("0000", "0001", etc.) as they are added to the key; the most recent value is named "0000" and when the next value is added, it is named "0000" and the previous value is "pushed down" to "0001", and so on. This way, looking at the value names, you can get a very quick view of the order in which the values were added, and there is no need for an MRUList (or MRUListEx) value.

In other instances, the values are assigned numbers as names (which may begin with the letters "MRU", depending upon the key and the application that uses them), and there will be an additional value named "MRUList" or "MRUListEx" that maintains the order in which the values were "used" (again, this depends upon the application). For example, consider a Registry key for which the first value added is named simply "a". At this point, the MRU-List value would indicate that the "a" value was the MRU value. At some point, several other values (b, c, etc.) are added, and the MRUList value indicates the order accordingly (c, b, a). However, at some point the user does something that reuses the first value (conducts a search for the same keyword, accesses the file, etc.); the MRUList value would now indicate that the MRU order is now "a", "c", "b". Even though all of the values keep their original names, the MRUList value indicates the order in which the values were "used."

Throughout this chapter, we'll be looking at a number of MRU lists, and in each case, we'll discuss the means for identifying the most recently accessed file or used item. The point is that while an MRU list may maintain a list of recently accessed objects, the means for identifying the most recently accessed object may vary and be different.

System Configuration Information

While most of the system configuration information found in the Registry is maintained in other hive files (as discussed in chapter: Analyzing the System Hives), the user's NTUSER.DAT hive file does contain some configuration information, as well, particularly as it applies to applications.

REDIRECTION

On 64-bit versions of Windows, 32-bit applications are redirected to another within the Registry (there's a similar function for the file system, but that is a topic that's beyond the scope of this book). Suffice to say that there are number of keys discussed in this chapter, as well as the previous one, that have corresponding values beneath the *Software\ Wow6432Node* subkey, such as the Run key discussed later in this chapter. Registry redirection is discussed at length at the Microsoft website and can be found online at https://msdn.microsoft.com/en-us/library/windows/desktop/aa384232(v=vs.85).aspx.

AutoStart

The autostart category refers to those locations within the user's hives that permit applications to start automatically (yes, I know that definition is somewhat circular), with no interaction from the user beyond logging in, or launching an application.

The Run Key

I usually refer to this key (the key path is \Software\Microsoft\ Windows\CurrentVersion\Run) as "the ubiquitous Run key," because it seems to be used so often by bad actors to ensure the persistence of some form of malware. Often times, this is predicated upon the privileges of the user account being infected; if the user account has administrator privileges, the malware may persist via a Windows service, but if the user account has normal user privileges, the malware may persist via the user's Run key.

Values beneath the Run key are all run asynchronously without any interaction from the user beyond logging into the system. Unless the application being run has some method for doing so, the user sees no notification that any particular program is running. Further, if the file pointed to by the value data doesn't exist (say, it was deleted), the user receives no notification, either.

With respect to the user's hive in particular, the functionality of this key is very often misrepresented in a variety of online sources, which tends to renew the cycle of this key being misunderstood. When an application persists via this key, by having a value beneath the key whose data points to the application executable, that application will only start following a system reboot *when the user logs in*. In a way, it's understandable how this sort of mistake is made, as Microsoft makes that statement themselves in their malware write-ups; for example, consider the write-up regarding Win32/Cypaux (found online at https://www. microsoft.com/security/portal/threat/encyclopedia/Entry.asp x?Name=Win32%2fCypaux#tab=2). In that write-up, the author states that persistence is achieved via the user's Run key and states that it's used to "ensure that its executable runs at each Windows start."

CORRELATING NEW VALUES

Many times when conducting forensic analysis of a system, I'll look at the contents of the Run key for a particular user and see several values beneath the key, sometimes as many as six or seven. The LastWrite time of the key tells me when the contents of the key were last modified, but there isn't anything that's readily available within the key structure that will tell me what specifically was modified.

CORRELATING NEW VALUES—Cont'd

One means for getting some context with respect to which value may have been added would be to create a timeline of system activity, including file system and Windows Event Log metadata, as well as Registry key LastWrite times. This may illustrate a cluster or series of artifacts that illustrate malware being installed on the system, malware that uses the user's Run key for persistence.

Another means for determining which value was added, or removed, would be to compare the contents of the key to what you find in the NTUSER.DAT hive for the user in a Volume Shadow Copy.

A good deal of malware can be seen using the user's "Run" key for persistence, particularly when the user account that gets infected has only normal user (not administrator) privileges. At the 2012 SANS Forensic Summit, Elizabeth Schweinsberg gave a presentation on Registry analysis (her presentation can be found online at http://digital-forensics.sans.org/summit-archives/2012/taking-registry-analysis-to-the-next-level.pdf). During her presentation, she shared some fascinating statistics on the use of the Run key by malware, which she collected by "trawling" the Symantec website for Registry keys. From what she was able to collect at the time, the "Run" key was used 42.2% of the time when malware persisted within the user's NTUSER.DAT. This is really very interesting, but at the same time, we have to keep in mind that it's not abundantly clear how the original data is collected, nor how the malware is executed in order to collect that data. For example, if the malware is executed with normal user privileges, it may be more likely that the malware will persist via the user's "Run" key.

As such, when examining the values beneath this key, you'd want to look for things such as odd file paths, with files in the root of the user profile (ie, C:\Users\harlan\), the user's "temp" folder (ie, C:\Users\harlan\AppData\Local\Temp), etc. Not only can the *user_run.pl* RegRipper plugin be used to extract the contents of the user's Run key, but other plugins can also be used to look for specific values. For example, the *ahaha.pl* plugin looks for indications of the malware that persists using the value name "360v", and the *reveton.pl* plugin looks for indications of the Reveton malware (a description of this malware can be found online at http://www.microsoft.com/security/portal/threat/encyclopedia/Entry.aspx?Name=Win32%2fReveton#tab=2) persisting via the user's Run key.

WHAT TO LOOK FOR

Sometimes folks will ask me what I tend to look for when looking at values beneath the Run key. Back in the early 2000s, my response was largely based on experience; there were value names or data values I could look

Continued

WHAT TO LOOK FOR—Cont'd

at that just didn't "feel right." Over time, as I worked a number of similar cases, what I saw as unusual would be something that I had seen before and knew to be "bad." Even now, at a first glance, I look for odd or random value names, data paths such as "C:\ProgramData", "C:\Users\user\AppData\Local", "C:\Users\user\AppData\Local\Temp", etc.

The RunOnce Key

The RunOnce key can be found in the path *Software\Microsoft\Windows\CurrentVersion\RunOnce.* Values beneath this key will be launched the next time the user logs in, and then the value will be deleted once the command has completed. However, according to Microsoft's Knowledge Base (KB) article 137367 (found online at https://support.microsoft.com/en-us/kb/137367), if the value name is prepended with an "!", the value will not be deleted once the command has completed. If this extra step is taken, the RunOnce key takes on the capabilities of the Run key described above.

The *user_run.pl* RegRipper plugin will collect values from both the Run and RunOnce keys, as well as the corresponding keys beneath the *Wow6432Node* key.

TEMPORAL PROXIMITY

The term "temporal proximity" is a Star Trek-y kind of term I first heard used in the fall of 2008 by Aaron Walters (of Volatility fame), and it refers to when response activities start in relation to the incident having occurred. I bring this up because keys such as the RunOnce key can really illustrate the importance of temporal proximity, as well as rapid incident detection and response. Something that differentiates the RunOnce key from the Run key is that items listed in the RunOnce key are run once. Any command line listed as a value beneath this key will be run the next time a user logs into the system and be deleted (before or after being run, per our previous explanation). The value of temporal proximity is also illustrated by issues such as deletions; when a Registry key is deleted, the space used by the key becomes part of the unallocated space of the hive file and may be reused (ie, overwritten) at some point (the same concept that applies to files in the file system). The sooner response activities are initiated, the more likely you are to have access "fresh" data.

Other AutoStart Locations

There are several other autostart locations similar to the Run key, which are listed as keys to check within the *user_run.pl* RegRipper plugin. Some of these locations can be referred to as "legacy" Run keys, but needless to say, they are still effective because they work. For example, one such key is the *Software\Microsoft*

Windows\CurrentVersion\Policies\Explorer\Run key, and it's corresponding key beneath the Wow6432Node subkey. Also, beneath the *Software\Microsoft\Windows NT\CurrentVersion\Windows* key, the "load" and "run" values also provide persistence locations that can be, and have been, used by malware authors.

The consulting company Cylance also has an interesting blog article available regarding persistence locations, which can be found online at http://blog.cylance.com/windows-registry-persistence-part-2-the-run-keys-and-search-order.

Program Execution

As was discussed in chapter "Analyzing the System Hives," those values within the Registry that serve as autostart locations also serve to provide information regarding program execution as well, as long as the condition for that location has been met. For example, in the previous section we discussed the Run key as an autostart location; as such, the user logging in would be the condition that needed to be met, and as such, would serve to indicate that the program had been executed.

Applets

Windows systems ship with a number of small applications (referred to as "applets") installed and readily available to users. These applets include RegEdit, MS Paint, the System Tray, and MS Write, and the key path is *Software\Microsoft\Windows\CurrentVersion\Applets*. Fig. 4.1 illustrates the contents of a user's Applets key.

As you can see in Fig. 4.1, the Paint and Wordpad applets include a subkey called "Recent File List", each of which provides an MRU listing of files that the user accessed via the applet. Fig. 4.2 illustrates what the contents of the "Recent File List" key beneath the *Applets\Paint* key might look like for a user.

As you can see in Fig. 4.2, the MRU values are listed, as we discussed with MRU values in general, there are no time stamps with each of the individual MRU entries. While you can see that the user accessed a file using a particular application (in this case, MSPaint), this data by itself will not tell you *when* the user accessed the file. To determine when the user accessed the file, you would need to look to additional information, perhaps even resources outside of the Registry (such as Jump Lists).

The RegEdit applet key does not include an MRU list, but it does include a LastKey value, as illustrated in Fig. 4.3.

These keys beneath the "Applets" key illustrate the user's use of the programs and therefore provide indications of program

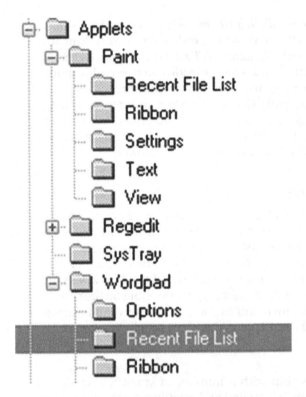

Figure 4.1 User's Applets key, showing subkeys.

Value	Type	Data
File1	REG_SZ	C:\Users\harlan\Desktop\herrcore.jpg
File2	REG_SZ	C:\Users\harlan\Desktop\usb.jpg
File3	REG_SZ	C:\Users\harlan\Desktop\tab.png
File4	REG_SZ	C:\Users\harlan\Desktop\tln.png
File5	REG_SZ	D:\books\WRF\ch3\2e\fig3.sticky.tif
File6	REG_SZ	C:\Users\harlan\Desktop\weather.jpg
File7	REG_SZ	C:\Users\harlan\Desktop\photo.PNG
File8	REG_SZ	D:\books\WRF\ch3\2e\fig3.3.TIF
File9	REG_SZ	D:\books\WRF\ch3\2e\fig3.amcache5.tif

Figure 4.2 MRU values beneath user's "Paint\Recent File List" key.

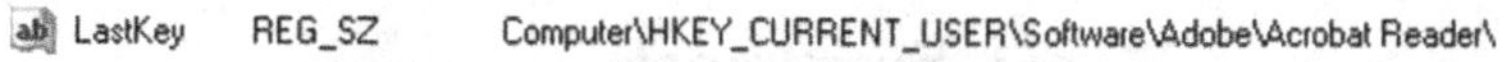

ab| LastKey   REG_SZ   Computer\HKEY_CURRENT_USER\Software\Adobe\Acrobat Reader\

Figure 4.3 Partial contents of user's LastKey value.

execution. As is the case with a number of artifacts, these keys, particularly those for the MSPaint and Wordpad applets, can also provide indications of user access to files. The LastKey value, however, can provide some very useful indications of user activity, particularly when individual indicators within a cluster are apparently absent.

THE LASTKEY VALUE AND ADMIN CLEANUP

I was performing forensic analysis of several systems during a targeted threat response engagement and ran across some anomalous findings on two particular systems. We had some indications that two specific systems had been infected with the malware in question, but what we weren't seeing was the persistence mechanisms; in this case, Registry keys associated with a Windows service. I started by looking for alternate means of persistence but then had a hunch and checked the administrator's LastKey value. In both cases, value contained the path to the service that followed the malware persistence path alphabetically. Doing some testing, I was able to easily verify that the administrator had opened the Registry Editor, navigated to the Windows services key used by the malware for persistence, and deleted it. Prior to closing the Registry Editor, the next key in alphabetical order was "in focus", and that was the key that was recorded in the LastKey value. Other artifacts on the system validated the finding that the administrator had taken steps to try to "clean up" the malware infection on those two systems.

SysInternals

Microsoft's SysInternals tools (found online at https://technet. microsoft.com/en-us/sysinternals/bb545021.aspx) include a number of very useful tools for administrators, and like many other utilities that are useful to administrators, they can also be useful to those with nefarious purposes. However, the tools include a small bit of functionality that can make them something of hindrance when employed but is extremely valuable for forensic analysts. In order to use the tools for the first time on a system, the user has to accept the end user license agreement (EULA); this is easily done by including the "/accepteula" argument at the command prompt or by clicking on the appropriate button that appears in the dialog box that appears if the "/accepteula" switch is not used. Not only do you have to employ this specific switch but also you have to spell it properly. When the EULA is accepted, a Registry key is created for the application in the user's hive, as illustrated in Fig. 4.4.

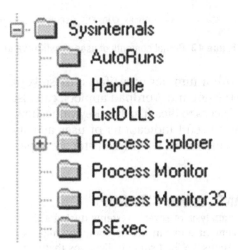

Figure 4.4 SysInternals tools listed in the NTUSER.DAT file.

If the strings.exe utility is used (I tend to use this particular utility quite a bit) and the EULA is accepted, then a key is created in the following path:

```
Software\SysInternals\Strings
```

The key usually has just one value ("EulaAccepted"), but the key's LastWrite time correlates to when the utility was run first run. How is this useful? Consider an investigation (violation of acceptable use policy, abuse of admin privileges, data breach) where the PSExec tool was used. This tool is a remote execution utility and allows someone with the appropriate privileges to run commands on remote systems. In a corporate environment, this might be a domain admin, or someone who has access to admin-level credentials on the remote systems. The PSExec tool is a command line tool and does not have a graphical user interface (GUI); regardless, it is a tool that is designed to run on Windows systems and has been used legitimately by system administrators to perform various functions. Unfortunately, it has also been used by dedicated adversaries to move laterally within a compromised network. When it's run for the first time from the source system, a Registry key (path is "Software\SysInternals\ PSExec") is created, leaving an indicator of the use of the tool.

COMMAND LINE TOOLS

I've been performing incident response and digital forensic analysis since about 1999 or so, and I've seen time and again that intruders are very familiar with the use of command line tools, particularly because the level of access required to use command line tools is relatively easy to achieve, and the use of such tools usually allows them to pass under

COMMAND LINE TOOLS—Cont'd

the radar of most system administrators. This is the reason why I highly recommend to...well, anyone who will listen...that they install a process creation monitoring tool such as Microsoft's own Sysmon or Bit9's Carbon Black. Either of these tools, when properly employed, provide a level of monitoring that is similar to having a video of a real-world crime occurring. Don't get me wrong...such tools are not the "silver bullet" for security, but in my experience, having such tools in place can enhance detection of an intrusion to significant levels and reduce the overall time for response from days and weeks to just minutes.

UserAssist

During a job interview a number of years ago, the interviewer asked me what my favorite Registry key was; if I had to answer that question today, I'd have to say that it is the UserAssist key. Oddly enough, the key name is pretty descriptive...the contents of this key assist the user. Okay, I know it's a stretch but bear with me; beneath this key (we'll address exactly where shortly) are Registry values that track a user's interactions via the Windows Explorer shell, primarily when the user clicks or double-clicks on certain items. This information is then used by the operating system to tailor the user experience; for example, like many other folks working in corporate America, I used to use a Windows XP SP3 laptop for work. Each morning when I would log in to the corporate network, I would click on the Start button, go to Programs, then to "Microsoft Office", and in the final menu, I click on Microsoft Outlook. After the first couple of times that I did this, when I got to that final menu, only the Microsoft Outlook choice was immediately visible; why would the operating system completely expand all of the menus in the path, when I'd demonstrated that I was primarily interested in only one or two items? It's a much better and preferable user experience to show those items I'm most interested in via customized menus based on my usage history. Given this, and the data included in the relevant values, would lead you to believe that this key should really be called "Forensics Assist"!

So, to begin, the UserAssist key (within the NTUSER.DAT hive) is located in the following path:

```
Software\Microsoft\Windows\CurrentVersion\Explorer\
UserAssist
```

Beneath this key (on all versions of Windows), you'll find two (I've seen three on a very few Windows systems; as I'll describe shortly, there may be more) keys with names that appear to be globally unique identifiers, or "GUIDs," as illustrated in Figs. 4.5 and 4.6.

Figure 4.5 Windows XP UserAssist key.

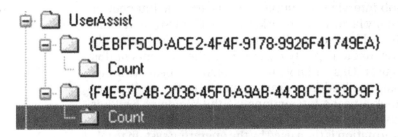

Figure 4.6 Windows 7 UserAssist key.

▌OTHER VERSIONS OF WINDOWS

I do not have access to an extensive library of Windows systems, but within the NTUSER.DAT file from one Windows 10 system, I saw nine subkeys (each with a name that looked like a GUID) beneath the UserAssist key; within the NTUSER.DAT hive from a Windows Server 2012 system, I counted a dozen subkeys with GUIDs for names. Clearly, there's a great deal of information being maintained in these keys, as well as a great deal of additional research that needs to be done.

As you can see in Figs. 4.5 and 4.6, each of the keys with GUIDs for names will have a subkey named "Count", and we're interested in the values located within the Count subkeys. Fig. 4.7 illustrates what these values look like in a Registry viewer.

The values illustrated in Fig. 4.7 don't look very useful, do they? Well, that's because the value names are encoded via the ROT-13 substitution algorithm; that is, each letter is swapped with the one 13 positions further down in the alphabet. To undo (decrypt) the algorithm, we simply reverse the substitution. Fortunately, the *userassist.pl* RegRipper plugin will handle this translation easily using the following code:

```
$value_name =~ tr/N-ZA-Mn-za-m/A-Za-z/;
```

Value	Type	Data
HRZR_PGYFRFFVBA	REG_BINARY	A9 C2 38 0E DB 04 00 00
HRZR_PGYPHNPbhag:pgbe	REG_BINARY	01 00 00 00 02 00 00 00 00 00 00 00 00 00 (
HRZR_HVFPHG	REG_BINARY	DB 04 00 00 AC 04 00 00 30 74 87 74 0A
HRZR_EHACNGU	REG_BINARY	DB 04 00 00 80 0F 00 00 00 10 F2 7A 0A
HRZR_EHACNGU:FO Nhqvtl ...	REG_BINARY	01 00 00 00 07 00 00 00 80 83 67 E7 0C (
HRZR_EHACNGU:P:\JVAQBJ...	REG_BINARY	DB 04 00 00 07 00 00 00 00 10 F2 7A 0A
HRZR_EHACNGU:Perngvir Cy...	REG_BINARY	01 00 00 00 07 00 00 00 F0 EE 77 E2 0C

Figure 4.7 UserAssist\...\Count key values.

Before we proceed, it's important at this point to mention that Didier Stevens has invested a considerable amount of time and effort in researching the values beneath the UserAssist key, particularly with respect to Windows 7. Without question, Didier deserves a great deal of credit for the current understanding of, and interest in, the contents of the UserAssist key within the computer forensics community. Didier's findings and tool can be found online at http://blog.didierstevens.com/programs/userassist/.

VIGENERE ENCRYPTION

During his research into the UserAssist key, Didier discovered that in the beta version of Windows 7, rather than ROT-13 "encryption," the value names were encrypted using Vigenere encryption, a polyalphabetic substitution cipher originally described by Giovan Battista Bellaso in 1553. The final release of Windows 7 switched back to the use of ROT-13 encryption. If nothing else, this illustrates how understanding the version of Windows that you're examining is absolutely critical.

According to a Microsoft employee I spoke with, the use of the encryption or obfuscation technique isn't to protect any sensitive information; rather, it's intended as a deterrent to prevent the user from modifying any information in the value name or data. From what I've seen over the years, this obfuscation technique does little more than obviate the use of text searches via a commercial forensic analysis framework and requires the analyst to parse the data first before running their search.

Okay, so how is all of this important? Well, remember that the operating system uses some method for keeping track of a user's actions (which items they click on, which shortcuts and applications they access, etc.) and then uses that information to provide an improved (beyond the default installation) experience to the user. Both testing and analysis indicate that the information embedded within the binary data associated with many of the values beneath the UserAssist key includes a 64-bit time stamp (ie, our familiar FILETIME structure), as well as a counter (referred to as a "run count") that appears to indicate how many times the user has interacted with the shell in the manner in which these values would be created or modified.

RUN COUNT

When the counter value embedded within the UserAssist value binary data was first examined, it appeared that the count actually started at 5, rather than 0. There seemed to be no apparent reason for this (the internals of any algorithms that may use this information are not known), Ovie Carroll and Bret Padres (of the CyberSpeak podcast fame; interestingly enough, after a long absence, Ovie recorded another podcast on August 31, 2015) came up with a very funny mnemonic device; the name "Gates" (as in "Bill Gates") contains five letters. Regardless of the reason apparently starting the count at 5, testing indicated that this was, in fact, the case; performing an action and then parsing the information on live system would result in a count value of 6 (the first time that the action was recorded, plus 5).

In short, the binary data can be parsed (by RegRipper plugins) to determine how many times the user had taken this action (ie, navigated through the Programs menu to launch MS Word, double-clicked a desktop icon, etc.) via the shell, and when they last did so. An important aspect of this is that in order to create/modify these values, the user needs to interact with the Explorer shell; that is, if the user clicks Start and then types "cmd" into the Run box on Windows XP, you don't get the same artifacts as if the user clicks Start, Programs, Accessories, and chooses "Command Prompt", and you won't be able to "see" what the user did in the command prompt.

Let's take a look at example; below is an excerpt from the output of the RegRipper *userassist.pl* plugin run against an NTUSER. DAT hive extracted from a Windows XP system:

```
{75048700-EF1F-11D0-9888-006097DEACF9}
Thu Feb 7 13:37:26 2008 Z
 UEME_RUNPATH:E:\FTK Imager.exe (1)
Thu Feb 7 12:41:42 2008 Z
 UEME_RUNPATH:C:\Program Files\Microsoft Office\OFFICE11\
WINWORD.EXE (120)
Thu Feb 7 11:27:41 2008 Z
 UEME_RUNPATH:C:\WINDOWS\regedit.exe (5)
Thu Feb 7 10:39:55 2008 Z
 UEME_RUNPATH:Lotus Notes 7.lnk (142)
 UEME_RUNPATH:C:\Program Files\Lotus\notes\notes.exe (142)
Thu Feb 7 10:38:38 2008 Z
```

```
  UEME_RUNPATH:C:\Program Files\AT&T Network Client\
NetClient.exe (147)
  UEME_RUNPATH:{5D5A8163-501D-4F38-8B17-23488A324D64} (146)
  UEME_RUNPATH:{AC76BA86-1033-0000-BA7E-100000000002} (112)
```

As you can see from the above excerpt, the *userassist.pl* plugin decrypts the value names beneath the UserAssist subkeys and then, where applicable, parses the associated binary data for the run count, and the last time the action was taken. First, we see the GUID that we mentioned which is one of the UserAssist subkeys; opening the Software hive from the system from which the NTUSER.DAT hive was extracted in Registry viewer (see chapter: Processes and Tools) and searching for that GUID, we find that it refers to a class identifier (CLSID) beneath the Classes key that points to "Active Desktop".

Next, we see an indication that on February 7, 2008, at approximately 13:37:26 Z (see the "Time References" sidebar), FTK Imager was launched from the E:\ drive. Well, that's where I placed a CD in the system and ran FTK Imager in order to collect specific files from the system, including the Registry hives. That reference begins with "UEME_RUNPATH", which indicates an executable file was accessed; in this case, by double-clicking the program icon as it appeared in Windows Explorer (opened to the CD, of course). According to the run count (ie, the number in parentheses after the application path), at this point, FTK Imager was only run once.

TIME REFERENCES

Most of the RegRipper plugins report time with "Z" or "UTC" at the end. The "Z" refers to Zulu, or Greenwich Mean Time (GMT). This is analogous to Universal Coordinated Time, or UTC. When performing analysis across multiple systems, or across multiple time zones, normalizing the time stamps to a common format and reference point can make that analysis much easier. I've had several cases where an intruder accessed systems within an organizations infrastructure that were dispersed across multiple time zones and normalizing all time stamps on all of the affected systems to UTC made it much easier to follow his trail, and more importantly, illustrate it to the customer.

Next, we see that regedit.exe was launched, and that Lotus Notes (our e-mail application at the time) was run for the 142nd time by double-clicking the Windows shortcut (on the desktop). Beneath that, at 10:38:38 Z, we see that the AT&T Network Client (VPN solution) was accessed, and that there are two GUIDs as well. Once again, opening the Software hive from this system in a Registry view application and searching for "{5D5A8163-501D-4F38-8B17-23488A324D64}", we find that this also appears as a subkey name beneath the Microsoft\Windows\CurrentVersion\Uninstall key, and that subkey contains a value named "DisplayName" set to "AT&T Network Client". The other GUID ("AC76BA86-1033-0000-BA7E-100000000002") appears in 24 locations (keys and values) throughout the Software hive and appears to refer to the Adobe Acrobat Reader version 7.0 installer.

Other entries may appear with different prefixes in the output of the *userassist.pl* plugin (and other tools). For example, rather than being preceded by "UEME_RUNPATH", some decoded values may begin with "UEME_RUNPIDL" (a "PIDL" is a pointer to an ItemIdList structure, which is used to identify objects in the Shell namespace [7]), referring to a folder or shortcut, and others may begin with "UEME_RUNCPL", which refers to Control Panel applets being clicked.

Personally, I've used the information within the UserAssist keys to great effect during a number of examinations. I've seen where users and intruders have installed and then run the password cracking tool named "Cain.exe", in order to collect passwords from a variety of applications; even after deleting the application, the entries in the UserAssist key persist. I've seen where programs were run from an external resource, such as a CD or thumb drive, because the user double-clicked the icon via the Windows Explorer shell. I've also seen where system administrators who stated that once a system had been confiscated and "secured," they "didn't do anything" had actually installed, run and then uninstalled two consecutive antivirus (AV) scanning applications, one after another. I guess they were just trying to be thorough… but their actions were "recorded" and accounted from some of the artifacts that I was seeing, as well as some I wasn't seeing. I've seen where intruders have installed malware on systems that we weren't immediately aware of, and this information helped us a great deal in our examination.

I've also examined systems where there were apparent disparities with time stamps recorded on the system, and in parsing the UserAssist key information, found "UEME_RUNCPL" entries referencing "timedate.cpl", the Date and Time Control Panel applet that allows the user to modify the system time. The user can change the system time in this manner by either double-clicking the Control Panel applet or by right-clicking the clock on the far right of the TaskBar and choosing "Adjust Date/Time" from the context menu that appears.

As we saw in figures 4.5 and 4.6, Windows 7 uses a different set of GUIDs for the UserAssist subkeys, and that's not all that's different. Those values that contain time stamp data are also formatted differently and appear to contain a great deal more information. Again, Didier Stevens has some testing and analysis in this area, in an attempt to identify the various pieces of information (ie, such as how long the application had focus, etc.), and reviewing some of what he's published, it's easy to see how an analyst can use them to support his findings during an examination. This is an area that will require significantly more research and testing.

One final note with respect to the UserAssist key; there have been two additional Registry values identified that may significantly affect the information maintained beneath the UserAssist subkeys. Both of these would be values added (they do not exist by default on any system I've seen) to a Settings key (beneath the UserAssist key). The first value, NoEncrypt, when set to a DWORD value of "1", can apparently be used to disable the ROT-13 encryption. The other value, NoLog, when set to a DWORD value of "1", can apparently be used to disable logging all together. Remember, though…if the logging or recording of user interaction data is disabled, the user experience will be significantly altered, as data used to enable customized menus based on usage history is no longer available. Now, I haven't seen either of these values during an engagement, but they are important for an analyst to be aware of, as the absence of entries beneath the UserAssist subkeys could be the result of deletion (manually or via an "evidence eraser" program or script) or through the addition of the NoLog value.

NOINSTRUMENTATION

Another Registry value mentioned in MS KB article 292504 (found online at https://support.microsoft.com/en-us/kb/292504) is "NoInstrumentation". This is a value that can be set via Group Policies and would be added to the user's CurrentVersion\Policies\Explorer key. When set to a DWORD value of "1", this value will "prevent the system from remembering the programs run, paths followed, and documents used"; apparently, this value may have more wide-ranging effects than simply disabling recording of information beneath the UserAssist key.

Application Compatibility Assistant

Windows systems have something referred to as the "program compatibility assistant" (PCA), which can be used to detect run-time issues in older applications. I won't go into detail in this section as to the specifics of how PCA works; if you want more information, one resource can be found online at http://blogs. technet.com/b/askperf/archive/2007/10/05/the-program-compatibility-assistant-part-two.aspx.

The user's NTUSER.DAT may contain information about applications that had run on the system and were monitored by PCA, even if PCA did not detect any issues with the application. For example, the key path *Software\Microsoft\Windows NT\Current*

Version\AppCompatFlags\Compatibility Assistant\Persisted is specifically intended to store a list of programs for which PCA came up, but no compatibility modes were selected. The values beneath this key point to applications that had been run on the system and for which PCA came up, but the contents of this key are not an MRU list, and there is no time stamp information associated with each value. As such, you can see that an application was run but not when it was run.

In December 2013, Corey Harrell wrote an excellent blog post that explains what PCA is and what it does (that post can be found online at http://journeyintoir.blogspot.com/2013/12/revealing-program-compatibility.html). In that post, Corey also mentioned the *Software\Microsoft\Windows NT\Current Version\AppCompat-Flags\Compatibility Assistant\Store* key, which appears to be similar to the Persisted key, but specifically for Windows 8, and meant to replace the use of the Persisted key. I should note that on the system on which I'm writing this book, both the Store and Persisted keys exist; the system was originally a Windows 7 system, but I upgraded (as opposed to doing a clean reinstall) to Windows 10.

Both of these keys (depending upon the version of Windows you're examining) may provide to be extremely valuable in terms of determining applications launched within the user context. As the values beneath these keys are generated by the operating system itself as the application executes within the ecosystem of the OS, they are not something that the application specifically controls. As such, a user running an unauthorized application may result in indicators that persist well beyond the deletion of the application itself and be valuable for forensic analysis.

Terminal Server Client

I've been involved in a number of incident response engagements where we found that a dedicated adversary was able to access an infrastructure through the use of Terminal Services; as such, their access to systems was via a remote desktop. As they were interacting with the Windows Explorer shell, we were able to follow their activities in much the same manner as if they had been sitting at the keyboard.

Essentially what we'd seen after developing a timeline of user activity is that the adversary had accessed some systems and then run the Terminal Server Client (formerly known as the Remote Desktop Protocol, or "RDP") to leap frog and move laterally to other systems within the infrastructure. This was very fortunate for us, as it not only helped us scope the incident but also provided a time frame for the access, allowing us to focus our analysis of the remote system to a specific time window. This can be extremely valuable when the adversary is using an administrator's account and accessing systems outside of the normal working hours for that administrator.

I wrote, and use, the *tsclient.pl* and *tsclient_tln.pl* plugins to collect information from the *Software\Microsoft\Terminal Server Client* subkeys, the latter doing so in a format useful for including in a timeline of system activity.

> ### REMOTE DESKTOP TOOLS
>
> Just as Hamlet said, "There are more things in heaven and earth...," there are other ways to access the desktop on remote systems, using applications such as WinVNC and its variants. The RegRipper plugins *realvnc.pl*, *vncviewer.pl*, and *winvnc.pl* can help an analyst determine if any of these tools had been used, and if so, which remote systems they were used to access.

Malware

As we've discussed throughout this chapter, as well as previous chapters, some malware will create Registry keys during their installation which they do not use for persistence. For example, the Symantec write-up on the Korplug backdoor malware from 2013 (found online at http://www.symantec.com/security_response/earthlink_writeup.jsp?docid=2015-030203-1048-99) describes the malware creating the "SXLOC.ZAP" value within the user's NTUSER.DAT hive. A Sophos technical paper (found online at https://www.sophos.com/en-us/medialibrary/PDFs/technical%20papers/plugx-goes-to-the-registry-and-india.pdf?la=en) on a similar variant from the same malware family describes the use of the same value. I wrote the *malware.pl* plugin to check for the keys and values associated with malware that left indications in the Registry hives not used for persistence.

There was some malware a while back that used an interesting means of persistence; I'm including it in this section simply because I couldn't find a more suitable location within the chapter. The malware was dubbed "Win32/KanKan" (a detailed analysis of the malware can be found online at http://www.welivesecurity.com/2013/10/11/win32kankan-chinese-drama/) and was found to use a Microsoft Office AddIn to persist on an infected system, ensuring that the malware would be loaded into memory each time the appropriate Office application (MS Word, Excel, etc.) was launched. I wrote the *kankan.pl* plugin specifically to look for and report on these addins.

Keep in mind that Registry values (and in some cases, keys) may be created as the malware interacts with the Windows operating system environment. These values are not created by the malware; there's nothing in the actual code for the malware that includes instructions to create these values or data entries. Rather, they're created as a result of the malware running within the Windows operating system environment.

File Access

There are a number of times when determining a user's access to files, or more specifically, the user account used to access files, can be paramount. This can be pertinent information during a human resources issue, access to illicit images or files case, as well as during data breach cases involving a targeted, dedicated adversary.

One of the great things about Windows systems from the perspective of a forensic analyst is that the systems record and save a great deal of information specific to actions taken via a user account. This can be valuable, as the information is maintained on the system long after the file has ceased to exist on the system.

RecentDocs

Windows systems do a very good job of tracking what documents a user has accessed, making them available in the Recent Documents menu, as illustrated in Fig. 4.8.

This list of documents can be very revealing about a user's activities. In most cases, such as in a corporate environment, the documents listed here will be legitimate, business-oriented documents. However, even in such environments, users may be found accessing documents that they shouldn't. Information about the documents that the user has accessed is maintained in the Recent-Docs key, which is found in the following path:

```
Software\Microsoft\Windows\CurrentVersion\Explorer\
RecentDocs
```

An example of RecentDocs key, as well as the subkeys and values, from a Windows XP (the structure of the data has not changed significantly on Windows 7 and Windows 10 systems) system is illustrated in Fig. 4.9.

As you can see in Fig. 4.9, the RecentDocs key itself contains numbered values (0, 1, etc.) that each contain binary data, as well as subkeys named for the various extensions of the files accessed. Each of these subkeys also contains numbered values with binary data as well. All of these keys contain a value named "MRUListEx",

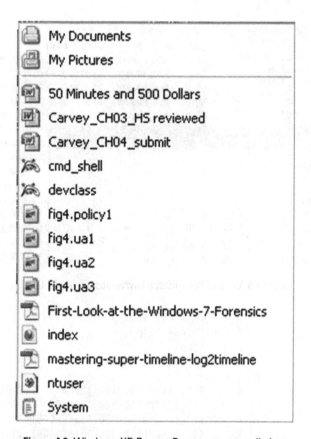

Figure 4.8 Windows XP Recent Documents menu listing.

which is a sequence of DWORD values that list the order in which the documents or files were accessed. Vista and Windows 7 record this information in the same way, and the recentdocs.pl RegRipper plugin can be used to parse the necessary information from the binary value data on all versions of Windows. An example of information retrieved by the recentdocs.pl plugin from a Windows 7 system appears as follows:

```
Software\Microsoft\Windows\CurrentVersion\Explorer\
RecentDocs\.jpeg
  LastWrite Time Sat Mar 13 22:25:46 2010 (UTC)
  MRUListEx = 2,1,0
  2 = anime_155.jpeg
  1 = 11.ca2.jpeg
  0 = roripara22_png.jpeg

Software\Microsoft\Windows\CurrentVersion\Explorer\
RecentDocs\.jpg
  LastWrite Time Tue Mar 16 15:43:58 2010 (UTC)
  MRUListEx = 3,1,2,8,9,4,0,6,5,7
```

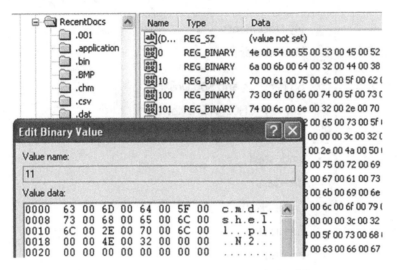

Figure 4.9 View of RecentDocs key/values via RegEdit.exe.

```
3 = Picnik collage.jpg
1 = hether-446.jpg
2 = 09.jpg
8 = 1211720515959.jpg
9 = 016.jpg
4 = 25517_1260411908194_1166566081_30636671_8251529_n.jpg
0 = 25517_1260297105324_1166566081_30636173_6335083_n.jpg
6 = 25517_1260297145325_1166566081_30636174_7038891_n.jpg
5 = 25517_1260297185326_1166566081_30636175_5223984_n.jpg
7 = 25517_1260297225327_1166566081_30636176_4397882_n.jpg
```

This example illustrates the user's access to .jpeg and .jpg files; in short, images. One thing you'll notice is that the plugin parses the MRUListEx value and then presents the files in the order in which they are listed in that value. Based on how the contents of these keys are maintained, we can see that anime_155.jpeg was accessed on Saturday, March 13, 2010 at approximately 22:25:46 (UTC), and that "Picnik collage.jpg" was accessed on Tuesday, March 16, 2010 at approximately 15:43:58 (UTC).

WHAT APPLICATION USES OR CREATED THAT FILE?

Many times while I'm perusing online forums, I'll see a question similar to, "what application is used to access/created this file?" Most of the time, the response is a reference to a Google search (or even a URL for lmgtfy.com) or to fileext.com. This may seem like the obvious answer, but it's not someplace I'd start. When I see a file extension listed on a file in an image, or in the RecentDocs key in the user's hive, and I'm interested in determining the application that is associated with that file extension

> ## WHAT APPLICATION USES OR CREATED THAT FILE?—Cont'd
>
> on the system, I'll run the *assoc.pl* RegRipper plugin against the Software hive (via rip.pl/.exe), redirect the output to a file, and then look to see what may be listed in the output file. This allows me to determine the file associations on that system; searching for this information via Google, while it may be useful, does not address the context of what applications are installed on the system being analyzed. The output of the assoc.pl plugin can also tell me about installed applications; for example, on a Windows 7 system, I found that all of the graphics files (.jpg, .img, .tif, etc.) were associated with the IrfanView application. So, not only did I now know that IrfanView was installed, but I now had another application to check for an MRU list of opened or saved files. From this same system, I also found that OpenOffice was installed rather than Microsoft Office. Searching via Google may provide useful leads, but examining artifacts on the system being examined will many times provide much-needed context.
>
> However, this information applies to the system itself; file association settings from the user profile (found in the user's USRCLASS.DAT hive) will supersede the system settings when the user logs in. This is covered in more detail in the "File Associations" section later in this chapter.

We can see from this that the values beneath the RecentDocs key and its subkeys will tell us what documents and files the user account was used to access (I say that, because that's all we know…we don't really know who was at the keyboard when the account was logged in…), as well as when the most recently access document was accessed (via the first item in the MRUListEx value and the key LastWrite time). A closer look at the binary data for the various values shows us the file name and a referenced Windows shortcut (.lnk) file, but not the full path to the file itself, so we don't know if the file was on the local hard drive, on a CD, thumb drive attached to the system, or on a network share.

ComDlg32

The key "ComDlg32" refers to common dialogs available on Windows systems. Rather than requiring developers to recreate or code from scratch some of those dialogs that are used frequently, these are actually provided for use through the Windows application programming interface (API). The path to the key is *Software\Microsoft\Windows\CurrentVersion\Explorer\ComDlg32*, and the keys of interest beneath this key differ slightly between Windows XP and Windows 7 and beyond. Figs. 4.10 and 4.11 illustrate the keys on Windows XP and Vista, respectively.

The OpenSaveMRU (on Windows XP and 2003; OpenSavePidMRU on Vista through Windows 10 systems) tracks files that the user account is used to access via the Open and Save As… common dialogs. You can see the use of these common dialogs when

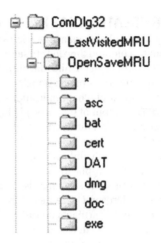

Figure 4.10 Windows XP ComDlg32 key.

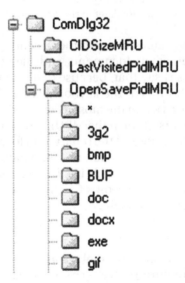

Figure 4.11 Windows Vista ComDlg32 key.

opening an application and clicking on the File menu item. From there, the drop-down menu will include Open and Save As... options, and choosing these options will launch the common dialogs. This key and its subkeys also track previously opened or saved files as an autocomplete feature, as illustrated in Fig. 4.12.

As you can see illustrated in Figs. 4.10 and 4.11, the Open-SaveMRU and OpenSavePidMRU keys contain subkeys that specify the extensions of the files opened or saved. In Fig. 4.10, we see a subkey named "asc", which refers to files used by the Pretty Good

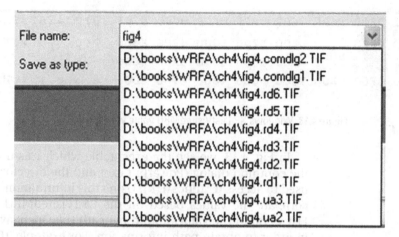

Figure 4.12 MS Paint Save As… dialog autocomplete listing.

Privacy (PGP) encryption application. Each of these keys contains values whose name letters and whose data points to the files in question. Each key also contains an MRUList value which is a string that lists the MRU order in which the files were accessed. As such, the LastWrite time of the key would correspond to the time that the first file referenced in the MRUList value was accessed. The Open-SavePidMRU subkey values are different, in that the values are binary data types and need to parsed appropriately to retrieve the file name; also, the subkeys each contain a value named MRUListEx (as opposed to a value named MRUList), which is also a binary data type and needs to be parsed appropriately as well.

One subkey beneath the OpenSaveMRU and OpenSavePid-MRU keys that stands out is the key named "*". This refers to files of any extension, or no extension, and also maintains the list of most recently accessed files for each type. For example, beneath the OpenSaveMRU key in Fig. 4.10 is a subkey named "zip", which contains six values. The most recently accessed file that ends with the ".zip" extension is not only listed in the MRUList value within that key, but it is also listed as a value in the "*" subkey.

The LastVisitedMRU (LastVisitedPidMRU on Vista and Windows seven systems) key serves a bit of a different function. This key tracks the application last used to access the files listed in the OpenSaveMRU key (and its subkeys), as well as the directory that was last accessed. The OpenSaveMRU values include the paths and file names; also, remember that the common dialogs (in this case Open and Save As…) are not applications in and of themselves but are instead accessed via other applications, such as MS Paint, Notepad, MS Word, the web browser, etc. Fig. 4.13 illustrates a LastVisitedMRU value.

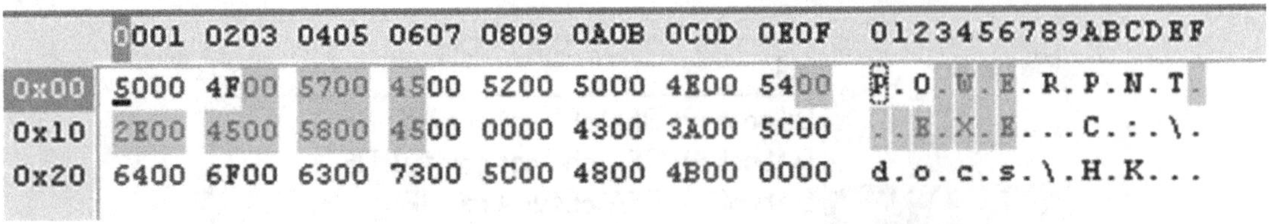

	0001	0203	0405	0607	0809	0A0B	0C0D	0E0F	0123456789ABCDEF
0x00	5000	4F00	5700	4500	5200	5000	4E00	5400	P.O.W.E.R.P.N.T.
0x10	2E00	4500	5800	4500	0000	4300	3A00	5C00	..E.X.E...C.:.\.
0x20	6400	6F00	6300	7300	5C00	4800	4B00	0000	d.o.c.s.\.H.K...

Figure 4.13 Windows XP LastVisitedMRU value viewed via RFV.

In Fig. 4.13, we see the executable which was used to access the common dialog (Powerpnt.exe) and the directory that it was used to access (C:\docs\HK). Using this information, we can then correlate the values based on the LastVisitedMRU key's MRU-List value to the values found beneath the OpenSaveMRU* key in order to obtain path information. For example, the first value referenced in the LastVisitedMRU MRUList value is "f", which points to Winword.exe, and includes the C:\docs\xcel directory in the binary data. We then go to the OpenSaveMRU* key, and the first value listed in the MRUList value is also "f", which in this case points to C:\docs\xcel\xcel.doc. However, remember that these are MRU keys, so we shouldn't expect to find a great deal of historical data that would allow us to track file paths back several weeks or months.

HISTORICAL DATA

Let's not forget that while some Registry keys (such as the ones that maintain MRU information) can show us not only the most recent documents that a user account had been used to access but also documents accessed in the past, analysts can also find further historical data in Windows XP System Restore Points or within Volume Shadow copies (as on Vista and Windows 7 systems).

Similar to the OpenSavePidMRU key values, the values listed within the LastVisitedPidMRU key (Vista through Windows 10) are binary data types and should be parsed appropriately. However, these values contain similar information as their counterparts on Windows XP and 2003 systems. The *comdlg32.pl* RegRipper plugin will extract and display the information from the values beneath the ComDlg32 key and its subkeys, but the caveat of continued research and input into the maintenance and development of the plugin (and others) to address new data types remains.

Microsoft Office File/Place MRUs

Most Windows systems, particularly those in a corporate environment, have the MS Office suite of products installed.

Thankfully, the MS Office applications maintain their own MRU lists, which are maintained in a path similar to the following:

```
SOFTWARE\Microsoft\Office\version\application name\File MRU
```

For MS Office 2010, the path for the "File MRU" key for Excel is *Software\Microsoft\Office\14.0\Excel\File MRU*. The path is similar for MS Office 2013 (version 15.0) applications, with the version listed as "15.0".

LIVEID ACCOUNTS

In some test scenarios, I've found the *File MRU* key path to be *Software\Microsoft\Office\15.0\Word\User MRU\LiveId_{hash}\File MRU* for the MS Word application that is part of the MS Office 2013 suite. This appears to be related to use of a Microsoft LiveID account and clearly will require additional research.

Something very useful about the values beneath these keys is that they have a time stamp value embedded within the value data for each of the MRU values. In 2011, Cameron Howell shared his code for the *office2010.pl* plugin, which not only parses the file path and name from the data, but it also parses and displays the time stamp. This plugin needs to be updated to include MS Office 2013 documents as well as MRU lists for LiveID accounts.

TrustRecords

For systems that do have MS Office installed, there may be another source of information available. When a user downloads an MS Office document from a network location, or from the Internet, and then opens the document, they see the yellow "Protected View" bar across the top of the document, as illustrated in Fig. 4.14.

The user can read the document even with the Protected View bar visible, but in order to edit (or print) the document, the user needs to click on the "Enable Editing" button. When they do so, an entry is created in the TrustRecords key. For MS Word, the path to the key is:

```
Software\Microsoft\Office\14.0\Word\Security\Trusted
Documents\TrustRecords
```

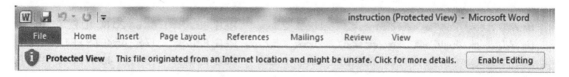

Figure 4.14 Enable Editing bar in MS Word.

Beneath this key is a value for each of the documents for which the user clicked the "Enable Editing" button. The first 8 bytes of the value data are a 64-bit FILETIME object that indicates the date and time that the user clicked on the button to enable editing of the document. As such, each value (ie, path to the document) has its own individual time stamp, as illustrated in Fig. 4.15.

MICROSOFT WORD

The TrustRecords key not only illustrates that the user accessed a particular file, and when, but it also illustrates the execution of the MS Word application.

An 18-page PDF document written by Dustin Hurlbut (available online at https://ad-pdf.s3.amazonaws.com/Microsoft_Office_2007-2010_Registry_ArtifactsFINAL.pdf) provides an extensive list of Registry artifacts associated with MS Office 2007 and 2010 and includes the TrustRecords artifacts.

Adobe Reader

On July 16, 2015, Jason Hale posted to his blog (found online at http://dfstream.blogspot.com/2015/07/adobe-readers-not-so-crecentfiles.html) detailing new values he'd found in the user's hive with respect to the Adobe PDF reader application. In short, he'd not only found that the number of previously viewed files was increased (that is, more keys were created and maintained), but also that several new values had been added to each key. Jason indicates in his post that as of version 11.0.07 of Adobe Reader application, there are a total of 100 subkeys that are maintained (up from the previous 5), one for each document the user opened. In addition, several values have been added to each subkey, including one for the page count of the document, as well as one for the size of the file itself. There is also a value named "sDate" that has been added, which appears to indicate the date at time for when the file was accessed. This value has a binary format but has a string format similar to "D:20150511165429-4′00″", which indicates that the file was accessed at 4:54:29 pm on May 11, 2015,

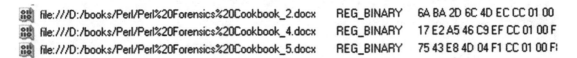

file:///D:/books/Perl/Perl%20Forensics%20Cookbook_2.docx	REG_BINARY	6A BA 2D 6C 4D EC CC 01 00
file:///D:/books/Perl/Perl%20Forensics%20Cookbook_4.docx	REG_BINARY	17 E2 A5 46 C9 EF CC 01 00 F
file:///D:/books/Perl/Perl%20Forensics%20Cookbook_5.docx	REG_BINARY	75 43 E8 4D 04 F1 CC 01 00 F:

Figure 4.15 TrustRecords values.

Chapter 4 CASE STUDIES: USER HIVES **159**

local time (the "-4" appears to indicate the time zone offset from GMT or UTC).

Why is this important? As the user views successive files, each previously viewed file is "pushed down," and the most recent one is written to the "c1" key. For example, on a system with a fresh installation of the application, the first file viewed would be written to the "c1" subkey; when the second file is viewed by the user, the information about the first file viewed is written to the "c2" subkey, and the information regarding the most recently viewed file is written to the "c1" subkey, and so on. What this means is that all of the subkeys (up to 100) will have the same LastWrite time, so that information will be of little value in a timeline that is meant to illustrate the user's activities. However, this new "sDate" value can be translated to a time stamp value, and that information can be used in a timeline.

DATA SOURCES

While data sources outside of the Registry are beyond the scope of this book, I think that it's important to point out that Jump Lists (available on Windows 7 through 10 systems) serve as excellent sources of MRU data when it comes to user access to files.

So far in this section, we've listed some of the locations within the Registry that are used to record a user's access to files. As with the rest of this book, this list should not be considered complete; there are far too many combinations of applications and versions to provide a complete list. What I've attempted to illustrate thus far in this chapter is that the Registry records a good deal of user activity, and in many cases, associates that activity with a time stamp, making the Registry an exceptional resource for forensic analysts.

User Activity

So far we've described a great deal of user activity that's recorded in the NTUSER.DAT file. As one might expect, there's even more information recorded in the Registry that can be categorized under "user activity." This category covers other activities that apply to actions the user took but don't fit into the previous categories.

TypedPaths

The TypedPaths key (*Software\Microsoft\Windows\Current-Version\Explorer\TypedPaths*) records paths that the user typed into Windows Explorer. On Windows 10, typing into the little box to the right of the Windows icon on the TaskBar, the one that usually says, "Search the web and Windows", will populate this key. The

Value	Type	Data
url1	REG_SZ	mspaint
url2	REG_SZ	Control Panel

Figure 4.16 TypedPaths key values.

values within this key have names such as "url1" and "url2", as illustrated in Fig. 4.16.

When the first entry is typed, the first value to be added to the key will be "url1". When the next entry is typed, the new value is named "url1", and previous value becomes "url2", and so on. As such, under normal circumstances, the LastWrite time of the key will correspond to when the most recent entry was typed.

Again, that's under normal circumstances and doesn't apply if the user modifies the key through the Registry Editor or through the use of code, such as a Visual Basic script. However, I have rarely seen this value manipulated in that manner; in fact, I don't recall a time when I've seen the content of this key manipulated specifically to obscure a user's activity. That does not mean that it could not happen, I just haven't seen it yet.

TypedURLS

Forensic analysts have long associated the values beneath the TypedURLs key in the user's NTUSER.DAT hive file with user activity. It's understood that when a user types in a website address in the Internet Explorer (IE) address bar, that URL is written to the URL1 value beneath the key.

In March 2011, Paul Nichols of Crucial Security posted an article (found online at http://crucialsecurityblog.harris. com/2011/03/23/typedurls-part-2/) regarding some potential issues with the accepted belief the values beneath the TypedURLs keys are modified solely by user activity. As the article points out, there is a default value listed beneath the key, and there are several malware variants that modify values beneath the key.

WRITING TO THE REGISTRY

While many Registry keys and values within the user's hives are modified when a user performs specific actions, it is important to remember that there may be other reasons for the data that you're seeing beneath specific keys. As has been mentioned several times throughout this chapter and the previous one, there are variants of malware that write directly to the Registry (as opposed to the operating system creating entries based on the presence of the malware), many for purposes other than persistence.

The contents of the TypedURLs key have proved fruitful during breach investigations, particularly when a dedicated adversary has access to the infrastructure via Terminal Services. In several instances, I've found the values beneath this key to be invaluable in determining an intruder's activities, particularly when they were accessing a web shell. The TypedURLs key contains values that appear as follows:

```
url19 -> http://pandora.com/
url20 -> http://192.168.1.1/
url21 -> \\fileserver
```

Much like the TypedPaths key, as the user types new URLs into the IE address bar, the most recently typed URL becomes url1, and each of the previous entries get "pushed down." As such, under normal circumstances, the LastWrite time of the TypedURLs key will correspond to when the user typed the contents of the url1 value into the IE address bar.

Another key that was found when Windows 8 was released and later determined to be associated with IE 10 is the "TypedURLsTime" key. Under normal circumstances (that is, without outside manipulation), each of the values beneath this key corresponds to value of the same name beneath the TypedURLs key and provides the date and time when the user typed the URL.

Searches

Users will often search for things (files by name, keywords within files, etc.) on their systems, as well as other systems, and on the Internet. Sometimes, they even do this using the built-in search capability that comes with Windows XP, as illustrated in Fig. 4.17.

When a user runs a search on Windows XP, the information about what is being searched for is maintained in the following Registry key:

```
Software\Microsoft\Search Assistant\ACMru
```

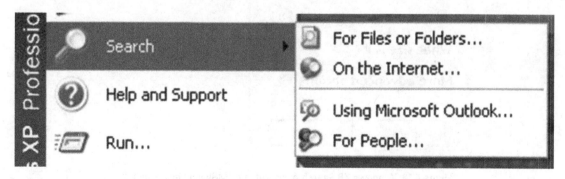

Figure 4.17 Windows XP Search.

Beneath this key are several subkeys, each of which is named for a number, and each of these numbers corresponds to a particular portion of the Search Assistant, as indicated as follows:

- 5001—contains list of terms entered via the "On the Internet…" search
- 5603—contains the list of terms entered via the Windows XP "For Files or Folders…" search
- 5604—contains list of terms searched for using the "A word or phrase in the file" search
- 5647—contains list of terms searched for using the "Computers or people" search

Fig. 4.18 illustrates the portion of the Search Assistant in which entries populate the 5603 and 5604 keys, respectively.

I have found this information has proven to be very useful during a number of examinations. For example, the values beneath these keys are also numbered in an MRU fashion: 000, 001, 002, etc. Therefore, the LastWrite time for the key itself lets us know when the search for the "000" value was conducted. Sometimes I find entries that are entirely normal for a particular

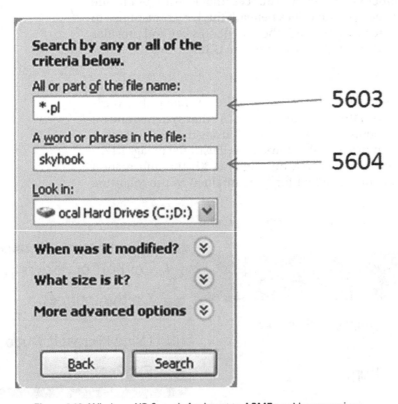

Figure 4.18 Windows XP Search Assistant to ACMRu subkey mappings.

user; in other cases, perhaps not so much. For example, I've seen where someone who had no business doing so was searching for terms such as "banking" and "passwords." I've also seen where someone has perhaps had trouble spelling, searching for "bankign."

On Vista systems, information about searches run by the user is maintained in a file and not within a Registry key. With Windows 7, information about what the user searched for is again recorded in the Registry, this time in the WordWheelQuery key. The full path to this key appears as follows:

```
Software\Microsoft\Windows\CurrentVersion\Explorer\
WordWheelQuery
```

Fig. 4.19 illustrates how the contents of this key appear in Windows Explorer on Windows 7.

The values within the WordWheelQuery key are binary data types that are numbered ("0", "1", etc.), and there is also an MRUListEx value that is also a binary data type. As with many MRUListEx values, the MRU list is maintained as 4-byte DWORD values in sequence, with the value 0xFFFF indicating the end of the list. As with the Windows XP ACMru key, the information in this key may shed some light as to the user's activity on the system.

The traditional approach to computer forensic analysis has relied heavily on file system time stamps and a few other artifacts

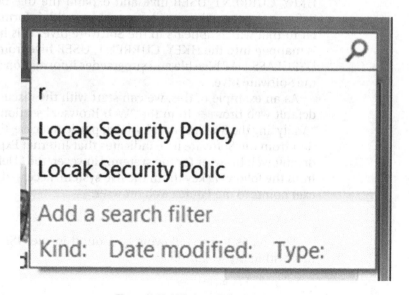

Figure 4.19 Windows 7 Search history.

(file contents) found on the system. However, systems are now often accessed via multiple user accounts, and the scope of many investigations has expanded beyond the boundaries and hard drive of just one system. Further, there are times when an analyst cannot trust file system time stamps, as either the updating of file last access times is disabled, or an intruder (or malware) modified those time stamps. As such, we need to look to other locations within the system to develop a better understanding of activity associated with a user account. The best place to start is within the Registry hive files within the user profile; there is the well-known NTUSER.DAT hive found in the root of the profile directory, and with more recent versions of Windows (Vista, Windows 7), the USRCLASS.DAT hive is seeing greater usage. In this chapter, we'll focus on discussing and demonstrating how activity associated with a user account ("user activity") is recorded in the user's hives, and how analysts can use that information to the benefit of their examinations.

File Associations

We discussed in chapter "Analyzing the System Hives" how file association information from within the Software hive can be used to answer questions regarding the relationship between file extensions and applications on a system. However, information about file associations is also maintained on a per-user basis, as well. If you open the Registry Editor on a live system to the HKEY_CURRENT_USER hive and expand the tree beneath the Software key, you'll see a Classes subkey with information similar to that which appears in the Software hive. This information is mapped into the HKEY_CURRENT_USER hive from the user's USRCLASS.DAT hive file and supersedes information available in the Software hive.

As an example of this, we can start with the discussion of the default web browser from the "Web Browser" section of chapter "Analyzing the System Hives". In that particular case, the information from the Software hive indicates that Internet Explorer is the default web browser for the system. However, the "Default" value from the following key (from the live system, accessed via regedit. exe) points to the Firefox web browser:

```
HKEY_CURRENT_USER\Software\Classes\http\shell\open\command
```

This maps to the following key found in the USRCLASS.DAT hive within my user profile:

```
http\shell\open\command
```

What this shows is that when I log into the system with my account, the system settings for file associations (and in this particular case, the default web browser) are superseded by settings found in my USRCLASS.DAT hive.

Note

As we've seen, there are a number of instances where Registry artifacts that indicate the installation or use of applications persist after the application is removed or deleted. This applies to many applications that simply have a GUI but do not require an installation routine (ie, the application files are simply copied to a directory). However, many applications that utilize an installation routine and set file associations in the Registry will also "undo" those settings when the application is uninstalled. This is yet another example of how Registry hives from System Restore Points (Windows XP) or Volume Shadow Copies, as well as deleted keys extracted from unallocated space within Registry hive files (via regslack.exe), can provide significant historical data from a system.

USRCLASS.DAT

Throughout the evolution of Windows systems, one of the things I've noted is that more and more has been "moved" to the USRCLASS. DAT hive. That's not to say that everything has…not at all. One example is the shellbags artifacts discussed later in this chapter; these artifacts were found in the NTUSER.DAT hive with Windows XP and 2003 systems and were "moved" to the USRCLASS.DAT hive in Vista systems, where they have remained. With the release of Windows 8 (and subsequently, Windows 8.1 and Windows 10), there appears to be the potential for even more data that may be relevant to investigators stored within this hive; I'm sure that as Windows 10 systems become more popular and in wider use, that data will be documented.

AutoStart

Within the user's USRCLASS.DAT hive, the location where we most often seen used to autostart programs (and subsequently, malware) is the *InProcServer32* key beneath the *CLSID* key; the full path within the hive is *CLSID\{GUID}\InProcServer32*, as illustrated in Fig. 4.20.

As with other autostart locations, this key path is most often used by legitimate applications but is also hijacked by malware. One such example is the malware downloader known as "Lurk," which was discussed in an article posted to the Dell SecureWorks

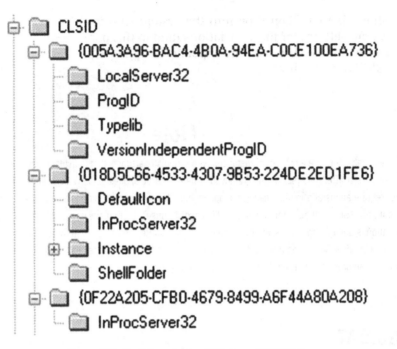

Figure 4.20 Partial contents of Windows 10 CLSID key.

website in November 2014 (found online at http://www.secureworks. com/cyber-threat-intelligence/threats/malware-analysis-of-the-lurk-downloader/). According to the article, the Lurk malware persists by hijacking the "(Default)" value beneath the *CLSID\ {A3CCEDF7-2DE2-11D0-86F4-00A0C913F750}\InProcServer32* key and pointing to the malware DLL rather than the Internet Explorer PNG image decoder. Performing a search via Google for the GUID shows us other malware that has been seen to use this same key path for persistence.

The RegRipper *inprocserver.pl* plugin can be used to search across the Software, NTUSER.DAT, and USRCLASS.DAT hive files for anomalous entries. If you open the plugin in an editor (Notepad, Notepad++, etc.) and look at the headers, you'll see that over time I've updated and modified the plugin; this is something that I'm sure will need to be done in the future as well, as our understanding of Windows 8, 8.1, and 10 progresses through new research and discovery.

Program Execution

There do not appear at this point to be a great many keys or values within the USRCLASS.DAT hive that contain information that would be associated with the "program execution" category. The MuiCache key is one of those Registry keys that seems as if it might be very useful, but for which there is very little documentation available. On Windows XP and 2003 systems, the path to the MuiCache key within the user's NTUSER.DAT hive is:

```
Software\Microsoft\Windows\ShellNoRoam\MUICache
```

On Vista systems and above, the key path is located in the user's USRCLASS.DAT hive, in the key path:

```
Local Settings\Software\Microsoft\Windows\Shell\MuiCache
```

So, how is this key useful? Several years ago, I was doing some research on specific malware samples and looking to see what some of the AV vendors had already documented with respect to the variants they'd seen. In some instances, I began to see references to malware creating a value (according to the AV vendor write-up) within the MuiCache key when run, and not being familiar with this key, I wanted to see if I could determine the reason for this value being created. As it later turned out, the malware wasn't creating the value…the value was being created by the operating system, as a result of how the malware was being launched within the testing environment. This proved to be very interesting and very useful.

We've already seen how we can track the user's activity on a system when they interact with the shell, whether they're conducting searches or launching applications. However, in some instances, we'll see that a command prompt was launched (as indicated by the UserAssist key or RunMRU entries) and then nothing afterward. In some instances, we may be able to get an idea of what the user may have done (or more correctly, what the user account may have been used to do…) by examining the contents of the MuiCache key. By default, when an account is first created (or shortly after it is first used) the MuiCache key may contain value names that start with "@". However, once the profile begins to be used, there may be additional entries that appear as illustrated in Fig. 4.21.

As you can see in Fig. 4.21, this key provides a sort of historic, persistent record of the applications that the user account has

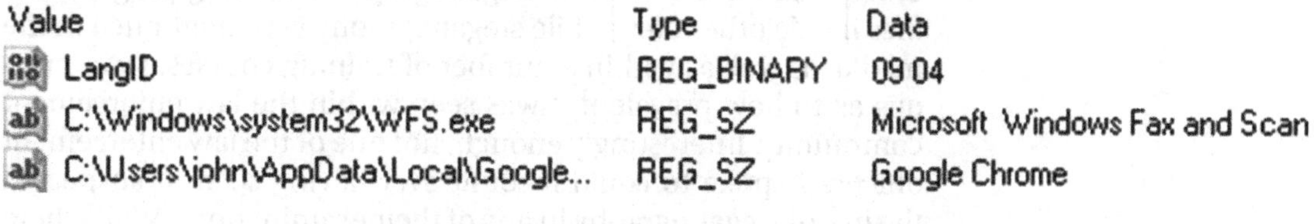

Value	Type	Data
LangID	REG_BINARY	09 04
C:\Windows\system32\WFS.exe	REG_SZ	Microsoft Windows Fax and Scan
C:\Users\john\AppData\Local\Google...	REG_SZ	Google Chrome

Figure 4.21 MuiCache key contents from a Windows 7 system.

been used to run, albeit without any sort of time stamp specific to each application. While conducting forensic analysis during an incident response engagement a number of years ago, I was parsing the NTUSER.DAT file from a compromised Windows 2003 system (using RegRipper's *muicache.pl* plugin), when I noticed that there were several unusual value names that referenced non-native executable files in the "C:\Windows\Tasks" directory. It appeared that the intruder was placing his toolset in this directory, as by default, when viewing the Tasks directory via the Windows Explorer shell on a live system (which is how most system administrators tend to do so), the .exe files do not appear in the viewing pane. This means that the intruder's tools are effectively hidden from view from most of the likely first responders, should any unusual activity be detected on the compromised system. It turned out that we were able to locate several of the tools in the Tasks directory, but several others had apparently been deleted. This provided an interesting indication of the intruder's other activities on the system (ie, they'd apparently added, used/run, and then deleted other command line tools) that remained persistent after the intruder had apparently deleted several of the tools used.

WINDOWS 10 SYSTEMS

During the course of writing this book, I was reviewing data in a USR-CLASS.DAT file extracted from a Windows 10 system and noticed that there wasn't an MUICache key in the "normal" location; however, I did see two additional keys, one at the path *Local Settings\ImmutableMuiCache*, and the other at *Local Settings\MuiCache*. I didn't see a great deal of particularly useful information beneath either of these keys, but that may have been because the profile hadn't been used to any great extent. That would also perhaps explain why the "normal" MUICache key did not appear to be present and simply reinforces that additional and continual research is required in the digital forensic analysis field.

Several years ago, I used to present pretty regularly at local High Tech Crime Investigation Association (HTCIA) conferences (our local chapter became known as the Regional Computer Forensics Group, or RCFG) and spoke to a number of law enforcement officers about the issue of steganography or hiding programs or files inside other files. While steganography was mentioned in the media, as well as within a number of training courses, I was curious as to how prevalent it was seen within the law enforcement community. Interestingly enough, not one of the law enforcement officers I spoke to could recount ever having seen or suspected the use of steganography in any of their examinations. While there are a number of freely available tools for embedding or hiding files (executable files, images, text, videos, etc.) within other file, many of them do not get installed on a system in the usual sense; instead, the application files are simply added to a directory by the user. The contents of the MuiCache key may indicate the use of steganography applications, particularly those that may have been copied to a system or run from external media, such as a CD or thumb drive.

Overall, the point of this is that, under most normal circumstances, values beneath the MuiCache key generally appear as a result of interaction of some kind with the shell. When an executable file path is found as a value name beneath this key, it appears to indicate that the user account in question was used to run the application. Follow-on analysis steps might be to attempt to locate the file within the file system (or unallocated space), a Prefetch file, or perhaps an MFT entry (particularly if the file path indicates that the file was on a local hard drive). This key can provide some very interesting indications of activities that occurred within the context of the user account.

File Access

The majority of locations within the user's hive files that provide indications of file access are found within the NTUSER.DAT, but there are some key paths within the USRCLASS.DAT hive that provide indications of the user accessing certain types of files.

Photos

In March 2013, Jason Hale posted to his blog (found online at http://dfstream.blogspot.com/2013/03/windows-8-tracking-opened-photos.html) regarding functionality inherent to Windows 8; specifically, when a user double-clicked an image file, it would be opened via the Photos application (or "tile") on what was referred to as the "Metro" desktop. Information regarding these files is buried deep within the user's USRCLASS.DAT hive file, including (but not limited to) the full path to the opened image file and a value named "Link" whose binary data is a variation on the Windows shortcut format. Yes, that's exactly what it sounds like; a value buried within the hive file contains what amounts to Windows shortcut, or *.lnk, formatted data.

Interestingly enough, Jason updated the blog post over a year later, stating that Windows 8.1 systems do not appear to record or maintain this data. This artifact is obviously different from the file access MRUs discussed previously in this chapter, but I wanted to include it here in case someone reading this book has to perform forensic analysis of a Windows 8 (not 8.1) system and is interesting in knowing which image files may have been accessed by a user.

Tip

This is yet another example of why knowing the version of Windows you're analyzing is important, and how sharing that information when you ask questions in online forums can prove fruitful.

Shellbags

As has been discussed thus far, with respect to versions of Windows beyond XP, a good bit of functionality has been added to the operating systems, functionality that makes Windows much more of a "user experience." As a result, some of the information recorded in order to enable the functionality was moved to the USRCLASS.DAT hive.

Perhaps the most notable artifact within the USRCLASS.DAT hive is referred to as *shellbags*. This artifact is referred to as "shellbags" due to the name of the one of the Registry keys involved; on Windows 7 through Windows 10 systems, the path to the artifacts is:

```
Local Settings\Software\Microsoft\Windows\Shell\BagMRU
```

Note

Again, with Windows XP and 2003 systems, the shellbags artifacts were maintained in the NTUSER.DAT hive, and you could even get directory listings of files from the Registry values, in some cases. That all changed when Windows Vista was released, and pretty much the only thing that's changed since then is that over time, new shell items have been released. As such, continual research in this area has been required, and Eric Zimmerman has put forth considerable effort into keeping abreast of new developments and artifacts in this area.

Once again…the version of Windows you're analyzing can play a significant role in determining what artifacts are available, and where those artifacts are located (within the file system, Registry, etc.).

Beneath this key path is a series of nested subkeys, as illustrated in Fig. 4.22.

Beneath the BagMRU key, and beneath the nested subkeys shown in Fig. 4.22, you'll find "MRUListEx" values along with numbered values (ie, 0, 1, 2, 3, etc.), as illustrated in Fig. 4.23.

As discussed previously in this chapter, the MRUListEx value simply indicates the order in which each of the numbered values

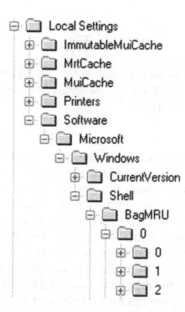

Figure 4.22 Windows 10 shellbags artifacts (via WRR).

Value	Type	Data
NodeSlot	REG_DWORD	0x00000001
MRUListEx	REG_BINARY	06 00 00 00 04 00 00 00 02 00 00 00 01 00 00
0	REG_BINARY	0C 00 01 00 84 21 DE 39 01 00 00 00 00 00
1	REG_BINARY	0C 00 01 00 84 21 DE 39 03 00 00 00 00 00
2	REG_BINARY	0C 00 01 00 84 21 DE 39 02 00 00 00 00 00
3	REG_BINARY	0C 00 01 00 84 21 DE 39 09 00 00 00 00 00
4	REG_BINARY	0C 00 01 00 84 21 DE 39 05 00 00 00 00 00
5	REG_BINARY	0C 00 01 00 84 21 DE 39 08 00 00 00 00 00
6	REG_BINARY	0C 00 01 00 84 21 DE 39 00 00 00 00 00 00

Figure 4.23 Description.

was accessed. For example, in Fig. 4.23, the first DWORD (ie, 4 byte) segment of the MRUListEx value data is "6", indicating that the item in the value named "6" was most recently accessed.

Now, the data associated with each of the numbered values is what's referred to as a "shell item." This is essentially a "blob" of binary data that contains considerable information about a specific object or element that is part of a complete path.

Tip

These "shell items" are used elsewhere on Windows systems, not only within the Registry (associated with other artifacts) but also within the file system. The most notable artifact within the file system that is made up of shell items, at least in part, is Windows shortcut or "LNK" files.

Depending on the type of data and where we are in the overall path, each of the data blobs can contain various bits of information about the item or object in question. For example, some shell items contain simply a GUID, and we can do a lookup of that GUID to determine if it refers to a special system folder, to the Control Panel, etc. Other shell items may refer to folders on the system, and the data blob may contain a name (ie, "system32"), in addition to file system time stamps for the folder (at the time that the object was accessed by the user), as well as the MFT reference number for that object. One of the extremely difficult aspects of parsing shell items is that doing so requires time and effort, as Microsoft doesn't provide a great deal of documentation for these data objects.

Parsing through the nested Registry keys, we can reassemble paths based on our understanding of the contents of the individual shell items. For example, we can parse and reassemble the shell items into a path to a folder (ie, "My Computer\D:\Tools\timeline"), to a zipped archive (ie, "My Computer\D:\Tools\md5deep-4.1.zip\md5deep-4.1"; zipped archives are treated as folders on Windows Vista and above systems), to Control Panel items (ie, "Control Panel\User Accounts\CLSID_User Accounts\Change Your Picture"), or to devices (such as "My Computer\Canon EOS DIGITAL REBEL XTi\CF\DCIM\334CANON" or "My Computer\DROID2\Removable Storage\dcim\Camera").

Tip

A great example of the differences between accessing a system via the command line interface (CLI) and via the GUI and the artifacts that are left through different interactions can be seen in a post at the Binary Zone blog from January 2015 (found line at http://www.binary-zone.com/2015/01/07/forensic-analysis-creating-user-gui-vs-cli).

Shellbags can also provide indications of program execution. How is that? Years ago, when I first started writing manuscripts for books, my publisher at the time had a methodology for transferring large files back and forth; rather than using email, they preferred the file transfer protocol, or "FTP." However, rather than operating at the command line (which most authors likely tend to *not* do), the publisher provided instructions for accessing FTP via the Windows Explorer shell. I read through the instructions a couple of times before attempting the process, and once I had transferred the files, I didn't think much more about it. Jump forward several years, and I was examining an image of a Windows server that had been accessed remotely via Terminal Services; yes, the password had been relatively trivial and easy to guess. My analysis indicated that the system had, in fact, been accessed several times, likely by different intruders. I could see where one intruder had used Internet Explorer to download and install the Firefox web browser and then used that browser to download other tools.

One of the goals of the analysis was to look indications of data exfiltration, so I began by looking for indications of access to various tools. In examining the Registry hives from the user profiles on the system, I parsed the shellbag artifacts and found some unusual entries that indicated that one intruder had accessed FTP servers via the Windows Explorer shell. Remembering the instructions from my publisher, I followed them again and connected to an FTP server that I know about…and found that doing so produced artifacts just like what I was seeing in my examination of the compromised Windows server!

While the shellbag artifacts do not explicitly illustrate access to files on Windows Vista through Windows 10 systems, they can provide indications of the user accessing folders, Control Panel applets, as well as external storage devices, including external hard drives, smartphones, and digital cameras. The shellbag artifacts can also show that a user accessed zipped archives, well after the archive itself has been deleted from the system, and they can also provide indications that the user accessed FTP sites via Windows Explorer. As with other artifacts, research into these artifacts is, and needs to be ongoing and continuous. Joachim Metz has compiled documentation regarding the format of various shell items and made that format specification available online, in PDF format, at https://docs.google.com/file/d/0B-VYGsDJPtZlVDNJQ3p-WX0M1b1k/edit. Willi Ballenthin provides a good description of shellbag artifacts via http://www.williballenthin.com/forensics/shellbags/. However, we're still discovering new things, as new versions of Windows and new applications are released. While I'm writing this chapter, there is no doubt in my mind that there are new shell items available in Windows 10, ones that we'll become familiar with as this version of Windows becomes more prominent and in more widespread use.

I use the RegRipper *shellbags.pl* plugin to parse shellbags arti-facts, and I do try to keep up with new shell items as they appear. Eric Zimmerman has been very helpful in this regard, not only in providing example data but also in sharing his ShellBag Explorer tool, which he described in a blog post which can be found at http://binaryforay.blogspot.com/2015/05/shellbags-explorer-061-released.html. Eric also provides copies of his tools for download via the web page http://binaryforay.blogspot.com/p/software.html.

BOOK CONTEST

Prior to actually writing this book, I wrote a post on my blog announc-ing a contest (the post can be found online at http://windowsir.blogspot.com/2014/10/wrf-2e-contest.html) in which I solicited stories from ana-lysts as to how Registry analysis helped them during an investigation. I offered up a free copy of the book once it was published to anyone who submitted their story, and that story was used in the book. By the time the context clock had run out, I had received only a single submission from an analyst who chose to remain anonymous. His story was that during an illicit images case examination of a Windows XP SP3 system, he had used the Shellbags entries (for Windows XP, those are found in the NTUSER.DAT hive file) to illustrate access to specific image files as well as knowledge of the directory contents. Additional information was used (cell phone records and call logs, work schedules, etc.) to determine which individual in the case had accessed the files in question.

While this is a summary of what was submitted, it does illustrate how Registry information, particularly those entries with time stamps, can be used to great effect and can have a significant impact on the analysis.

Summary

Hopefully, what I've been able to illustrate in this chapter is that there is a great deal of information in the user's hives (NTUSER.DAT, and on Vista and above systems, USRCLASS.DAT) that will provide indications of not only what the user did but also when they did it. This can help demonstrate that a system was in use during a specific period; for example, the creation date and last modification time of the NTUSER.DAT file will provide indications of when the user account was first used to log into the system and when it last logged out, respectively, but information from many of the keys (including key LastWrite times and data derived from binary and string values) will provide indications of actions the user took and when they took them. An analyst can use all of this information to develop an understanding of and add context to other activity found on the system. As with the other hive files, analysis of the user's hives can also assist in determining if the system was infected with malware, or if the user (or an intruder) was responsible for the observed activity.

By now, through these four chapters, I hope that I've been able to illustrate the immense value of Registry analysis. Over the years, I've tracked user and intruder activity, provided information to obviate the "Trojan Defense," and even exonerated falsely accused employees, all by incorporating Registry analysis in my overall examination.

REGRIPPER

Introduction

Since it was first released, RegRipper has been downloaded a great number of times and seems to be used by a great many analysts. However, I tend to wonder just how many analysts really *use* RegRipper to get the most from the Registry hives they're examining, as opposed to those that simply run the tool because they heard someone say that they should. There's much more available to an analyst when employing a tool such as RegRipper, and the purpose of this chapter is to provide a foundation not only of how to employ RegRipper, but also how to get the most out of using RegRipper.

Over the years, I've written a number of blog posts and discussed RegRipper in a number of forums (conference presentations, etc.). In some cases, I've written blog posts to answer individual questions I've received, and in other cases, I've written blog posts to address somewhat more "collective" questions, the kinds of things I see over and over again. My intent for adding this chapter to this book is to consolidate a lot of that information in one location.

What Is RegRipper?

From our discussion in chapter Processes and Tools, you could say that RegRipper is a "superparser" for the Windows Registry. RegRipper is a framework that runs various plugins, individually or in groups, where the plugins are used to extract specific data from within the Registry hive files, parse and translate that data as necessary, and then display the results for the analyst. RegRipper is not a viewer application; you cannot load a hive file into RegRipper and browse through the structure. What you can do is parse binary value data to display contents that would not be visible in a viewer application. For example, you can decode such things as ROT-13 encoded value names for display, and you can format parsed and decoded data in whatever manner fits the needs of your analysis.

Tip

In the fall of 2014, I decided to put RegRipper in one easy-to-reach location, and I created a project page on GitHub. If you're at all interested in the latest, most up-to-date version of RegRipper or any of the plugins, you can get them from https://github.com/keydet89/RegRipper2.8.

RegRipper started its life as a couple of Perl scripts I'd written in order to retrieve specific data from hives during exams. I had thought at the time, why should I continue to open the hive file in a viewer and navigate to the key or value of interest when it's quicker to just have a computer program do it for me? So a couple of Perl scripts became a couple more, and then a few more, and pretty soon I was getting to the point where I was running out of short names for the scripts. I was also getting to the point where I felt like I needed some way to better manage the scripts, not only just keeping them but keeping track of which script extracted what data. The idea I came up with was to continue using the Perl programming language but develop a way to combine all of the common elements of the scripts into a framework so that I didn't have to continually rewrite those elements. The result was a command line tool that would run the various scripts, but in no particular order. Over time, I added a graphical user interface (GUI), and the ability to run groups of scripts, or "plugins," in a specific order. Since RegRipper was first released, a number of plugins have been added, and others have been removed or modified.

RegRipper itself is written in Perl, and the plugins are Perl code as well. RegRipper is distributed as Perl source code, and the archive also includes Windows executable files for both the RegRipper GUI tool, as well as the command line tool (rip.exe), both of which were "compiled" using Perl2Exe (found online at http://www.indigostar.com/perl2exe.php). As such, the dynamically linked library (DLL) file that is included with the distribution, named p2x5124.dll, must be in the same folder as the .exe files for RegRipper (rr.exe, rip.exe) so that the applications can be successfully launched.

RegRipper is not only available as a standalone download, but it is also available in Linux-based forensic application distributions

such as PlainSight (found online at http://www.plainsight.info/
features.html) and the SANS Investigative Forensic Toolkit (aka
SIFT), which can be found online at http://digital-forensics.sans.
org/community/downloads. Slight modifications to the original
code for the command line component of RegRipper allowed it
to also run on Linux systems; these modifications were incorporated into the RegRipper GUI as well. RegRipper is also included
in the Autopsy framework (found online at https://github.com/
sleuthkit/autopsy).

Most analysts utilize the RegRipper GUI, by either opening a
command prompt, navigating the directory where RegRipper was
copied, and typing "rr" at the command line, or by double-clicking the yellow "pearl" (not "Perl," "pearl") icon for "rr.exe". Either
one will open the RegRipper GUI, which is illustrated in Fig. 5.1.

Once the RegRipper GUI appears, you select a hive file by clicking the "Browse" button to the right of the "Hive File" text field,
and an output report file, and then select the appropriate profile

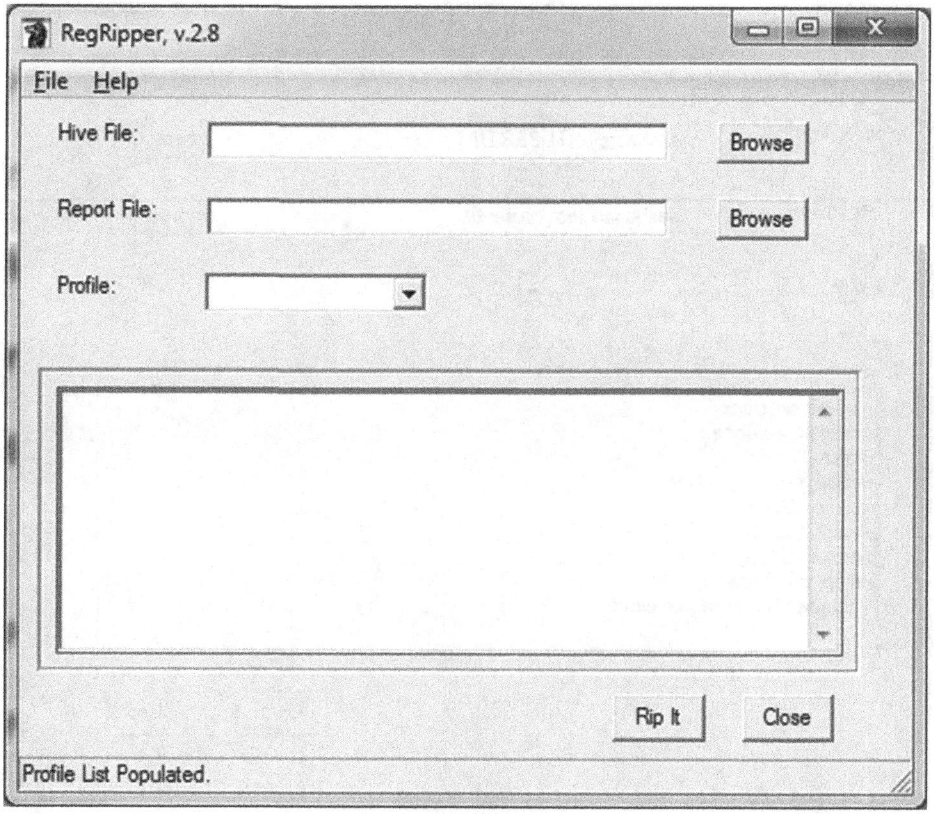

Figure 5.1 RegRipper GUI.

from the "Profile:" drop-down list. Clicking the "Rip It" button will run the plugins within the selected profile, in order, against the hive file, write the output of each plugin to the report file, and report progress information in the large text field.

When RegRipper completes running all of the plugins against the selected hive file, you will see something similar to what is illustrated in Fig. 5.2.

As you can see in Fig. 5.2, RegRipper displays a running status of the plugin being run in the large text window, and when the tool has completed running all of the plugins in the profile, the word "Done" appears in the status bar at the bottom of the main window. You can also see in Fig. 5.2 that the tool reported that "4 plugins completed with errors." What many folks don't realize is that when the RegRipper GUI is used, this tool maintains a log file of its own activity. In the "Report File" text field, you can see that the output of all of the plugins will be written to a file named "D:\cases\jason\test_ntuser. txt". Once the tool has completed, you will also find a file named

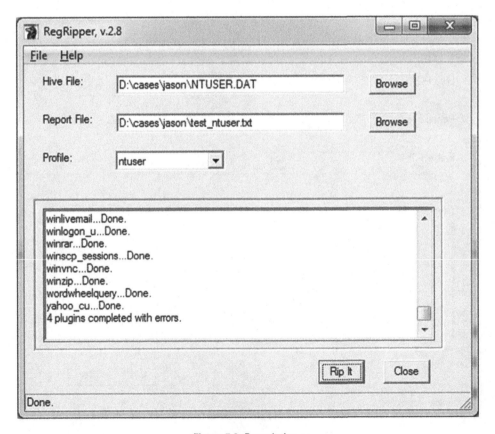

Figure 5.2 Description.

"test_ntuser.log" in the same folder; this is the file that contains the log of activity. This file is intended to log the hive file that RegRipper is being run against, each hive file that is run against the hive file, and any significant errors. This log file maintains a record of which plugins (including the version of each plugin) were run against the hive and allows the log file to be included as part of an analyst's case notes. Each line of the log file starts with the date/time stamp of the entry. If a plugin encounters an error, that error is also recorded in the log file and can be used for troubleshooting purposes.

Warning

The RegRipper GUI allows you to run groups of plugins, or profiles, against a hive file. It doesn't allow you to run individual plugins against a hive file, unless you want to use a profile that contains just one plugin. The capability for running one plugin against a hive file wasn't included in the RegRipper GUI, as it's not terribly efficient, and the capability exists with the command line RegRipper component (rip.exe).

Plugins

Plugins are small Perl scripts that are run by RegRipper and perform specific functions. These are the bits of code that do all of the work of RegRipper: accessing the appropriate key path(s), extracting metadata from the key structures, accessing values, parsing and displaying data, etc. As they are Perl scripts, plugins end with the ".pl" file extension.

Tip

By design, if you are running RegRipper by using the Windows executable files (rr.exe, rip.exe), you do not need to have Perl installed on your system. Even though the plugins are Perl code and are not "compiled" in the same manner as the main RegRipper components, you still do not need Perl installed in order to run the complete set of plugins.

Most plugins are intended for specific hives; the data that they collect are only found in one hive. In some cases, the data that you may be looking for may be found in either the Software hive or the NTUSER.DAT hive, with the only difference in extracting the desired data from one hive or the other is a slight variation in the path to that data. In cases such as these, it is trivial to have a plugin that can be run against either hive file and "fail silently" (that is, not report an error) if one path does not succeed in finding the data.

Some plugins are intended to extract very specific data, making them very "tactical," while others are more general or "strategic" in nature. For example, the regin.pl plugin checks the System hive file for specific values known to be indicative of the Regin malware. The renocide.pl plugin checks the Software hive for a specific key known to be indicative of the Renocide malware. These plugins are very "tactical," as they check for specific keys or value data. On the other hand, the svc.pl plugin accesses the Services key in the System hive and extracts (and displays) data from all of the subkeys, making no attempt to filter the data.

Some plugins can be run across all hives. For example, the findexes.pl plugin was written to look for binary data types (values with data of type 0 or 3) that start with "MZ", the first 2 bytes of a Windows portable executable file. The rlo.pl plugin was written to check any hive file for any key and value names that contain the right-to-left override Unicode control character. The fileless.pl plugin was written to check any hive file for indications of the Poweliks malware; throughout the growth of the malware, it employed different persistence mechanisms that spanned multiple hives, while the value data itself remained similar enough to be detected through the use of a simple regular expression.

Profiles

Profiles within RegRipper are found in the "plugins" folder and are not Perl code. Rather, profiles are text files with no extension; for example, rather than "profile.txt", they are named simply "profile". These files contain just a list of plugins to be run, one on each line. If you choose to run RegRipper using a profile, each of the plugins listed in the profile is run in the order in which they appear in the file.

When you launch the RegRipper GUI, you'll be able to see the available profiles by exposing the drop-down menu for the "Profile:" listbox, as illustrated in Fig. 5.3.

You can create your own profiles for your own use or to share with others. I know several folks who've done this, and I've done it upon occasion. I don't include those in the RegRipper distribution because I've found that it tends to confuse some of those who download and run RegRipper; with too many plugins available, there appears to be confuse as to which ones to run. However, we do discuss how to create your own profiles in detail later in this chapter. Creating your own profile is as easy as opening Notepad and typing the name of each plugin that you want to run against a hive file on one line.

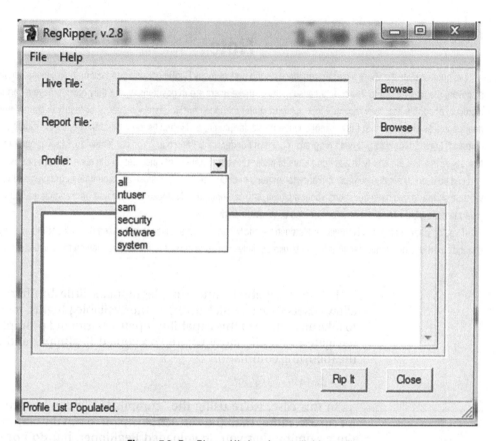

Figure 5.3 RegRipper UI showing available profiles.

Getting the Most Out of RegRipper

I know that to many users, RegRipper seems like a pretty static tool; most users download the tool, run it using GUI, and generally don't do a great deal to really push RegRipper beyond the tool that they downloaded. However, RegRipper is actually pretty flexible and, when used in conjunction with other tools (see chapter Processes and Tools) and analysis processes, can also be a very dynamic framework.

Finding Out About Plugins

Finding out about the plugins that you have available to you is a relatively straightforward affair. One way to do this is to simply open Windows Explorer, click through the directory structure until you get to where the plugins are located, and open them up one at a time in Notepad.

Note

I've noticed over the years a certain reticence on the part of many RegRipper users to take on the responsibility of discovery themselves. I find this odd, because many of these users are in positions where they have to have a certain modicum of confidence; they regularly interact with senior management, interview suspects, or testify in court. I will hear people ask (or, hear that they asked) about a particular plugin, and when I suggest that they open the plugin file in Notepad, I immediately get, "I don't program" or "I don't understand Perl code." You don't have to. Many programming languages provide the ability to add comments to code; these are statements included in the code that are not executed and can be used to provide context or clarity to sections of code. I tend to make use of comments in the plugins I've written, so that if you have questions about a plugin, you can open it in Notepad without fear of changing it (if all you're going to do is read it) to get a little better idea of what the code is doing.

If you do open a plugin in Notepad or Notepad++, and when you go to close it, are asked if you want to save any changes (perhaps due to an inadvertent key stroke), simply choose to close the file without saving the current contents.

I built a capability into rip (RegRipper's little brother) that allows users to get a quick listing of the available plugins. In order to take advantage of this capability, open a command prompt and navigate to the directory where you copied RegRipper and type the following command:

```
C:\perl\rr>rip -l
```

In this case, we're using the "compiled" Windows executable for rip.exe, rather than the Perl script (rip.pl) to run the command. I'm assuming that you downloaded RegRipper, but do not have Perl installed, which is perfectly acceptable.

An excerpt of the output of the command appears as follows:

```
265. typedurls v.20080324 [NTUSER.DAT]
 - Returns contents of user's TypedURLs key.
266. typedurlstime v.20120613 [NTUSER.DAT]
 - Returns contents of user's TypedURLsTime key.
267. typedurlstime_tln v.20120613 [NTUSER.DAT]
 - Returns contents of Win8 user's TypedURLsTime key (TLN).
```

Again, this is just an excerpt; at the time of this writing, my installation of RegRipper has 315 plugins.

So, what the command does is that it goes to the plugins folder (by default, "plugins"), locates all files that end in ".pl", and extracts information from them. The information that you see displayed (name, version number, hive that the plugin is intended for, and a description) is all embedded within the plugin file itself. Of course, there may be more extensive information available in the headers or comments of the plugin file, which you can view by opening the plugin file in Notepad or Notepad++.

Another way to run the same command is to add the "-c" switch, which when used with the "-l" switch (for listing the plugins) will format the output as comma-separated values (CSV), suitable for opening in Excel.

```
C:\perl\rr>rip -l -c
```

You'll notice that the output is displayed on the console. To get this into an Excel file, simply redirect the output to a file as follows:

```
C:\perl\rr>rip -l -c > plugins.csv
```

You can now open the resulting file in Excel, or even Notepad, if you wish. Once you have the output in Excel, you can sort on names, versions, or hive files. Or, you can extend the command line you're using to produce only a list of plugins intended to be run against the NTUSER.DAT hive file by typing:

```
C:\perl\rr>rip -l -c | find "NTUSER" /i > ntuser_plugins.
csv
```

Again, you can open the resulting file in Excel and sort on any of the columns. This is a great way to get a listing of plugins that are run against a particular hive (replace "NTUSER" with any other hive name, or "ALL") so that you can create your own custom profiles, which will be discussed later in this chapter.

Tip

In April, 2013, Adam (aka "Hexacorn") wrote a Perl script that you could run across the plugins that you have available, and it would produce a nice HTML report illustrating the keys that were checked by each plugin. I haven't run it, but I do think that it was a great way to address an issue (or solve a problem) that at least one analyst had encountered. The Perl script (named "3r.pl", for "RegRipper Ripper") can be found online at http://hexacorn.com/tools/3r.pl, and an example of the output of the script, run at the time that the script was created, can be found online at http://hexacorn.com/tools/3r.html.

Creating New Plugins

I promised that you don't have to be a programmer to use or get the most out of RegRipper, and that's still true. However, even without extensive programming skills, you can create your own plugins. As an example, Corey Harrell (author of the "Journey into IR" blog, found online at http://journeyintoir.blogspot.com) created his own plugin by copying the contents of an available plugin into another plugin file, and changing specific items within the code (ie, Registry key path, value, etc.) to meet his needs. I've used this same "cut-and-paste" approach myself to create more than a few plugins. Let's say that I read something online regarding malware that creates a particular Registry key during installation; knowing the hive file in which the key is located is the first step. I then just open a plugin that extracts data from the same hive file, copy as much of the contents as I need, paste that into another file, and start making the necessary changes for the plugin I want to produce.

Since I first released RegRipper, my request has always been that if someone has a question about RegRipper or a plugin, ask it. Similarly, if someone needs a plugin modified, or a new one created, the best approach is to contact me with a concise description of what you're looking for (maybe include some examples) and provide sample data for testing. In some cases, when someone has asked for assistance in that manner, I've been able to turn around new or updated plugins in 1–4 hours. I have had people ask me for new plugins but be either unwilling or unable to provide sample data, and I really don't want to send someone a plugin that I haven't had an opportunity to test. My goal is to provide a plugin that they can use, not something that the only response is that "it doesn't work."

To my knowledge, there are no "hidden" repositories of RegRipper plugins. For the foreseeable future, the RegRipper distribution will continue to be located online at https://github.com/keydet89/RegRipper2.8. Over the years, a few analysts have provided plugins of their own, and others have requested updates to plugins, as well as providing the necessary data to develop and test the plugin. The most notable case for the latter is the *ares.pl* plugin; I don't have many opportunities to work cases involving peer-to-peer (P2P) file sharing applications, and a district attorney shared an NTUSER. DAT file with me along with a request to update the *ares.pl* plugin in order to address the data that they'd seen.

Tip

I understand that sharing data from cases can be hard to do; however, the instances where someone has shared hive files from actual cases have predominantly been from law enforcement. Not long ago, Cindy Murphy, a detective from Wisconsin who is extremely well known for her extensive knowledge of mobile device forensic analysis, shared Registry hive files from a Windows Phone 8 with me, and from these I was able to determine that many of the current RegRipper plugins worked just fine on these hives. In another instance, a district attorney shared a hive file with me that allowed me to update a plugin.

Create Your Own Profiles

Both the RegRipper GUI tool (rr.exe) and the command line tool (rip.exe) make use of profiles, which are simply files that contain a list of plugins to run. A profile file has no extension; it does *NOT* end in ".txt" nor any other extension.

An easy way to see which profiles you have available is to open a command prompt and navigate to the folder that contains the plugins and type the following command:

```
C:\Perl\rr\plugins>dir /os | more
```

What this command does is list the files within the folder, using a sort order based on the size of the files, listing the smallest files first. This is an effective means of listing the profiles, as you'll see, because the profiles are much smaller than the plugins. An excerpt of the output from the above command, run on the system I use to develop RegRipper, appears as follows:

```
03/29/2013 02:43 PM 77 sam
03/29/2013 02:43 PM 93 usrclass
03/29/2013 02:43 PM 104 security
08/07/2014 04:27 PM 107 all
04/03/2013 09:55 AM 568 system
07/16/2013 06:44 AM 660 software
09/05/2013 07:15 AM 1,259 ntuser
08/21/2014 02:34 PM 1,351 at_tln.pl
07/13/2010 12:45 PM 1,465 skype.pl
```

Notice that the smallest file is "sam", which is only 77 bytes in size. Using the "type" command, you can send the contents of the file to the console, and you'll see what appears as follows:

```
# 20120528 *ALL* Plugins that apply on SAM hive,
alphabetical order
  samparse
```

As you can see, there really isn't much to the "sam" profile, as it points to only one plugin, samparse.pl. In fact, the vast majority of the 77 bytes of the file are consumed by the visible comment. That's right, lines beginning with "#" are comments and as such are not processed as commands by RegRipper.

Similarly, the "all" profile contains the following lines:

```
# 20120528 *ALL* Plugins that apply on any HIVES,
alphabetical order
  baseline
  findexes
  regtime
  rlo
  del
```

The "all" profile contains plugins that can be run against any hive. I know...the file name isn't entirely imaginative, but it is deceptively descriptive.

Once you've created your new profile, be sure to test it by running it against whatever hives you have available. You can do this by closing and relaunching the RegRipper UI and selecting the new profile from the drop-down list. An alternative to this approach is to use rip.exe to run the profile against a hive file using a command similar to the following:

```
C:\perl\rr>rip -r d:\cases\local\ntuser.dat -f new_ntuser_
profile
```

If you want to see all of the output from the above command, be sure to redirect the output to a file, using the appropriate redirection operator; either ">" to create a new file or ">>" to append the information to a new file.

Tip

In chapter Processes and Tools, we discussed various tools you could use, and we discussed those tools as they pertained to different analysis processes. One of the tools we discussed for diff'ing two hive files—displaying the differences between two hives—was a script that shipped as part of the Parse::Win32Registry Perl module. An alternative means to doing the same sort of analysis, albeit on a smaller scale, would be run create a profile, run that same profile against two hive files, and then use native text-based differencing tools such as *fc.exe* or *comp.exe* to compare the output files.

Extending RegRipper

When it comes to getting the most out of RegRipper, another approach to consider is what Corey Harrell came up with in creating "auto_rip", which can be found online at http://journeyintoir. blogspot.com/2013/05/unleashing-autorip.html. Note that at the end of the blog post, Corey provides a download location for the auto_rip script, which he describes as a wrapper script for using RegRipper.

Corey has long been a proponent for "artifact categories," which is a method for classifying various artifacts based on their applicability to various aspects of analysis. For example, if your analysis goals are to determine, as best you could, all of the programs that had been run on a computer system, or all of the applications that had been launched by a specific user, there are a number of data sources and artifacts within a Windows system where you can focus your analysis. The "give me everything, including the kitchen sink" approach to analysis can quickly become overwhelming due to the sheer volume of data, and the concept of "artifact catego-ries" allows an analyst to focus on specific data sources and arti-facts that will provide the analyst with information pertinent to that analysis. As we saw in chapters Analyzing the System Hives and Case Studies: User Hives, there are several keys and values within the Registry that allow an analyst to focus on specific infor-mation about which applications were run on a system, which falls under the "program execution" category. Sometimes, various categories can be very similar; for example, there are "program execution" artifacts that will provide information about applica-tions that a user launched, as well as "autostart" artifacts that will provide information about applications that were automatically launched when the user took a specific action, such as logging into the system, logging out, or running an application.

Corey developed auto_rip to be a means for using RegRipper to get information specific to various artifact categories. His blog post lists the various supported categories and even includes the ability to run RegRipper across multiple hive files and retrieve information that pertains to all of the supported categories. This can be extremely valuable to an analyst who has a very clear pic-ture in their mind regarding what their analysis goals are and what questions they are trying to answer. Corey's efforts have extended the ability to use RegRipper not in a single step but rather in a quantum leap.

What to Do When Something Goes Wrong

As with any software, there is the possibility that something will not go as planned or expected. If you get an error message or some other message that you didn't expect to see when you ran RegRip-per, there are a couple of things you can check.

First, check to ensure that you ran the plugin against the appro-priate hive file. The plugins are written in Perl, which means that for the most part, they're text files and can be opened in an editor, such as Notepad (native to Windows installations) or Notepad++ (avail-able online from http://notepad-plus-plus.org/). Near the begin-ning of each plugin, there's a Perl hash structure named "%config" that contains metadata for the plugin; within this structure is a value named "hive" that indicates for which hive (or hives, as the case may be) the plugin is intended. This value is illustrated in Fig. 5.4.

Second, check the hive file itself; is it a hive file? Open the hive file in a hex editor and check to see if the first 4 bytes are "regf", and go to offset 4096 (0x1000 in hexadecimal) and check to see if the first 4 bytes at that offset are "hbin". Most importantly, check to ensure that the hive file itself is not full of zeros.

```perl
package shellbags;
use strict;
use Time::Local;

my %config = (hive          => "USRCLASS\.DAT",
              hivemask       => 32,
              output         => "report",
              category       => "User Activity",
              osmask         => 20, #Vista, Win7/Win2008R2
```

Figure 5.4 Plugin metadata.

If everything looks good and checks out at this point, check the log file. Remember earlier in this chapter (see Fig. 5.2), we discussed the fact that when you run the RegRipper GUI, it creates a log file of activity? Whichever file name you chose for the output file (the file should end with the ".txt" extension) a log file with same name, albeit with the ".log" file extension, will be created in the same folder. If you run into issues with the output of RegRipper, be sure to check this file out. Open it in Notepad or Notepad++ and scroll through it. Do any of the plugins report errors?

Here's an example of an error I found in a log file:

```
Tue Mar 3 16:19:06 2015: Error in compatassist:
PLEASE SEE THE PERL2EXE USER MANUAL UNDER "Can't locate
somemodule.pm in @INC"
FOR AN EXPLANATION OF THE FOLLOWING MESSAGE:
  Can't locate plugins\compatassist.pl in @INC (@INC
contains: PERL2EXE_STORAGE
  C:\Perl\rr C:\Users\harlan\AppData\Local\Temp/p2xtmp-1900)
at C:\Perl\rr\rr.exe line 274.
```

So what does all this mean? Well, this one is pretty easy. See the part where it says "Can't locate plugins\compatassist.pl...?" If I navigate to the plugins folder (via a command prompt) and type "dir compatassist.pl", I get "File not found". Basically, what this error means is that a plugin was included in the profile, but the plugin doesn't exist in the plugins folder. This one is an easy fix...simply open the profile in Notepad and remove the reference to the plugin.

If you still can't figure out what's wrong, feel free to contact me. My e-mail address is included in the header of the plugins that I have written (which is most of them), so you should have no trouble reaching me. I tend to discourage folks from publishing their questions and concerns to random websites, for the simple fact that it would be highly unlikely that I would see them. Whatever information you can share (beyond, "it doesn't work") about the version of the operating system you were using (as well as the one from which the Registry hive files were extracted), the hive files themselves, the plugins you were running, etc., will only serve to provide me with a better view into what the issue might be and allow me to provide an answer, and possibly even a solution, in a more timely manner.

Summary

RegRipper can be an extremely useful and valuable tool in an analyst's toolkit. RegRipper provides capabilities not available in viewer applications, allowing analysts to parse binary data structures and decode encoded values (or value names). RegRipper can also be used to translate binary data, allowing analysts to parse a globally unique identifier (GUID) out of binary value data and provide for a lookup of what that GUID refers to, displaying it in a human-readable manner.

However, the real power of RegRipper comes from the community of analysts who use and extend the tool, by writing tools such as auto_rip, or by writing their own plugins, and then sharing those tools and plugins with other analysts. To many, the Registry seems like a dark, foreboding abyss, but by working together and sharing knowledge through frameworks such as RegRipper, we can pierce that veil of mystery.

INDEX

Note: Page numbers followed by "f" indicate figures, "t" indicate tables and "b" indicate boxes.